Contents

Lesson 14

Lesson 15

Getting Started

Adobe® Acrobat® 7.0 is the essential tool for universal document exchange. You can use Acrobat Standard or Acrobat Professional to create virtually any document in Adobe Portable Document Format (PDF), preserving the exact look and content of the original, complete with fonts and graphics.

You can distribute your PDF documents by e-mail or store them on the World Wide Web, an intranet, a file system, or a CD. Other users can view and review your work, regardless of the platform they work on. You can add interactive elements such as custom hyperlinks and sound clips, streamline your document review process with Acrobat comments, and add digital signatures.

But Acrobat 7.0 goes far beyond PDF creation and simple document enhancement. With Acrobat 7.0, you can manage a broad range of essential business activities. You can convert a wider variety of documents into Adobe PDF files and assemble them into one compact, comprehensive Adobe PDF document that can be easily shared. And performance and security enhancements make sharing documents faster, easier, more secure, and more flexible.

In Acrobat Professional, you also have tighter integration with more professional and engineering applications, support for 3D objects, more powerful forms creation capability, and the ability to include anyone with the free downloadable Adobe Reader® 7.0 software in the electronic document review process.

About Classroom in a Book

Adobe Acrobat 7.0 Classroom in a Book® is part of the official training series for Adobe graphics and publishing software. The lessons are designed to let you learn at your own pace. If you're new to Adobe Acrobat, you'll learn the fundamental concepts and features you'll need to master the program. If you've been using Acrobat for a while, you'll find Classroom in a Book teaches many advanced features and includes lessons targeted specifically for technical and print professionals.

The lessons in this edition include information on the popular Adobe Acrobat features, including:

- Using the Organizer to manage your PDF files.

- Single-click creation of Adobe PDF files.

- Repurposing the content of Adobe PDF files for use in other applications.

- Editing PDF documents.

- Creating multimedia presentations.

- Improved work flows and tools for reviewing and commenting on Adobe PDF documents, including the ability to invite users of Adobe Reader to participate in the review and commenting process.

- Tools for making your documents more accessible.

- Forms creation.

- New measuring tools designed for engineering and technical users.

- Enhanced document security.

Although each lesson provides step-by-step instructions for specific projects, there's room for exploration and experimentation. You can follow the book from start to finish or do only the lessons that match your interests and needs.

Acrobat Professional and Acrobat Standard

This book covers both Acrobat Professional and Acrobat Standard. Where a tool or feature described in this book is specific to Acrobat Professional, the information is italicized and called out with an icon as shown below.

Acrobat Professional offers several tools and features that are not available in Acrobat Standard. You need to upgrade to Acrobat Professional if your work includes the following:

- *Preflighting documents, working with color separations, and delivering final print production output as Adobe PDF.*

- *Creating interactive forms.*

- *Converting layered and large-format engineering drawings to Adobe PDF.*

- *Inviting users of Adobe Reader to participate in email-based and web-based reviews and allowing them to save forms data.*

- *Modifying the reflow order of objects on a page to optimize the accessibility of documents.*

- *Embedding 3D content.*

Prerequisites

Before beginning to use *Adobe Acrobat 7.0 Classroom in a Book*, you should have a working knowledge of your computer and its operating system. Make sure you know how to use the mouse, standard menus and commands, and how to open, save, and close files. If you need to review these techniques, see the printed or online documentation included with your system.

Installing Adobe Acrobat

Before beginning to use *Adobe Acrobat 7.0 Classroom in a Book*, make sure that your system is set up correctly and that you've installed the required software and hardware. You must purchase Adobe Acrobat 7.0 software separately. For system requirements, see the Adobe website at http://www.adobe.com/products/acrobat/main.html.

You must install the application from the Adobe Acrobat 7.0 CD onto your hard drive; you cannot run Acrobat 7.0 from the CD. Follow the onscreen installation instructions.

Starting Adobe Acrobat

You start Acrobat just as you would any other software application.

- On Windows, choose Start > Programs or All Programs > Adobe Acrobat 7.0 Standard. or Adobe Acrobat 7.0 Professional.

- On Mac OS, open the Adobe Acrobat 7.0 Standard folder or the Adobe Acrobat 7.0 Professional folder, and double-click the program icon.

Note: *To run Acrobat 7.0 Standard or Acrobat 7.0 Professional on Mac OS, you must have Mac OS X, version 10.2.8 or later.*

The Adobe Acrobat application window appears. You can now open a PDF document or create a new one and start working.

Copying the Classroom in a Book files

The *Adobe Acrobat 7.0 Classroom in a Book* CD includes folders that contain all the electronic files for the lessons. Each lesson has its own folder, and you must copy the folders to your hard drive to do the lessons. To save room on your drive, you can install only the necessary folder for each lesson as you need it, and remove it when you're done.

To install the Classroom in a Book files:

1 Insert the *Adobe Acrobat 7.0 Classroom in a Book* CD into your CD-ROM drive.

2 Create a folder named AA7_CIB on your hard drive.

3 Copy the lessons you want to the hard drive:

• To copy all of the lessons, drag the Lessons folder from the CD into the AA7_CIB folder.

• To copy a single lesson, drag the individual lesson folder from the CD into the AA7_CIB folder.

4 If you are working on Windows 2000, you may need to unlock the lesson files. To unlock the lesson files, right click the Lessons folder in the AA7_CIB folder on your system, and select Properties from the context menu. In the Properties dialog box, deselect Read-only option (under Attributes), and click Apply. In the Confirm Attributes dialog box, select the option Apply Changes to This Folder, Subfolders and Files. Then click OK and OK again. (If you are copying one lesson at a time, you will need to unlock each lesson folder as you copy it to your system.)

Note: If, as you work through the lessons, you overwrite the lesson files, you can restore the original files by recopying the corresponding lesson folder from the Classroom in a Book CD to the AA7_CIB folder on your hard drive.

Additional resources

Adobe Acrobat 7.0 Classroom in a Book is not meant to replace documentation provided with the Adobe Acrobat 7.0 program. Only the commands and options used in the lessons are explained in this book. For comprehensive information about program features, refer to these resources:

• The How To pages, which give overviews of popular tasks and concise steps for completing common tasks. To open the How To pages, choose Help > How To or click the Help button (⊘) on the Acrobat toolbar, and then select a topic area.

- The Complete Acrobat 7.0 online Help included with the Adobe Acrobat 7.0 software, which you can view by choosing Help > Complete Acrobat 7.0 Help or clicking the Help button ( ) on the Acrobat toolbar and choosing Complete Acrobat 7.0 Help. This guide contains a complete description of all features.

- The Adobe website (www.adobe.com/products/acrobat/), which you can view by choosing Help > Acrobat Online if you have a connection to the World Wide Web.

Adobe certification

The Adobe training and certification programs are designed to help Adobe customers improve and promote their product proficiency skills. The Adobe Certified Expert (ACE) program, which is designed to recognize the high-level skills of expert users, is the best way to master Adobe products. For information on Adobe-certified training programs, visit the Partnering with Adobe website at http://partners.adobe.com/.

Lesson 1

Lesson 1

1 Introducing Acrobat

Acrobat makes it easier to connect people, paper, and applications in all types of settings, from a personal work environment to multinational business environments. Acrobat helps you create and manage electronic documents quickly and easily, and enhanced security helps keeps your documents safe. Regardless of the operating system, Adobe Reader is all that users need to access the PDF files you send them.

In this lesson, you'll do the following:

• Look at the differences between electronic documents designed for printing and viewing online.

• Identify the types of formatting and design decisions you need to make when creating an electronic publication.

• Explore Organizer, which is a new Adobe Acrobat feature designed to help you manage your PDF files.

This lesson will take about 45 minutes to complete.

If needed, copy the Lesson01 folder onto your hard drive.

Note: Windows 2000 users may need to unlock the lesson files before using them. For information, see "Copying the Classroom in a Book files" on page 4.

About Adobe PDF

Adobe Portable Document Format (PDF) is a universal file format that preserves all of the fonts, formatting, colors, and graphics of any source document, regardless of the application and platform used to create it. Adobe PDF files are compact and can be shared, viewed, navigated, and printed exactly as intended by anyone with the free Adobe Reader. You can convert almost any document to Adobe PDF using Acrobat Standard or Acrobat Professional software.

• Adobe PDF preserves the exact layout, fonts, and text formatting of electronic documents, regardless of the computer system or platform used to view these documents.

• PDF documents can contain multiple languages, such as Japanese and English, on the same page.

• PDF documents print predictably with proper margins and page breaks.

• PDF files can be secured to prevent undesired changes or printing, or to limit access to confidential documents.

• The view magnification of a PDF page can be changed using controls in Acrobat or Adobe Reader. This feature can be especially useful for zooming in on graphics or diagrams containing intricate details.

About Acrobat Standard and Acrobat Professional

Acrobat lets you create, work with, read, and print Portable Document Format (PDF) documents.

Creating Adobe PDF

Your workflow and the types of documents you use determine how you create an Adobe PDF file.

• Use Distiller® to convert almost any file to Adobe PDF, including those created with drawing, page-layout, and image-editing programs.

• Use Acrobat PDFMaker to create Adobe PDF files from within third-party applications, such as Microsoft Office applications. Simply click the Convert to Adobe PDF button (📌) on the authoring application's toolbar.

 In Acrobat Professional, you can also use Acrobat PDFMaker to create Adobe PDF files directly from within Micorosoft Project and Visio files and from within Autodesk AutoCAD files on Windows.

• Use the Create PDF commands to quickly convert a variety of file formats to Adobe PDF and open them in Acrobat. You can convert files one at a time or convert several different types of files at once and consolidate them into one compact Adobe PDF file.

• Use an application's Print command and the Adobe PDF printer to create Adobe PDF directly from within popular authoring applications.

• Scan paper documents and convert them to Adobe PDF.

• Use the Create PDF from Web Page command to download web pages and convert them to Adobe PDF.

 In Acrobat Professional, you can use specialized prepress tools to check color separations, preflight PDF files to check for quality concerns, adjust how transparent objects are imaged, and color-separate PDF files.

Lesson 3, "Converting Microsoft Office Files;" Lesson 4, "Converting Other File Types to Adobe PDF;" Lesson 5, "Creating Adobe PDF from Web Pages;" and Lesson 15, "Using Adobe Acrobat for Professional Publishing" give step-by-step instructions for creating Adobe PDF using several of these methods.

Working with PDF files

Working with PDF files has never been easier.

• Add hyperlinks, electronic bookmarks, and page actions to create a rich online experience. (Lesson 7, "Modifying PDF Files" and Lesson 8, "More on Modifying PDF Files.")

In Acrobat Professional, you can modify the reflow order of objects on a page to optimize the accessibility of your PDF documents for users with assistive technology.

• Use the powerful content repurposing tools to re-use content in other applications by saving text in other file formats, extracting images in image formats, and converting PDF pages to image formats. The new Select tool makes it even easier to extract text, tables, and images. (Lesson 8, "More on Modifying PDF Files.")

• Convert Microsoft Outlook email messages to Adobe PDF with one click. [Lesson 3, "Converting Microsoft Office Files (Windows)."]

• Use built-in or third-party security handlers to add sophisticated protection to your confidential PDF documents, preventing users from copying text and graphics, printing a document, or even opening a file. Add digital signatures to approve the content and format of a document. Send files in secure eEnvelopes. In Acrobat 7.0, you can create named security policies for easy re-use. And you can apply advanced security and control with the Adobe LiveCycle™ Policy Server. (Lesson 11, "Adding Signatures and Security.")

• Add comments and files, and markup text in a totally electronic document review cycle. All the review and commenting tools are in one toolbar. You can import comments back into some types of source documents. And with Acrobat Professional, you can invite users of Adobe Reader to participate in electronic reviews. (Lesson 10, "Using Acrobat in a Document Review Cycle.")

• Create sophisticated multimedia presentations. With Acrobat Professional, you can embed 3D objects in Adobe PDF files. (Lesson 12, "Creating Multimedia Presentations.")

• Create PDF forms. You can create XML-based forms with the Adobe LiveCycle Designer software included with Acrobat Professional. (Lesson 16, "Creating Forms with Adobe LiveCycle Designer.")

• Use the Organizer feature to manage your PDF files. (Lesson 1, "Introducing Acrobat.")

Reading PDF files

You can read PDF documents using Adobe Reader, Acrobat Elements, Acrobat Standard, or Acrobat Professional. You can share your PDF documents using network and web servers, CDs, DVDs, and disks.

Adobe PDF on the World Wide Web

The World Wide Web has greatly expanded the possibilities for delivering electronic documents to a wide and varied audience. Because web browsers can be configured to run other applications inside the browser window, you can post PDF files as part of a website. Your users can download or view these PDF files inside the browser window using Adobe Reader.

When including a PDF file as part of your web page, you should direct your users to the Adobe website so that the first time they look at a PDF document, they can download Adobe Reader free of charge if necessary.

PDF documents can be viewed one page at a time and printed from the web. With page-at-a-time downloading, the web server sends only the requested page to the user, decreasing downloading time. In addition, the user can easily print selected pages or all pages from the document. PDF is a suitable format for publishing long electronic documents on the web. PDF documents print predictably, with proper margins and page breaks. (For information on optimizing your files for the web, see Lesson 8, "More on Modifying PDF Files.")

You can also download and convert web pages to Adobe PDF, making it easy to save, distribute, and print web pages. (For more information, see Lesson 5, "Creating Adobe PDF from Web Pages.")

Adding Adobe Reader installers

Adobe Reader is available free of charge for distribution with your documents, making it easier for users to view your PDF documents. It's important either to include a copy of the Reader installers on your CD (if that's how you're distributing your documents) or to point users to the Reader installers on the Adobe website at www.adobe.com.

If you're including the Reader installers on a CD-ROM, you should include a ReadMe text file at the top level of the CD that describes how to install Reader and provides any last-minute information. If you're posting the Reader installers on a website, include the Reader installation instructions with the link to the down-loadable software.

If you're distributing documents on the web, you'll probably want to point users to the Adobe website for the downloadable Reader software.

You may make and distribute unlimited copies of Adobe Reader, including copies for commercial distribution. For complete information on distributing and giving your users access to Adobe Reader, visit the Adobe website at http://www.adobe.com/products/acrobat/.

A special logo is available from Adobe for use when distributing Adobe Reader.

Looking at some examples

Publishing your document electronically is a flexible way to distribute information. Using Adobe PDF, you can create documents for printing, for multimedia presentations, or for distribution on a CD or over a network. In the first part of this lesson, you'll take a look at some electronic documents designed for printing on paper and at some designed for online reading.

1 Start Acrobat.

2 Choose File > Open. Select Introduc.pdf in the Lesson01 folder, and click Open.

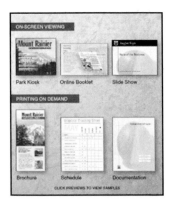

The views of the various documents in this overview represent links to the corresponding electronic documents. The top three images link to documents designed to be both distributed and viewed electronically; the bottom three images link to documents intended to be distributed online, but also printed out for reading.

3 Click the Schedule image in the bottom row to open the corresponding PDF file.

This document is a work schedule that has been converted to Adobe PDF for easy electronic distribution.

4 Move your pointer (🖑) over the bottom left of the document pane, and notice that the page size is a standard 8.5-by-11 inches, a suitable size for printing on a desktop printer. The page size display disappears when you move the pointer away from the area.

You might glance at the schedule online, but you'd probably want to print out a hard-copy version for handy reference.

5 Click the Previous View button (◉) in the status bar to return to the overview in the Introduc.pdf document.

Notice that the Previous View button moves you between files as well as between pages.

Another example of a publication designed for printing is the Documentation file. This text-intensive document is much easier to read in printed format than online.

6 Click the Documentation image in the bottom row to look at the file. Notice that this file opens with bookmarks visible. You can click any of these bookmarks to move to the relevant section in the document. When you are finished looking at the document, click the Previous View button as many times as necessary to return to the Introduc.pdf document.

7 Click the Slide Show preview in the top row to open that document.

This document is a marketing presentation designed to be shown and viewed exclusively onscreen. Notice that the presentation opens in Full Screen mode to occupy all available space on the monitor. All the Acrobat toolbars and menus have disappeared.

8 Press Enter or Return several times to page through the presentation. The colorful graphics, large type size, and horizontal page layout have been designed for optimal display on a monitor.

The Full Screen preference settings in Acrobat let you control how pages display in this mode. For example, you can have a full-screen document with each page displayed automatically for a certain number of seconds.

9 Press the Escape key to exit Full Screen mode.

You can set your Full Screen preferences to ensure that you always have navigation controls, even in full screen view. In Acrobat, choose Edit > Preferences (Windows) or Acrobat > Preferences (Mac OS), and select Full Screen in the left pane of the Preferences dialog box. Under Full Screen Navigation, check the Show Navigation Bar option. Click OK to apply your change. Whenever you open a document in full screen view from here on you will have Next Page, Previous Page, and Exit Full Screen View buttons at the bottom left of your document pane.

10 Click the Previous View button until you return to the overview in the Introduc.pdf document.

An online help publication and an electronic catalog are further examples of documents for which onscreen viewing is suitable and even preferred. Electronic publishing offers intuitive navigational features, such as hypertext links, which are well-suited for publications meant to be browsed or used as quick reference guides.

Designing documents for online viewing

If you've decided to put your documents online, you need to make the design and production decisions that will help make the publication attractive and easy to use. If you're simply converting an existing paper document to electronic format, you'll inevitably weigh the benefits of reworking the design against the time and cost required to do so. If your publication will be viewed onscreen and on paper, you'll need to make the design accommodate the different requirements of both.

First you'll take a look at a document designed to be browsed online but printed out for closer reading.

1 In the Introduc.pdf file, click the Brochure image at the bottom of the page to open the corresponding document.

This document is a printed brochure that was converted unchanged to electronic format. Converting a document to Adobe PDF is a good way to distribute it cheaply and easily. It also enables you to use features such as hypertext links to make navigation of the online brochure both easy and intuitive.

2 If necessary, click the Fit Page button (⬍) to view the entire page. Click the Next Page button (▶) in the status bar at the bottom of the document window a couple of times to page through the brochure.

Notice that while the online brochure is useful for quick browsing and printing of selected pages, it is not designed to be comfortably read onscreen. The long and narrow pages are inconveniently shaped for the screen, and the small image and type sizes make reading a strain for the user.

Now you'll look at the same brochure redesigned and optimized for online reading. The topics in the brochure have been reorganized as a series of nested and linked topic screens that lead the reader through the document.

3 Click the Previous View button (⬅) until you return to the Introduc.pdf file, and click the Park Kiosk image at the top of the page to open that document.

4 If necessary, click the Fit Page button to view the entire page.

Notice that the horizontal page orientation is well-suited for display on a monitor.

5 Click About the Park to activate that link.

The About the Park topic screen appears, with its own list of subtopics. Notice how the larger image and type sizes make this document easier to view than the online brochure.

Notice also the use of sans serif fonts in the publication. Sans serif fonts have simpler and cleaner shapes than serif fonts, making them easier to read onscreen.

6 Click Flora & Fauna to jump to that topic screen. Then click Lowland Forest to view a specific information screen about the Olympic Elk in this region.

Notice that the pages of the original brochure have been redesigned to accommodate a navigational structure based on self-contained, screen-sized units.

The formatting considerations of onscreen publications—fonts, page size, layout, color, and resolution—are the same as those of other kinds of publications; however, each element must be reevaluated in the context of onscreen viewing. Decisions about issues such as color and resolution, which in traditional publishing may require a trade-off between quality and cost, may require a parallel trade-off between quality and file size in electronic publishing. Once you have determined the page elements that are important to you, you need to choose the publishing tools and format that will best maintain the desired elements.

7 Click the Previous View button until you return to the Introduc.pdf file.

8 Click the Online Booklet image to see another example of a PDF document designed for online viewing. Again, you can use the Next Page button and the Previous View button to page through the document.

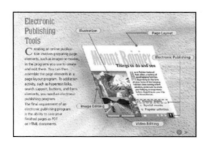

9 Choose Window > Close All to close any open PDF files.

In this part of the lesson, you have examined a variety of electronic documents designed in different file formats for different purposes. Later on in this book, you'll get some hands-on practice in creating and tailoring electronic documents. Now though, you'll take a few minutes to look at the powerful new Organizer feature in Acrobat 7.0.

Using Organizer

Acrobat has always listed your most recently opened file at the bottom of the Acrobat File menu. In Acrobat 7.0, however, you have a far more powerful tool for locating and managing your files. Acrobat 7.0 offers the Organizer, which not only gives the history of PDF files you have accessed by date, but lets you group your PDF files into collections and favorites, and browse through documents page-by-page, without having to open them to find exactly what you're looking for.

When you've found the file you're looking for, you can use the buttons on the Organizer toolbar to open your file, print it, email it, or send it for review. You can even consolidate multiple PDF files into one PDF file from within Organizer. As you work through later lessons in this book, you'll learn more about the functions of the buttons on the Organizer toolbar. (These buttons work in the same way as the equivalent buttons in Acrobat.) In this lesson, you'll review the basics of the Organizer feature.

First you'll look at how you can use Organizer to give you fast and easy access to all of your PDF documents.

1 To open Organizer, click the Organizer button (⊞) on the Acrobat toolbar.

2 Select Today under History in the left pane.

The Organizer window has three panes:

• The Categories pane (on the left) that lists the files that you have opened recently (History), the files stored on your system, and collections of files that you create. You can't rename folders in the History section, Favorite Places, or My Computer. You can name collections, as you'll see shortly.

• The Files pane (in the center) lists all the files contained in any category you select in the Categories pane.

- The Pages pane (on the right) displays a thumbnail of each page of any document you select in the Files pane.

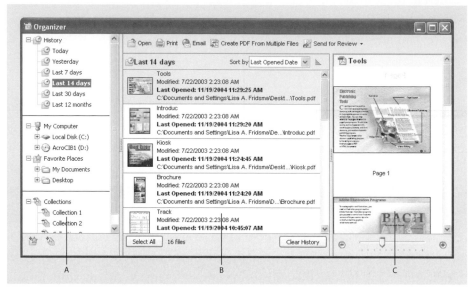

***A.** Categories pane   **B.** Files pane   **C.** Pages pane*

Using the History component to locate PDF files

First you'll look at the History component of the Categories pane.

1 Make sure that you have selected the Today label under History. You cannot edit or delete these History categories.

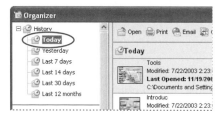

All the files that you opened in this lesson (assuming that you have worked through the lesson to this point) are listed in the Files pane, with the last file that you opened, Tools.pdf, listed first and highlighted. Look at the Pages pane. All the pages in the Tools.pdf file are shown as page thumbnails.

2 Drag the slider at the bottom of the Pages pane to enlarge or reduce the view. (You can also click the Zoom In and Zoom Out icons to achieve the same effect.) We dragged the slider to the left until all the pages were displayed without having to use the scroll bar.

3 Double click on any page in the Pages pane to open the Tools.pdf file at that page. In Acrobat, use the Next Page button (▶) on the Acrobat status bar to page through the document.

4 When you're finished, click the Organizer button (⊟) on the Acrobat toolbar to return to the Organizer.

You just opened a PDF file directly from the Pages pane of the Organizer. You can also open PDF files by double-clicking any file name in the File pane.

5 Click the arrow next to the Sort By button at the top of the Files pane to see the criteria that you can use to sort the files within your History category. Select Filename to list files alphabetically.

Now you'll see how you can use Organizer to quickly scan for a particular page in a file.

6 Since you are displaying Today's History, you're displaying all the files that you used today in the Files pane. To display all the pages of all the files that you used today in the Pages pane, click the Select All button at the bottom of the Files panel. Use the scroll bar to scroll through the pages. It may take a few moments for the display to catch up with the scroll bar, depending on your system.

7 Drag the pointer on the Zoom bar at the bottom of the Pages pane to reduce or magnify the view of the pages in the Pages pane.

8 When you are finished, in Acrobat, choose Window > Close All to close any files that you have opened.

The Clear History button clears the Files pane. This operation cannot be undone.

Creating a collection

Now you'll create a collection. A collection can be any number of PDF files, and the files do not have to be in the same folder or even on the same system. For the purpose of this lesson, you'll create a collection that contains all the files in the Lesson01 folder.

Organizer gives you several empty Collections icons to get you started. You can rename these collections or you can add new collections as necessary.

First you'll name your collection and then you'll add the files from the Lesson01 folder to the collection.

1 Right-click (Windows) or Control-click (Mac OS) on the Collection 1 icon. From the context menu, choose Rename Collection and type in a name for your new collection. We type in **My_Lesson_1.** Then click outside the Collection label.

2 Right-click (Windows) or Control-click (Mac OS) again on the Lesson 1 collection icon, and choose Add Files from the context menu.

3 In the Select Files to Add to Your Collection dialog box, navigate to the Lesson01 folder. Click on Introduc.pdf, and then click Add. (You cannot add folders.)

4 Right-click (Windows) or Control-click (Mac OS) again on the Lesson 1 collection icon again, and choose Add Files from the context menu. Open the Samples folder and Ctrl-click (Windows) or Command-click (Mac OS) on each file name in the Samples folder to select all the files listed, and then click Add again.

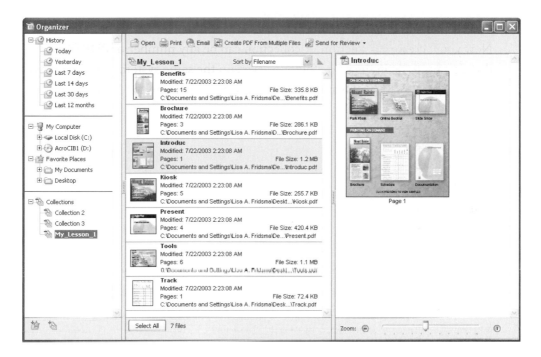

The Files pane lists the name, file size, number of pages, date last accessed, and physical location of each file that you added. (Files do not have to be on your system; they can be on a network or on the web.)

You can determine the actual physical location of a file in Windows Explorer or in the Finder by right-clicking (Windows) or Control-clicking (Mac OS) on the file icon in the Files pane, and choosing Show in Explorer (Windows) or Show in Finder (Mac OS).

You can add any other file or files to your collection from another location on your system by simply right-clicking (Windows) or Control-clicking (Mac OS) on the collection name (My_Lesson_1) in the Collections pane, and selecting Add Files from the context menu. Similarly you can delete files from a collection by selecting the file in the Files pane, right-clicking (Windows) or Control-clicking (Mac OS), and choosing Remove From <<*collection name*>> from the context menu.

5 When you're finished, click the close button in the Organizer window.

In this Classroom in a Book, the lesson files are organized in folders, so you don't need to use the capabilities of Organizer to keep track of your PDF lesson files. When you start creating your own PDF files and receiving files from other people, you'll find that Organizer is a powerful management tool.

6 Exit or Quit Acrobat.

Review questions

1 Describe some of the features of Acrobat 7.0.

2 How do electronic documents designed for printing differ from documents optimized for online use?

3 What kinds of media can you use to distribute PDF documents?

4 What kinds of fonts or typefaces and type sizes are best suited for onscreen display?

Review answers

1 Acrobat 7.0 Standard is used for creating, modifying, printing, and viewing PDF documents. Among the things you can do with Acrobat are add hyperlinks, electronic bookmarks, and page actions to PDF documents; add security to prevent users from copying text and graphics, printing a document, or even opening a file; digitally sign documents; and add comments and files, and markup text.

2 Documents designed for paper output are often longer, text-intensive documents. Online documents are preferably redesigned for optimal display on a monitor and may contain more graphics and screen based navigational features.

3 You can distribute PDF documents via floppy disk, CD, electronic mail, corporate intranet, or the World Wide Web. You can also print PDF documents and distribute them as printed documents.

4 Large fonts or typefaces with simple, clean shapes display most clearly on the screen. Sans serif fonts are more suitable than serif fonts, which contain embellishments more suitable for the printed page.

2 Getting to Know the Work Area

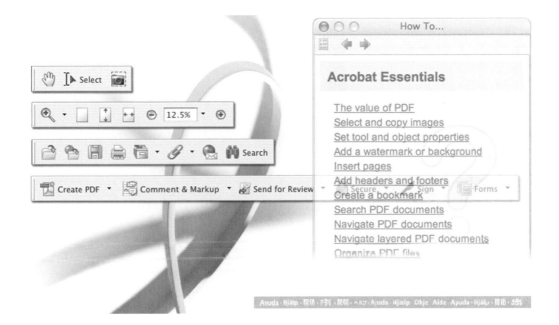

In this lesson, you'll familiarize yourself with the Complete Acrobat 7.0 Help, the Acrobat toolbars, and the Acrobat work area. You'll learn how to navigate through an Adobe PDF document, paging through an online document using controls built into Adobe Acrobat 7.0. You'll also get some tips on printing help topics.

In this lesson, you'll learn how to do the following:

- Work with Acrobat tools and the navigation pane.
- Page through an Adobe PDF document using Acrobat's built-in navigational controls.
- Change how an Adobe PDF document scrolls and displays in the document window.
- Change the magnification of a view.
- Retrace your viewing path through a document.
- Use the Complete Acrobat 7.0 Help and the How To pages.

This lesson will take about 60 minutes to complete.

If needed, remove the previous lesson folder from your hard drive and copy the Lesson02 folder onto it.

Note: *Windows 2000 users may need to unlock the lesson files before using them. For information, see "Copying the Classroom in a Book files" on page 4.*

Opening the work file

You'll practice navigating through a PDF version of a document. This document was created using Adobe FrameMaker® and then converted to Adobe PDF.

1 Start Acrobat.

2 Choose File > Open. Select Illus_Excerpt.pdf in the Lesson02 folder, and click Open. Then choose File > Save As, rename the file **Illus_Excerpt1.pdf**, and save it in the Lesson02 folder.

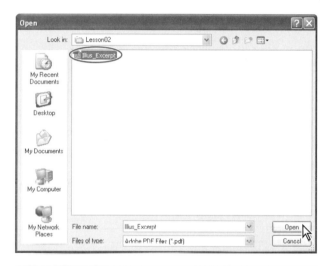

On Windows

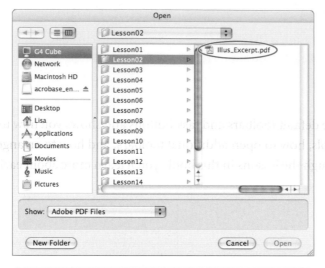

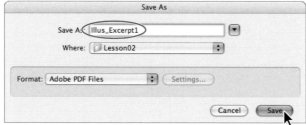

On Mac OS

Using the Acrobat tools, toolbars, and task buttons

When you first launch Acrobat, a default set of toolbars and task buttons are displayed. The toolbars contain commonly used tools and commands for managing your Adobe PDF files, scrolling, zooming, selecting text and images, and rotating pages. Task buttons on the toolbar give you access to additional commands and toolbars.

This section introduces the default toolbars and task buttons and shows you how to select tools, including hidden tools, how to open additional toolbars, and how to arrange the toolbars. As you work through the lessons in this book, you'll learn more about each tool's specific function.

The majority of tools, toolbars, and task buttons are available in both Acrobat Professional and Acrobat Standard. If a particular tool, toolbar, or task button is available only in Acrobat Professional, this information will be highlighted in a note of this type. This type of note will also be used to identify differences in features between Acrobat Professional and Acrobat Standard.

Reviewing the toolbars

To see the name of a toolbar, position the pointer over the toolbar's separator bar. The separator bar is located at the beginning of each toolbar.

Separator bar   *Toolbar name*

The basic toolbars—File, Tasks, Basic, Zoom, Rotate View, Search the Internet, and Help, are described below.

The File toolbar contains the Open, Create PDF from Web Page, Save, Print, Organizer, Attach a File, Email, and Search buttons.

Click the arrow next to the Organizer or Attach a File button to see a menu of commands, associated tools, and toolbars.

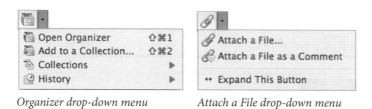

Organizer drop-down menu   *Attach a File drop-down menu*

The Tasks toolbar contains the Create PDF, Comment & Markup, Send for Review, Secure, Sign, and Picture Tasks buttons. (The Picture Tasks button is only available when you open documents that contains pictures created with the Adobe Photoshop® family of products, or when you open a PDF file created by Acrobat from a JPEG source file.)

The Forms task button is available in Acrobat Professional only, and only users of Acrobat Professional can create forms. Users of Adobe Reader and Acrobat Standard can fill in forms. Users of Acrobat Standard can save completed forms. (Users of Adobe Reader can save filled-in forms if the creator of the form assigned special rights to the form.)

Click the arrow next to any task button, such as the Create PDF button, on the Acrobat toolbar to show a menu of commands, associated tools, toolbars, and links to the How To pages for that task.

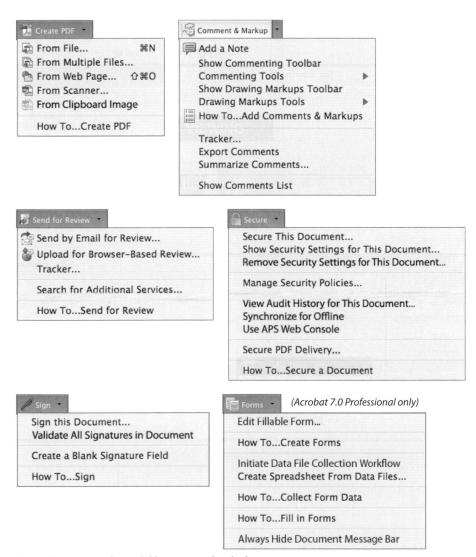

Note: *The commands available may vary by platform.*

The Basic toolbar contains the Hand, Select, and Snapshot tools.

The Zoom toolbar contains the Zoom In and hidden zoom tools, Actual Size, Fit Page, and Fit Width buttons, the Zoom Out button, the magnification menu, and the Zoom In button.

The Loupe tool ( ) and the Pan & Zoom window ( ) on the Zoom In menu are available in Acrobat Professional only.

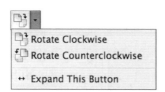

The Rotate View toolbar contains the Rotate Clockwise and Rotate Counterclockwise tools.

The Search the Internet Using Yahoo toolbar

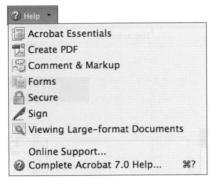

*The Help task button lists the help topic
areas and links to online support and online help.*

Selecting tools

The default tool in Acrobat is the Hand tool (🖐).

1 To select a different tool, you click the tool icon in the toolbar. A selected tool usually remains active until you select a different tool.

2 Click the Actual Size button (▢) to display the page at 100%.

3 Click the Zoom In tool (🔍). Notice that when you move the pointer into the document pane, the pointer changes to a magnifying glass (🔍).

4 Click anywhere in the document pane. The view of the document is magnified.

5 Click the arrow next to the Zoom In tool, and select the Zoom Out tool (🔍).

6 Click in the document pane again. The view of the document returns to 100%.

💡 *The presence of an arrow or small triangle to the right of a tool icon indicates the presence of hidden tools. Click the small triangle next to a tool name to reveal the hidden tools. Click outside the drop-down menu to close the menu without selecting a tool.*

You can also zoom in and out using the Zoom In and Zoom Out buttons on the Zoom toolbar. With these buttons, the magnification changes by a preset amount with each click.

*Clicking the Zoom In and Zoom Out
buttons changes the magnification by a
preset amount.*

7 Click the Zoom Out button once, and note the change in the magnification value.

8 Click the Zoom Out button again to decrease the magnification.

9 Now click the Zoom In button twice to return to a magnification of 100%.

The Zoom In and Zoom Out tools offer greater control over the area to be magnified and the level of the magnification. The Zoom In and Zoom Out buttons offer useful shortcuts for increasing and decreasing the degree of magnification. You'll learn more about page view magnification later in this lesson (see "Changing the page view magnification").

💡 *You can temporarily revert to the Hand tool while you have another tool selected by pressing the space bar. When you release the space bar, your other tool is the selected tool again.*

10 Select the Hand tool.

Using the Tools menu

You can also access hidden tools using the Tools menu. In the prior section, you used the arrow next to the Zoom In tool (🔍) to reveal the Zoom Out tool (🔍). Now you'll use the Tools menu to access the same tool.

1 Choose Tools > Zoom > Zoom Out. When you move the pointer into the document pane, the hand changes to the magnifying glass containing a minus sign.

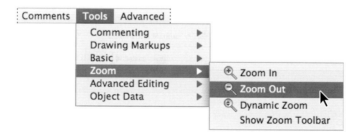

2 Select the Hand tool (✋).

Take a few minutes to explore some of the tools you can access from the Tools menu. The Tools menu offers a convenient way to access many of the hidden tools without crowding the toolbar area with unnecessary toolbars. When you are finished, be sure to reselect the Hand tool.

Docking toolbars

You can display hidden tools in a toolbar and dock the toolbar in the main toolbar area.

1 Click on the arrow next to the Zoom Out tool (![magnifying glass icon]). When the list of additional tools appears, click Show Zoom Toolbar.

The Zoom tools are displayed on a floating toolbar. You can leave the floating toolbar as is, or dock it with the other toolbars.

2 To dock a floating toolbar, drag it by its separator bar or title bar and drop it in the toolbar area.

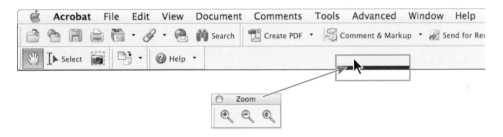

You can drag toolbars to a new location in the toolbar area. You can also drag toolbars from the toolbar area into the document pane or navigation pane. The toolbar area holds up to three rows of toolbars.

Practice moving toolbars in and out of the toolbar area.

🔆 *If your toolbar area becomes cluttered as you expand some of the hidden toolbars, you can create more space by hiding the tool button labels. Choose View > Toolbars > Show Button Labels to hide or show all the labels or to restore the default labels. Acrobat also automatically hides labels selectively as the toolbar area becomes full.*

Using keyboard shortcuts to select tools

You can set your Acrobat preferences so that you can use a keyboard shortcut to select a tool.

1. Choose Edit > Preferences (Windows) or Acrobat > Preferences (Mac OS), and select General in the left pane.

2. Click the check box next to the Use Single-Key Accelerators to Access Tools option. A checkmark appears in the box when this option is selected.

3. Click OK to apply the change.

Now when you position the cursor over a tool, you'll see a letter in parentheses following the tool name. This is the keyboard shortcut for that tool.

4. With the Hand tool selected, move the cursor over the Zoom In tool and notice that the tooltip now contains the letter "Z." This is the keyboard shortcut.

5. Move the cursor into the document pane, and press "Z" on the keyboard. The cursor changes from a hand to a zoom tool.

6. Click the Hand tool or press H on the keyboard to return to the Hand tool.

Customizing toolbars

You can customize your toolbars, putting the ones you use most frequently together in the most convenient location.

1 To hide a toolbar, make sure that you have the Hand tool (✋) selected, and then choose View > Toolbars, and choose a name of a toolbar (such as Basic) from the menu. A checkmark appears next to the name of any toolbar that is currently visible. Selecting a checked toolbar name hides that toolbar. Selecting an unchecked toolbar name displays that toolbar. Try hiding and showing different toolbar combinations.

You can also show or hide a toolbar by right-clicking (Windows) or Control-clicking (Mac OS) in the toolbar area, and then selecting the toolbar name from the context menu.

2 To show the Basic toolbar again (if you hid it in step 1), right-click (Windows) or Control-click (Mac OS) in the toolbar area and choose Basic from the menu.

3 To move a toolbar, drag it by the separator bar. Release the mouse button when the toolbar is located in its new position. Try dragging a toolbar to another location in the toolbar area or into the document pane. For example, drag a toolbar from the upper row to the lower row. Then drag the bar back to its original location and reattach it.

Locking toolbars

If you customize the arrangement of toolbars in the toolbar area, you can save your arrangement by locking the toolbars. Locking the toolbars preserves your arrangement, even after you close and restart Acrobat. (You cannot lock the position of a floating toolbar.)

1 To preserve the arrangement of toolbars in the toolbar area, choose View > Toolbars > Lock Toolbars.

When toolbars are locked, the separator bars are hidden. We recommend that you don't lock toolbar configurations until you're confident of the toolbars that you'll use most often.

2 To unlock toolbars, choose View > Toolbars > Lock Toolbars again.

Resetting toolbars

After you have rearranged the toolbars, you can revert to the Acrobat default toolbar arrangement any time by choosing View > Toolbars > Reset Toolbars.

Experiment with expanding and collapsing toolbars, and repositioning them.

When you're finished with this section, we recommend that you reset the toolbars before continuing.

Using the navigation pane and tabs

Acrobat provides a navigation pane that helps you organize and keep track of a document's bookmarks, page thumbnails, comments, signatures, and attachments, for example, in a series of tabs. Tabs can be docked inside the navigation pane or floated over the work area. They can also be grouped with other tabs. This section introduces the navigation pane and shows you how to display tabs. As you work through later lessons in this book, you'll learn more about each tab's specific function.

Displaying the navigation pane and tabs

You can display the navigation pane and its tabs in a variety of ways. Experiment with these techniques:

• To show the navigation pane as you work, click the tab that you want to view, or click on the vertical bar that separates the document pane from the tab display. To close the navigation pane, click the active tab (the tab that you are currently viewing), or click on the vertical separator bar between the navigation pane and the document pane.

• To show or hide a tab, choose the tab's name from the View > Navigation Tabs menu. If the navigation pane is closed, no names are checked on the menu. If the navigation pane is open, the name of the tab that is currently active is checked.

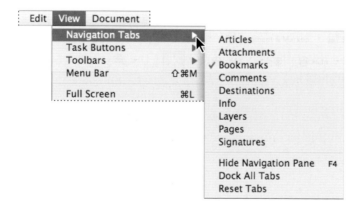

Changing the navigation pane display

You can change the navigation pane display in a variety of ways.

If necessary, click the separator bar to open the navigation pane, and then experiment with several techniques for changing the display of the navigation pane:

• To change the width of the navigation pane while it's visible, drag the vertical separator bar between the document pane and the navigation pane.

• To bring a tab to the front of a group of tabs, click the tab's name.

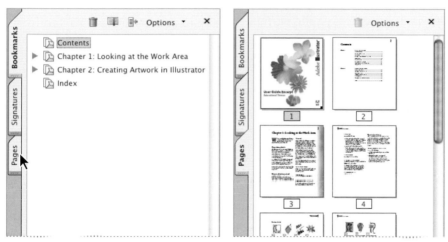

Click a tab to bring it to the front.

• To move a tab to its own floating window, drag the tab into the document pane. To return the tab to the navigation pane, drag the tab back into the navigation pane.

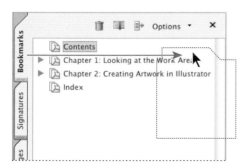

- To display the Options menu for a tab, click the Options button at the top of the tab. Then drag down to select a command. To hide the Options menu without making a selection, click anywhere in the blank space in the navigation pane.

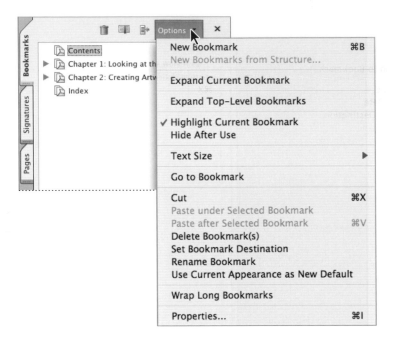

💡 *The Comments List in the Comments tab has a unique set of buttons and commands that help you manage comments in a PDF document. For information on using this tab, see Lesson 10, "Using Acrobat in a Document Review Cycle." The Attachments tab lists any files attached to the PDF.*

Using context menus

In addition to menus at the top of your screen, context menus display commands relevant to the active tool, selection, or tab.

1 If necessary, click on the vertical separator bar between the navigation pane and the document pane to open the navigation pane, and click the Bookmarks tab.

2 Position the pointer over the Contents bookmark in the Bookmarks tab and right-click (Windows) or Control-click (Mac OS). After you have looked at the commands available in the context menu, click in a blank area anywhere outside the context menu to close it without choosing a command. You'll learn more about these commands in later lessons.

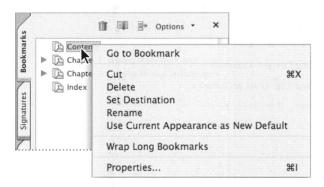

About the onscreen display

Take a look at the Zoom toolbar located at the top of the document window.

The magnification shown in the Zoom toolbar does not refer to the printed size of the page, but rather to how the page is displayed onscreen. Acrobat determines the onscreen display of a page by treating the page as a 72 ppi (pixels-per-inch) image. For example, if your page has a print size of 2-by-2 inches, Acrobat treats the page as if it were 144 pixels wide and 144 pixels high (72 x 2 = 144). At 100% view, each pixel in the page is represented by 1 screen pixel on your monitor.

To see the printed size of your page, move your cursor into the bottom left of the document pane.

How large the page actually appears onscreen depends on your monitor size and your monitor resolution setting. For example, when you increase the resolution of your monitor, you increase the number of screen pixels within the same monitor area. This results in smaller screen pixels and a smaller displayed page, since the number of pixels in the page itself stays constant. The following illustration shows the variation among 100% displays of the same page on different monitors.

Pixel dimensions and monitor resolution

Regardless of the print size specified for an image, the size of an image onscreen is determined by the pixel dimensions of the image and the monitor size and setting. A large monitor set to 640-by-480 pixels uses larger pixels than a small monitor with the same setting. In most cases, default PC monitor settings display 96 pixels per inch, and default Macintosh monitor settings display approximately 72 pixels per inch.

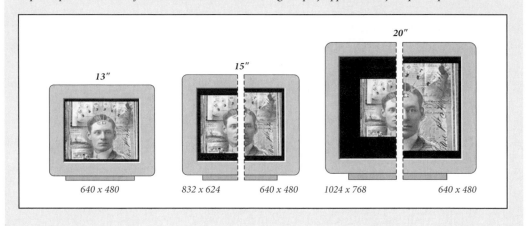

Setting up a work area

As you become more familiar with Acrobat, you'll want to rearrange your toolbars so that the tools you use most often are always close at hand and the tabs in the navigation pane are arranged for easy access.

Organizing the toolbars

You'll start work with the default toolbar arrangement. As you progress through the lessons, you'll open and close additional toolbars as needed.

1 Choose View > Toolbars > Reset Toolbars to return to the default toolbar configuration.

If the Reset Toolbars command is grayed out, check that you don't have your toolbars locked. The toolbars should *not* be locked while you are working on these lessons.

2 Choose View > Toolbars > Show Button Labels, and verify that there is a check mark next to the Default Labels command. The tool button labels should be visible.

Using the navigation controls in the status bar

Acrobat provides a variety of ways for you to move through and adjust the magnification of a PDF document. For example, you can scroll through the document using the scroll bar at the right side of the window, or you can turn pages as in a traditional book using the navigation controls in the status bar at the bottom of the document window. You can also jump to a specific page using the status bar at the bottom of the window or the page thumbnails in the Pages tab.

You can add a Navigation toolbar to the toolbar area by choosing View > Toolbars > Navigation, and then docking the Navigation toolbar in the toolbar area.

Browsing the document

1 If needed, click the vertical separator bar between the navigation pane and the document pane or click the current tab to hide the navigation pane. And if you're not on the first page of the document, click the First Page button (◄) in the status bar.

2 Click the Fit Width button (↔) to resize your page to fit the width of your screen.

3 Make sure that the Single Page button (▫) on the status bar is selected.

4 With the Hand tool (✋) selected in the toolbar, position your pointer over the document. Hold down the mouse button. Notice that the hand pointer changes to a closed hand when you hold down the mouse button.

5 Drag the closed hand up and down in the window to move the page up and down on the screen. This is similar to moving a piece of paper around on a desktop.

Drag with Hand tool to move page.   *Result*

6 Press Enter or Return to display the next part of the page. You can press Enter or Return repeatedly to view the document from start to finish in screen-sized sections.

7 Click the Fit Page button (⬍) to display the entire page in the window. If needed, click the First Page button to go back to page 1.

8 Position the pointer over the down arrow in the scroll bar, and click once.

The document scrolls automatically to display all of page 2. In the next few steps, you'll control how PDF pages scroll and display.

9 Click the Continuous button (▤) in the status bar, and then use the scroll bar to scroll to page 3 of 54.

The Continuous option displays pages end to end like frames in a filmstrip.

10 Now click the Continuous - Facing button (⊞) in the status bar to display page spreads, with left- and right-hand pages facing each other, as on a layout board.

Continuous option   *Continuous - Facing option*

11 Click the First Page button (|◄) to go back to the beginning of the document.

In keeping with the conventions of printed books, a PDF document always begins with a right-hand page.

12 Click the Single Page button (□) to return to the original page layout.

You can use the page box in the status bar to switch directly to a specific page.

13 Move the pointer over the page box until it changes to an I-beam, and drag across to highlight the current page number.

14 Type **15** to replace the current page number, and press Enter or Return.

You should now be viewing page 15.

The scroll bar also lets you navigate to a specific page.

15 Begin dragging the scroll box upward in the scroll bar. As you drag, a page status box appears. When page 3 appears in the status box, release the mouse.

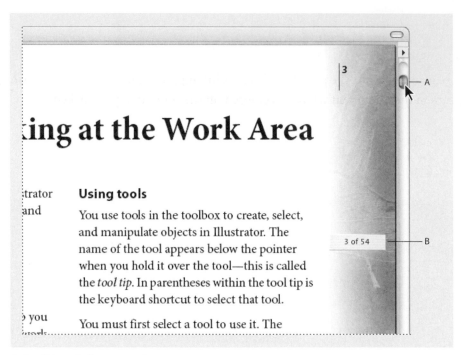

*A. Scroll box **B.** Page status box*

You should now be back at the beginning of Chapter 1 in the document.

Browsing with page thumbnails

Page thumbnails are miniature previews of your document pages that are displayed in the Pages tab, which is docked in the navigation pane to the left of the document pane.

In this part of the lesson, you'll use page thumbnails to navigate and change the view of pages. In Lesson 7, "Modifying PDF Files," you'll learn how to use page thumbnails to reorder pages in a document.

1 Click the Fit Width button ( ) to view the full width of the page. You should still be looking at page 3.

2 Click the Pages tab in the navigation pane to open the Pages tab and bring it to the front.

Page thumbnails for every page in the document are displayed automatically in the navigation pane. The page thumbnails represent both the content and page orientation of the pages in the document. Page-number boxes appear beneath each page thumbnail.

You may need to use the scroll bar to view all the page thumbnails.

3 Click the page 5 thumbnail to go to page 5.

The page number for the page thumbnail is highlighted, and a full-width view of page 5 appears in the document window, centered on the point that you clicked.

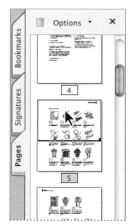 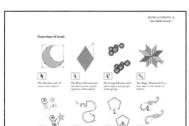

Take a look at the page 5 thumbnail. The rectangle inside the page thumbnail, called the page-view box, represents the area displayed in the current page view. You can use the page-view box to adjust the area and magnification being viewed.

4 Position the pointer over the lower right corner of the page view box. Notice that the pointer turns into a double-headed arrow.

5 Drag to shrink the page-view box, and release the mouse button. Take a look at the Zoom toolbar and notice that the magnification level has changed to accommodate the smaller area being viewed.

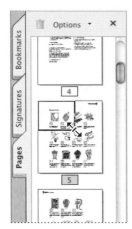
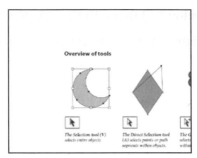

Drag lower right corner of page-view box up and to the left.   *Result*

6 Now position the pointer over the bottom border of the page-view box. Notice that the pointer changes to a hand.

7 Drag the page-view box within the page thumbnail, and watch the view change in the document window.

8 Drag the page-view box down to focus your view at the bottom of the page.

Page thumbnails provide a convenient way to monitor and adjust your page view in a document.

9 Click the Pages tab to hide the navigation pane.

Changing the page view magnification

You can change the magnification of the page view using controls in the toolbar, or by clicking or dragging in the page with the Zoom In tool ( ) or Zoom Out tool ( ).

1 Click the Fit Width button ( ). A new magnification appears in the Zoom toolbar.

2 Click the Previous Page button ( ) twice to move to page 3. Notice that the magnification remains the same.

3 Click the Actual Size button ( ) to return the page to a 100% view.

4 Click the arrow to the right of the magnification pop-up menu in the Zoom toolbar to display the preset magnification options. Drag to choose 200% for the magnification.

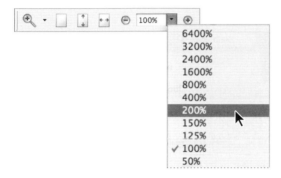

You can also enter a specific value for the magnification.

5 Move the pointer over the magnification box in the Zoom toolbar, and double-click to highlight the current magnification.

6 Type 75 to replace the current magnification, and press Enter or Return.

Double-click to highlight magnification.   *Type in new magnification, and press Enter or Return.*

7 Now click the Actual Size button (☐) to display the page at 100% again.

Next you'll use the Zoom In tool to magnify a specific portion of a page.

8 Select the page number in the status bar at the bottom of the document pane, and type 5, and press Enter or Return to go to page 5. Then click to select the Zoom In tool (🔍) in the toolbar.

9 Click once in the top right section of the page to increase the magnification. Notice that the view centers around the point you clicked. Click in the top right section of the page once more to increase the magnification again.

10 Hold down Ctrl (Windows) or Option (Mac OS). Notice that the zoom pointer now appears with a minus sign, indicating that the Zoom Out tool (🔍) is active.

11 With Ctrl or Option held down, click in the document to decrease the magnification. Ctrl-click or Option-click once more to decrease the magnification again, and then release Ctrl or Option.

The page should be displayed at 100% again.

Now you'll drag the Zoom In tool to magnify the image.

12 Position the pointer near the top left of the image, and drag over the page as shown in the following illustration.

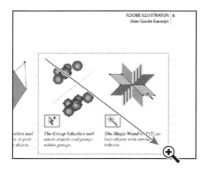

Marquee-zooming

The view zooms in on the area you enclosed. This is called *marquee-zooming*.

13 Click the Fit Page button( ).

Using the Dynamic Zoom tool

The Dynamic Zoom tool lets you zoom in or out by dragging the mouse up or down.

1 Click the arrow next to the Zoom In tool, and choose Dynamic Zoom from the menu.

2 Click in the document pane, and drag upward to magnify the view, and drag down to reduce the view.

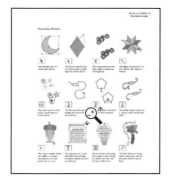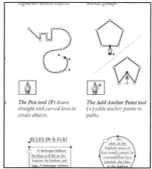

3 When you're finished, click the Hand tool, and then click the Fit Page button ( ).

You can switch from the Zoom In or Zoom Out tool to the Dynamic Zoom tool by pressing the Shift key. When you release the Shift key, you switch back to the Zoom In or Zoom Out tool.

For information on using the Loupe tool and the Pan & Zoom window, see Lesson 13, "Using Acrobat's Engineering and Technical Features."

Following links

In a PDF document, you don't always have to view pages in sequence. You can jump immediately from one section of a document to another using custom navigational aids such as links.

One benefit of placing a document online is that you can convert traditional cross-references into links, which users can use to jump directly to the referenced section or file. For example, you can make each item under the Contents list into a link that jumps to its corresponding section. You can also use links to add interactivity to traditional book elements such as glossaries and indexes. In this lesson you'll follow links; in later lessons, you'll create links.

Now you'll try out an existing link.

1 Click the Previous Page button (◀) in the status bar as many times as necessary to return to the Contents page (page 2).

2 Move the pointer over the Creating Artwork in Illustrator heading in the Contents. The Hand tool changes to a pointing finger, indicating the presence of a link. Click to follow the link.

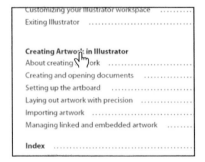

This entry links to the chapter on Creating Artwork in Illustrator.

3 Click the Previous View button (⊙) to return to your previous view of the Contents.

You can click the Previous View button at any time to retrace your viewing path through a document. The Next View button (⊙) lets you reverse the action of your last Previous View.

In this section, you have learned how to page through a PDF document, change the magnification and page layout mode, and follow links. In later lessons, you'll learn how to create links and create and use other navigational features, such as bookmarks, page thumbnails, and articles.

Printing PDF files

When you print Adobe PDF files, you'll find that many of the options in the Acrobat Print dialog box are the same as those found in the Print dialog boxes of other popular applications. For example, the Acrobat Print dialog box, lets you print a page, an entire file, or a range of pages within a PDF file. (On Windows, you can also choose print from the context menu.)

Here's how you can print non-contiguous pages or portions of pages in Acrobat.

1 In the Illus_Excerpt1.pdf document, click the Pages tab if necessary and click the page thumbnails corresponding to the pages you want to print. You can Ctrl-click (Windows) or Command-click (Mac OS) page thumbnails to select non-contiguous pages, or Shift-click to select contiguous pages.

2 If you have a printer attached to your system and turned on, choose File > Print. Make sure the name of the printer attached to your system is displayed. If you have selected pages in the Pages tab, the Selected Pages option will be selected automatically in the Print dialog box.

3 Click OK or Print to print your selected pages. Click Cancel to abort the printing operation.

4 Click the Pages tab to close the navigation pane.

If you have an Internet connection and a web browser installed on your system, you can click Printing Tips in the Print dialog box to go to the Adobe website for the latest trouble-shooting help on printing.

For information on printing comments, see Lesson 10, "Using Acrobat in a Document Review Cycle."

If your PDF file contains odd-sized pages, you can use the Page Scaling option in the Print dialog box. The Fit to Printer Margins option scales each page to fit the printer page size. Pages in the PDF file are magnified or reduced as necessary. The Tiling options print oversize pages on several pages that can be assembled to reproduce the oversize image.

Printing over the Internet

You can send Adobe PDF documents to printers and fax machines in the PrintMe network or securely store PDF files online for on-demand printing.

To print over the Internet:

1. Save the document, and then choose File > PrintMe Internet Printing.

2. Follow the instructions in the URL provided.

—From the Complete Acrobat 7.0 Help.

Opening the How To pages

In this section of the lesson, you'll learn how to open the How To pages when you need information on a feature or when you need help with the steps for completing a task.

1 To open the How To pages, choose Help > How To, and select a topic area from the menu. We selected Acrobat Essentials.

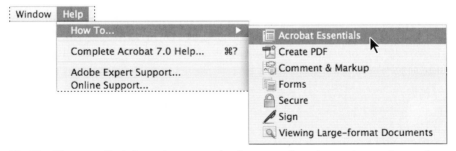

The How To pages offer information on popular features and step-by-step instructions on how to complete common tasks.

The Acrobat Essentials How To page opens to the right of the document pane and displays a list of topics on which help is available. To get information on a listed topic, simply click the link for that topic.

2 To get information on how to create a bookmark, click the Create a Bookmark link.

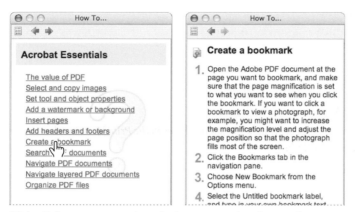

Click a link to get an overview of a feature or review the steps for completing a task.

You'll learn more about creating bookmarks in Lesson 7, "Modifying PDF Files."

Notice that after the step-by-step instructions, the How To page gives additional links to the section on creating bookmarks in the Complete Help and to a related Help topic, Magnifying and Reducing the View.

If you want the How To pages to open each time you launch Acrobat, make sure the Show How To Window at Startup option on the How To home page is selected. To return to the How To home page, click the How To ... Home Page button ( ) on the How To toolbar. The option is selected when the box contains a check mark.

Now you'll see how easy it is to open and use the Acrobat online Help.

Linking to the online Help

1 Click the "<u>Creating bookmarks</u> in complete Help" link towards the bottom of the How To page.

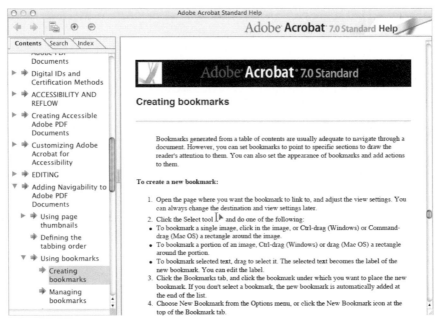

The How To pages have direct links to the Complete Acrobat 7.0 Help.

The online Help opens (in a separate window) at the Creating Bookmarks topic.

You'll learn how to use the online Help later in this lesson (see "Using the Complete Acrobat 7.0 Help" in this lesson). For now, you'll close the online Help and return to the How To pages.

2 Click the Close button to close the online Help.

Navigating the How To pages

The How To pages have their own navigation bar at the top of the page. You'll use this navigation bar to return to the list of How To topics.

1 In the How To navigation bar, click the Back button ( ).

Now you're back at the list of topics available under Acrobat Essentials. However, Acrobat Essentials is only one of several topics for which there are How To pages.

2 Click the Home Page button ( ) to return to the list of topic areas.

You can use the Back or Forward buttons to retrace your path through the How To pages at any time. Note, however, that anytime you click the Home Page button, you erase the Back/Forward history.

3 Click the Comment & Markup link to see the list of related How To pages.

The How To page opens and displays a list of tasks related to reviewing and commenting. Use the scroll bar on the right of the How To pages to scroll down the list if necessary.

4 Under the Create Comments heading on the How To pages, click the Add a Note Comment link.

5 Click the Back button ( ) at the top of the How To page once to return to the complete list of commenting and markup topics. Click the Forward button ( ) to return to the steps explaining how to add a note comment.

Use the Back and Forward buttons to navigate through the How To pages.

Add a note comment if you wish, using the steps on the How To page to guide you.

6 If you've added a comment, you can right-click (Windows) or Control-click (Mac OS) the note, and choose Delete or Delete Comment to remove the comment.

The step-by-step procedures presented in the How To pages provide limited background information on procedures. For more in-depth information, you should always use the Complete Acrobat 7.0 Help.

Closing the How To pages

1 When you've finished experimenting, click the Home Page button ( ) at the top of the How To pages.

Clicking the Home Page button always returns you to the primary list of topic areas, which also contains the link to the complete help system.

2 Click the Hide button on Windows or the Close button on Mac OS to close the How To pages.

3 If necessary, click the Close button on the Commenting toolbar to close the toolbar.

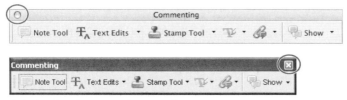

Click the Close button to close a toolbar.

Using the Complete Acrobat 7.0 Help

This book and the lessons in this book focus on commonly used tools and features of Acrobat 7.0. You can get complete information on all the Acrobat tools, commands, and features for both Windows and Mac OS systems from the Complete Acrobat 7.0 Help, an accessible HTML-based help system. The Complete Acrobat 7.0 Help is easy to use because you can look for topics in several ways:

- Scan the table of contents.

- Search for keywords.

- Use the index.

- Jump from topic to topic using related topics links.

Opening the Complete Acrobat 7.0 Help

1 Choose Help > Complete Acrobat 7.0 Help, or click the Help button on the Acrobat toolbar and choose Complete Acrobat 7.0 Help from the menu.

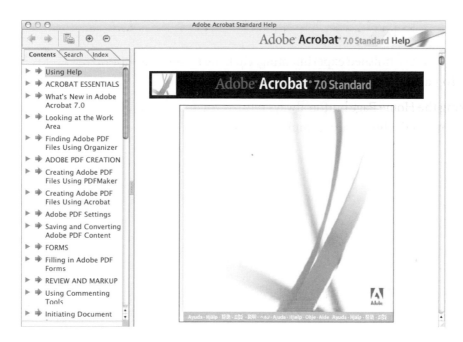

Acrobat Help opens in your browser. The help content is displayed in the right panel—the topic frame; the navigation information is displayed in the left panel—the navigation frame.

2 Click the Using Help link in the navigation pane to see the topic pages on how to use the Complete Acrobat 7.0 Help.

3 Click the Using Acrobat Online link in the navigation pane to read about the type of help you can get from the Adobe website.

4 Click the Zoom In button (⊕) at the top of the navigation frame to enlarge the image area if necessary.

You can drag the Help screen around on your desktop (using the title bar), and you can resize the Help screen on Windows by dragging any corner or on Mac OS by dragging the bottom right corner.

5 When you are finished reading the information, click the Previous Topic button (◀) in your browser as required to return to the first page of the help system.

6 Click the Using Help bookmark in the Contents panel to see the help topics available. Clicking a link automatically expands the link in the navigation frame.

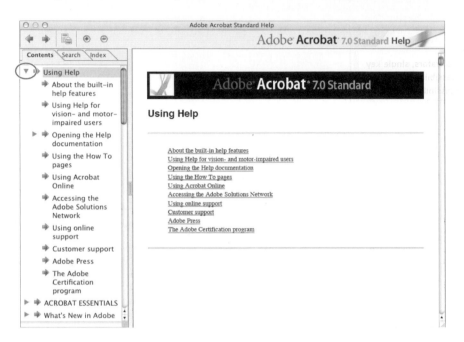

7 Use the scroll bar on the right of the navigation frame to scroll through the headings. Click on any of these major topic headings to open a list of secondary topic headings in the topic frame.

You can collapse or expand any topic listing in the Contents navigation frame.

If you can't find the topic you need in the Contents tab, try using the index.

Using the index

1 Click the Index tab in the navigation frame.

2 You can use the scroll bar in the navigation frame to move through the index, or you can start to type your keyword or keywords into the text box. We typed in **watermarks**.

Notice how the display moves to display entries that correspond to the letter sequence that you are typing in.

3 Click the plus sign or arrow next to the "watermarks" entry to expand the entry. Then expand the "adding" entry. Click the entry "Adding watermarks and backgrounds." You may need to scroll down the list to see the expanded index entry.

The topic frame displays the information on adding watermarks and backgrounds.

Using the Search feature

If you can't find the information that you need using the Contents listing or the Index, you can use the Search feature.

1 Click the Search tab at the top of the navigation frame to start a search.

2 Type in the word or words you want to search for. We typed in **Multiple Files** because we want to know more about the commands under the Create PDF button (▨).

Note: The search is not case-sensitive.

If you use multiple words in the search field, the search results will return all topics that contain one or all the search words. For this reason, you should be as precise as possible about the search word or phrase that you use.

3 Click the Search button.

The search results are listed in the navigation frame.

The search may take a few seconds to complete.

4 Move your pointer over the first topic listed, "Creating Adobe PDF files from multiple files." The topic looks promising, so click the link to view the help topic. Occurrences of the search word or words are highlighted.

You can view the help topics onscreen, or you can print them.

Printing help topics

1 To print a help topic, simply click the Print Topic button (📑) on the Help toolbar, and click the Print button or OK button in the Print dialog box.

2 Click the browser Close button to close the online Help.

3 Exit or quit Acrobat.

Printing the complete online Help

Your Acrobat application CD contains an Adobe PDF file of the complete Acrobat 7.0 online help in a printable format. You can print a page, a range of pages, or the entire file.

Now that you're familiar with the Acrobat work area, you can move through the lessons in this book and learn how to create and work with Adobe PDF files.

Review questions

1 How do you select a hidden tool?

2 Name several ways in which you can move to a different page.

3 Name several ways in which you can change the view magnification.

4 How do you reset the toolbars to their default configuration?

5 How would you find a topic in the Complete Acrobat 7.0 Help?

Review answers

1 Do one of the following:

• Select a hidden tool by holding down the mouse button on the arrow or triangle next to the related tool until the additional tools appear, and then drag to the tool you want.

• Choose Tools, and choose the appropriate category from the menu. Then choose the tool from the listing.

• Display the expanded toolbar by holding down the mouse button on the arrow or triangle next to the tool, and then choosing the command to show the toolbar or expand the button.

2 You can move to a different page by clicking the Previous Page or Next Page button in the status bar; dragging the scroll box in the scroll bar; highlighting the page box in the status bar and entering a page number; or clicking a bookmark, page thumbnail, or link that jumps to a different page.

3 You can change the view magnification by clicking the Actual Size, Fit Page, or Fit Width buttons in the toolbar; marquee-zooming with the Zoom In or Zoom Out tool; choosing a preset magnification from the magnification menu in the Zoom toolbar; or highlighting the entry in the magnification box and entering a specific percentage.

4 Choose View > Toolbars > Reset Toolbars.

5 You can look for a topic using the Acrobat 7.0 online Help contents listing. You can also look in the index using keywords, and you can search for words or phrases in the Complete Acrobat 7.0 Help using the Search command.

3w | Converting Microsoft Office Files (Windows)

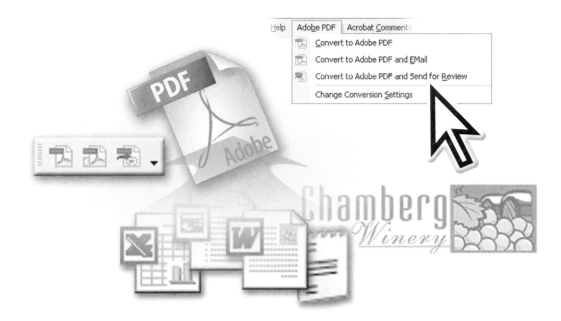

Acrobat is designed to work efficiently with your Microsoft Office applications. You can create Adobe PDF files and email them without ever leaving your Microsoft application. Friends and colleagues can open your documents reliably, regardless of what platform they work on. If Microsoft Outlook is your email program, you can convert emails and folders of emails to Adobe PDF.

This lesson is designed for Windows users who have Microsoft Office applications such as Microsoft Word, Microsoft PowerPoint, Microsoft Excel, and Microsoft Outlook installed on their computer. You need to have one or more of these applications installed on your system to use this lesson. If you do not use these Microsoft Office applications, you should skip this lesson and move on to Lesson 4, "Converting Other File Types to Adobe PDF."

For information on converting files in other Microsoft applications such as Internet Explorer, Microsoft Project, and Microsoft Visio to Adobe PDF, see Lesson 5, "Creating Adobe PDF from Web Pages" and Lesson 13, "Using Acrobat's Engineering and Technical Features."

In this lesson, you'll learn how to do the following:

- Convert a Microsoft Word file to Adobe PDF.
- Convert Word headings and styles to Adobe PDF bookmarks.
- Convert Word comments to Adobe PDF notes.
- Add password protection to your Adobe PDF files.
- Change the Adobe PDF conversion settings.
- Convert a Microsoft Excel file and send it for review online.
- Convert a file and attach it to an email in Microsoft Outlook.

This lesson will take about 60 minutes to complete.

If needed, remove the previous lesson folder from your hard drive, and copy the Lesson03\Win folder onto it.

Note: *Windows 2000 users may need to unlock the lesson files before using them. For information, see "Copying the Classroom in a Book files" on page 4.*

About PDFMaker

PDFMaker, which is installed automatically when you install Acrobat, is used to create Adobe PDF files from within Microsoft applications. Convert to Adobe PDF buttons and an Adobe PDF menu are added automatically to the Microsoft toolbars and menu bars. You use this Adobe PDF menu and these buttons to control the settings used in the conversion to Adobe PDF, to email your PDF file, and to set up an email review process without ever leaving your Microsoft application. For complete information on which Microsoft applications are supported and which versions of the Microsoft applications are supported, visit the Adobe website (www.adobe.com).

PDF files created using PDFMaker are often substantially smaller than the source file. (Complex Excel files may be an exception.)

Acrobat adds buttons and a menu to your Office application that let you quickly convert a file to Adobe PDF.
A. *Convert to Adobe PDF*
B. *Convert to Adobe PDF and Email*
C. *Convert to Adobe PDF and Send for Review*

Note: *If you don't see the Acrobat buttons and menu, choose View > Toolbars in your Microsoft Office application, and make sure that PDFMaker 7.0 is checked.*

Acrobat installs essentially the same buttons and commands for creating PDF files, creating and emailing PDF files, and creating and emailing PDF files for review in Word, PowerPoint, and Excel. There are, however, some application-specific differences in the Acrobat/Microsoft Office interface. For example, PDFMaker for Excel offers the ability to convert an entire workbook, an option that isn't available in Word or PowerPoint. Despite these application-specific differences, you should be able to complete all sections in this lesson, even if you have only one Microsoft Office application, such as Word, installed on your system. Just follow the steps in each section, avoiding the application-specific steps, and use the lesson file for the Microsoft Office application that you have. (However, you do need to have Microsoft Outlook installed to complete the section on "Converting and attaching a file in Microsoft Outlook" in this lesson.)

Converting a Microsoft Word file to Adobe PDF

Word is a popular authoring program that makes it easy to create a variety of types of documents. Very often, users of Word apply styles to create headings and create hyperlinks to make their documents more usable. In a review process, users may also add Word comments. When you create an Adobe PDF document from your Word document, you can convert these Word styles and headings to Acrobat bookmarks and convert comments to Acrobat notes. Hyperlinks in your Word document are preserved. Your Adobe PDF file will look just like your Word file and retain the same functionality, but it will be equally accessible to readers on all platforms, regardless of whether or not they have the Word application.

About the Microsoft Word file

First you'll look at the Word file that you'll convert to Adobe PDF.

1 Start Microsoft Word.

2 Choose File > Open. Select the file Our_Wines.doc, located in the Lesson03\Win folder, and click Open. Then choose File > Save As, rename the file **Our_Wines1.doc**, and save it in the Lesson03\Win folder.

3 Choose Whole Page from the Zoom menu so that you can view the entire page.

4 Place the pointer on the heading "ABOUT THE WINES," and click to create an insertion point. Notice that the Word style is titled "Chamberg Title." (If necessary, open the Styles and Formatting panel by choosing Format > Styles and Formatting to view the styles and formatting options.)

Click in the heading or select the heading to display the name of the Word style.

5 Now place the pointer on the heading "PinotNoir," and click to create an insertion point. Notice that the Word style is titled "Chamberg Heading."

You'll use this information to convert your Word styles to bookmarks in Adobe PDF.

Notice also that a Word comment has been added to the document, requesting that a spelling error be corrected. In the next section you'll verify that this comment converts to an Acrobat comment in the PDF document.

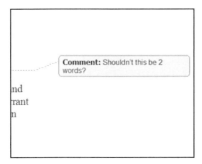

Word comments are converted automatically to Adobe PDF comments.

Converting Word headings and styles to PDF bookmarks

If your Word document contains headings and styles that you want to convert to bookmarks in Adobe PDF, you must identify these headings and styles in the Acrobat PDFMaker dialog box. Word Heading 1 through Heading 9 styles are converted automatically and maintain their hierarchy. You do not need to change the Adobe PDF Conversion Settings to convert these nine styles to Adobe PDF bookmarks. Because the headings used in Our_Wines1.doc aren't formatted using Headings 1 through 9, you'll need to make sure that the styles used convert to bookmarks when you create the Adobe PDF file.

1 On the Word menu bar, choose Adobe PDF > Change Conversion Settings.

The Acrobat PDFMaker dialog box is where you define the settings that control the conversion of your Microsoft application files to Adobe PDF. The tabs available in this dialog box vary with the Microsoft Office application that you are using. Because you are using Microsoft Word, the Word tab and the Bookmarks tabs are available in the Acrobat PDFMaker dialog box. Later in this lesson, you'll open the Acrobat PDFMaker dialog box from within PowerPoint and Excel. With these applications, you'll see only the Settings and Security tabs in this dialog box.

💡 *To learn more about a setting in the Acrobat PDFMaker dialog box, place your cursor over the option. A brief explanation of the option is displayed.*

2 Click the Bookmarks tab.

This tab is where you determine which Word headings and styles are converted to Adobe PDF bookmarks. The author of Our_Wines1.doc used styles to format headings, and now you'll make sure that these Word styles are converted to PDF bookmarks.

3 Scroll down the list of bookmarks and styles, until you see the styles Chamberg Title and Chamberg Heading.

4 Move your pointer over the empty square in the Bookmarks column opposite Chamberg Title, and click in the empty box.

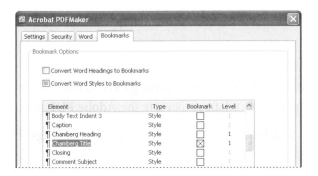

A cross appears indicating that a bookmark will be created for this style. Notice that the level is automatically set to 1. This is the hierarchical level of the PDF bookmark.

5 Move your pointer over the empty square in the Bookmarks column opposite Chamberg Heading, and click in the empty box.

Again, a cross appears indicating that a bookmark will be created for this style. Notice again that the level is automatically set to 1. Because this level of heading is subordinate to the main heading, "About the Wines," you'll change the level setting so that the PDF bookmarks are nested to show the correct hierarchy.

6 Click on the number 1 in the Level column opposite Chamberg Heading, and select 2 from the menu. Changing the level to 2 nests these bookmarks under the first-level "About the Wines" bookmark.

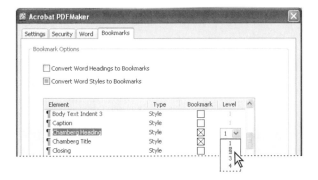

7 Click OK to accept the settings and close the dialog box.

Any settings that you make in the Bookmarks tab apply only to the conversion of Word documents.

Converting Word comments to PDF notes

You needn't lose any comments that have been added to your Word document when you convert the document to Adobe PDF. Your converted Word comments become part of any Acrobat review process, as described in Lesson 10, "Using Acrobat in a Document Review Cycle."

Now you'll make sure that the comment in your Word document is converted to a note in the Adobe PDF document.

1 On the Word menu bar, choose Adobe PDF > Change Conversion Settings again.

2 Click the Word tab in the Acrobat PDFMaker dialog box, and check the Convert Displayed Comments to Notes in the PDF option.

3 In the Comments window, you'll now see one comment to be included. Make sure that the box in the Include column is checked.

4 To change the color of the note in the Adobe PDF document, click repeatedly on the icon in the Color column to cycle through the available color choices. We chose blue.

5 To have the note automatically open in the PDF document, click in the box in the Notes Open column. You can always close the note in the PDF document later if you wish.

Set the color of your Adobe PDF notes and specify whether they are automatically opened.

Any settings that you make in the Word tab apply only to the conversion of Word documents.

Later in this lesson, you'll see the Adobe PDF note created from the Word comment. First though, you'll limit access to the PDF document in its review stage.

Adding security to your Adobe PDF file

There are several ways you can apply security to your Adobe PDF documents. You can add password security to prevent unauthorized users from opening, changing, or even printing your document, you can limit access to the PDF document to a predefined list of users, and you can certify the status of a document. You'll learn more about this in Lesson 11, "Adding Signatures and Security."

In this lesson, you'll add password security to your document to prevent unauthorized users from opening the document.

1 Click the Security tab in the Acrobat PDFMaker dialog box to review the security settings that you can apply to the PDF document that you create.

You'll see that no security is specified for the Adobe PDF document that you will create. However, since this is a copy for internal review only, you'll add password protection so that only users with the password can open the document, minimizing the chance that the document might be released to the public prematurely.

2 Click in the Require a Password to Open the Document box. The option is selected when the box contains a checkmark.

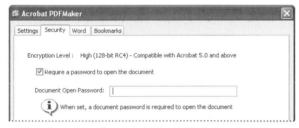

Set security options for your Adobe PDF document.

Now you'll set the password that opens the document.

3 In the Document Open Password text box, type in your password. We entered **wine123**. Be sure not to forget your password. You'll need to share this password with your colleagues, otherwise they won't be able to open your document.

Next you'll review the general conversion settings.

4 Click the Settings tab.

Before you can review the general conversion settings, you have to confirm the password that you just set by re-entering it.

5 Re-enter your password. We entered **wine123.** Click OK to clear the confirmation dialog box.

About document security

When creating Adobe PDF documents, authors can use the following methods to enhance document security:

• *Password security. You can add passwords and set security options to restrict opening, editing, and printing PDF documents.*

• *Certification security. Encrypt a document so that only a specified set of users have access to the documents.*

• *Adobe Policy Server. Apply server-based security policies to PDF documents. Server-based security policies are especially useful if you want others to have access to PDF documents only for a limited time.*

• *Document certification. When an author digital signature is added, editing changes are restricted and detected.*

Tip: *If you often use the same security settings for a set of PDF documents, consider creating a security policy to simplify your workflow.*

—From the Complete Acrobat 7.0 Help.

Changing the conversion settings

Later in the lesson, you'll use a different set of conversion settings to create a smaller file that is more suitable to be emailed as an attachment. For this part of the lesson though, you'll use the default settings for the conversion.

Note: *Conversion settings made in the Settings tab and the Security tab of the Acrobat PDFMaker dialog box remain in effect until you change them. If you apply password protection in the conversion process, for example, you should be sure to remove the password protection setting in the Acrobat PDFMaker dialog box unless you want that security to apply to subsequent conversions.*

1 In the Acrobat PDFMaker dialog box, click the arrow next to the Conversion Settings menu.

This menu lists the predefined conversion settings used to create Adobe PDF files. For users of Acrobat Standard, these predefined settings are sufficient. If you need to customize the conversion settings you can use the Advanced Settings button to access the Adobe PDF Settings dialog box. Lesson 6, "Customizing Quality and File Size," describes how to customize the Adobe PDF Settings. Any customized settings that you have created are also listed in this menu.

To see an explanation of the default conversion settings, choose the name of a conversion set in the Conversion Settings menu. A description is displayed next to the information icon. Use the up and down scroll arrows to move through the text if the description exceeds two lines.

For information on the PDF/A and PDF/X setting, see Lesson 15, "Using Adobe Acrobat for Professional Publishing."

A description of each default conversion setting is displayed below the Conversion Setting menu.

2 Choose Standard from the Conversion Settings pop-up menu.

3 Verify that the View Adobe PDF Result option is checked. When this option is checked, Acrobat is launched automatically and the Adobe PDF file that you create is displayed as soon as the conversion is complete.

4 Make sure that the Enable Accessibility and Reflow with Tagged PDF option is on (checked). Creating tagged PDF makes your files more accessible.

5 Click OK to apply your settings.

6 Now you've defined the settings to be used for the conversion, you're ready to convert your Word file to Adobe PDF, but first you'll save your file.

7 Choose File > Save to save your work in the Lesson03\Win folder.

Converting your Word file

1 Simply click the Convert to Adobe PDF button () on the Word toolbar.

2 In the Save Adobe PDF As dialog box, name and save your file. We named the file **Our_Wines1.pdf** and saved it in the Lesson03\Win folder.

Your file is converted to Adobe PDF. The status of the conversion is shown in the Acrobat PDFMaker message box. Because you applied password security to prevent unauthorized users from opening your document, you need to enter the password that you set earlier in this section before the document opens in Acrobat.

3 In the Password dialog box, enter your password and click OK. We entered **wine123**.

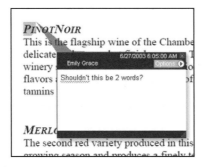

Acrobat displays your converted file. Notice that the Word comment has been converted to an open Adobe PDF note.

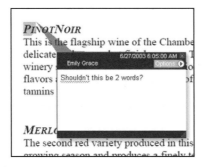

4 After you have read the note, click the close box on the note to close it.

5 Click the Bookmarks tab in the navigation pane, and notice that bookmarks have been created automatically and follow the hierarchy of the Word document. Click the Sparkling Wine bookmark to go to the associated text.

6 When you have finished reviewing the file, choose File > Close to save and close your work.

7 Choose File > Exit to close Acrobat.

8 In Word, choose Adobe PDF > Change Conversion Settings.

9 In the Acrobat PDFMaker dialog box, click the Security tab and click in the Require a Password to Open the Document box to turn the option off, and click OK. If you don't turn this option off, all documents that you create using Acrobat PDFMaker from now on will require entry of the password before you can open them.

10 Exit Microsoft Word.

For information on using the Convert to Adobe PDF and Email button (📄), see "Converting and emailing a PowerPoint presentation" in this lesson. For information on using the Convert to Adobe PDF and Send for Review button (📄), see "Converting an Excel document and starting a review" in this lesson.

💡 *You can convert multiple files of different file types and consolidate them into one PDF file using the Create From Multiple Files command in Acrobat. For more information, see Lesson 4, "Converting Other File Types to Adobe PDF" and "Exploring on your own" at the end of this lesson.*

Converting and emailing a PowerPoint presentation

PowerPoint presentations are an effective way to deliver your message, but not every place that you visit has a system available with Microsoft PowerPoint installed on it, nor does every person that you'd like to share your presentation with have this software. Converting your PowerPoint presentation to Adobe PDF allows you to show the presentation on any system that has the free Adobe Reader software installed. Similarly, you can email a PDF version of your presentation to anyone who has Adobe Reader. They'll see your presentation as you created it. And the PDF file is almost always substantially smaller than the source file.

In this section of the lesson, you'll convert a PowerPoint presentation to Adobe PDF and email it without ever leaving your PowerPoint application.

💡 *If you don't have PowerPoint installed on your system (but you do have Word), you can use the Convert to Adobe PDF and Email button in Word to convert and email the Our_Wines.doc file. Open Our_Wines.doc in Word, skip the "About the PowerPoint file" section and go directly to the "Checking the conversion settings" section later in this lesson.*

About the PowerPoint file

1 Start Microsoft PowerPoint.

2 Choose File > Open. Select the file Welcome.ppt, located in the Lesson03\Win folder, and click Open. Then choose File > Save As, rename the file **Welcome1.ppt**, and save it in the Lesson03\Win folder.

First you'll review the PowerPoint file.

3 Choose View > Slide Show, and press Enter to move to the second page.

On the second page, notice the fly-in bullets and the locators on the map. All these elements will appear in the Adobe PDF file that you create. (The fly-in animation is not preserved, but all the information is present.)

The fly-in information is preserved.

4 Press the Esc key to return to the normal PowerPoint view.

Checking the conversion settings

You'll check the default Adobe PDF Settings first to make sure they are appropriate for your needs.

1 Choose Adobe PDF > Change Conversion Settings.

2 In the earlier part of this lesson, when you converted a Word file, the Acrobat PDFMaker dialog box had four tabs—Settings, Security, Word, and Bookmarks. With PowerPoint, the dialog box has only the Settings and Security tabs.

3 In the Acrobat PDFMaker dialog box, click the Security tab.

No security is set for the conversion, which is correct because you want anyone to be able to open and view your PDF file. If you did want to add security, you would do so in the same way as described in "Adding security to your Adobe PDF file" earlier in this lesson.

4 Click the Settings tab.

Because you're going to email the file to various people, you want the file to be as small as possible.

5 Click the arrow next to the Conversion Settings to open the menu, and choose Smallest File Size.

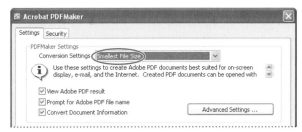

Choose the predefined Conversion Settings that give the smallest file size.

To customize the conversion settings, you would click the Advanced Settings button. For information on customizing the conversion settings, see Lesson 6, "Customizing Quality and File Size."

6 Select the Save Animations in Adobe PDF option.

Note: A few features aren't converted when you create a PDF file from a PowerPoint file: If a PowerPoint transition doesn't have an equivalent transition in Acrobat, then a similar transition is substituted in the PDF file. If there are multiple animation effects in the same slide, a single effect is used instead.

You'll use the default settings for all the other conversion options. Note that the option to use PDF Layout Based on PowerPoint Printer Settings is checked. For example, if you're using Microsoft Power Point and choose Handouts from the print dialog box, the resulting PDF file will be based on the Handouts version of the presentation.

 Always make sure that the Enable Accessibility and Reflow with Tagged PDF option is on (checked). Creating tagged PDF makes your files more accessible.

7 Click OK to apply the settings and close the dialog box.

Converting and emailing the presentation

Now you're ready to convert your PowerPoint presentation to Adobe PDF and email it in one easy step.

1 On the PowerPoint toolbar, click the Convert to Adobe PDF and Email button (▣).

2 In the Save Adobe PDF File As dialog box, click Save to save the file as **Welcome1.pdf** in the Lesson03\Win folder.

The conversion to Adobe PDF is shown in a progress window.

Your default email application is opened automatically, and your Adobe PDF document is attached. All you have to do is fill out recipient information and type a message.

3 In the newly opened email message window, type in recipient information, a subject line, and a message if you wish. We suggest that you send the message to yourself as a test.

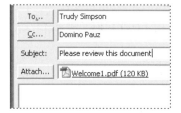

4 When you're ready to send the message, click Send or Send Message.

That's all there is to it. You've created a PDF version of your PowerPoint presentation and emailed it without ever leaving PowerPoint. The PDF version of your presentation is also saved on your hard drive. Now you'll check your PDF file.

5 If you emailed the PDF file to yourself, open your email application and open the PDF attachment. If you didn't email the PDF file to yourself, double-click the Welcome1.pdf file in the Lesson03\Win folder.

6 If necessary, click the Single Page button (▢) on the status bar to view the presentation one page at a time. Then use the Next Page button (▶) and the Previous Page button (◀) to navigate between the pages.

In a later lesson, you'll learn how to create a PDF file that opens in full-screen view so that your PDF files look just like PowerPoint presentations. (See Lesson 12, "Creating Multi-media Presentations.")

7 When you're finished reviewing the Welcome1.pdf file, close the file and exit Acrobat.

8 Close the Welcome1.ppt file and exit PowerPoint.

Converting an Excel document and starting a review

In the prior section, you saw how easy it is to create a PDF file from a Microsoft Office application—PowerPoint—and email it to friends or colleagues without ever leaving your Microsoft Office application. In this section, you'll create a PDF file from an Excel document and start a formal review process in which the PDF file is emailed to selected reviewers. In addition to managing the email process, the Acrobat email review process also offers powerful file management and comment management tools to facilitate the review.

If you don't have Excel installed on your system, you can use the Convert to Adobe PDF and Send for Review button in Word to convert and start an email review of the Our_Wines.doc file. Open Our_Wines.doc in Word, and go directly to the "Checking the conversion settings" section later in this lesson.

About the Excel file

1 Start Microsoft Excel.

2 Choose File > Open. Select the file Projections.xls, located in the Lesson03\Win folder, and click Open. Then choose File > Save As, rename the file **Projections1.xls**, and save it in the Lesson03\Win folder.

Now you'll review the Excel file. Notice that the first sheet has case-lot projections for red-wine sales.

3 Click the Sheet 2 button at the bottom of the Excel spreadsheet. The second sheet has case-lot projections for white wines.

When you create your PDF file, you'll need to convert both these sheets.

Converting the entire workbook

If you convert an Excel file to Adobe PDF by simply clicking the Convert to Adobe PDF button on the Excel toolbar, you'll convert only the active worksheet. If you want to convert all the worksheets in a book, you must first select the Convert Entire Workbook option.

Note: *Your Excel worksheet will be automatically sized for your printer page size. You don't need to worry about defining a custom page size.*

Choose Adobe PDF > Convert Entire Workbook. The Convert Entire Workbook option is on when there is a checkmark; it is off when there is no checkmark. (The default is off.)

Checking the conversion settings

The settings used by Acrobat PDFMaker to convert Excel files are set in the same way as for Word and PowerPoint.

1 Choose Adobe PDF > Change Conversion Settings.

2 In the Acrobat PDFMaker dialog box, choose Smallest File Size from the Conversion Settings menu because you're going to be emailing the PDF file.

To customize the conversion settings, you would click the Advanced Settings button. For information on customizing the conversion settings, see Lesson 6, "Customizing Quality and File Size."

You'll use the default values for all the other conversion settings.

Make sure that the Enable Accessibility and Reflow with Tagged PDF option is on (checked). When you create tagged PDF, you can more easily copy tabular data from PDF files back into spreadsheet applications. For more information, see "Exploring on your own" in this lesson. Creating tagged PDF also makes your files more accessible.

Now you'll check that no security is specified for the file.

3 In the Acrobat PDFMaker dialog box, click the Security tab.

No security is set for the conversion, which is correct because you want anyone to be able to open and view your PDF file. If you did want to add security, you would do so in exactly the same way as described in "Adding security to your Adobe PDF file" in this lesson.

4 Click OK to apply the conversion settings and close the dialog box.

Now you'll convert your Excel file and send it for review.

Starting an email-based review

When you send a file for review by email using the Convert to Adobe PDF and Send for Review button (⬛), you package your PDF file in an FDF (File Data Format) setup file. When the recipient opens this setup file, the PDF file opens, together with instructions for adding and returning comments. When you in turn open comments returned by your reviewers, the comments are automatically added to a master copy of the PDF file.

You can also use the Tracker feature to invite additional reviewers to join the process or to send reminders to reviewers. If you're using Acrobat Professional, you can invite users of Adobe Reader to participate in the review. For more information on using Acrobat in the reviewing and commenting process, see Lesson 10, "Using Acrobat in a Document Review Cycle."

1 Click the Convert to Adobe PDF and Send for Review button (⬛).

First you'll be prompted to save the file.

2 In the Save Adobe PDF File As dialog box, and click Save to save the file as Projections1.pdf in the Lesson03\Win folder.

The Send By Email For Review dialog box opens to guide you through the process.

3 In the Identity SetUp dialog box, enter any personal identification information that you want to share with reviewers. We entered a name and email address. Click complete. (The Identity Setup dialog box opens only the first time you execute this process.)

4 In the Getting Started panel, check that the correct file name is displayed, and click Next.

5 In the Invite Reviewers panel, enter the email addresses of the people you want to send the file to. Click the Address Book button to open your email address book. Highlight a name, and click To to move the name to the Message Recipients panel. You can enter as many addresses as your email application supports. Click OK when you have selected all the required recipients.

6 Click the Customize Review options button if you want to specify a different email address for reviewers to return their comments to, if you want Acrobat to automatically display the Drawing Markup tools when a recipient opens the PDF file, and most importantly if you're using Acrobat Professional, to allow users of Adobe Reader 7.0 to participate in the review process. Click OK when you have made your choices.

 Only users of Acrobat Professional 7.0 can extend additional usage rights to allow users of Adobe Reader to join a review.

7 Click Next to customize your email message in the Preview Invitation panel.

8 Click Send Invitation to complete the process.

9 Close the Projections1.xls file, and exit Microsoft Excel.

You cannot experience the email review feature without the help of at least one other participant. We encourage you to experiment with this feature when you have a document to review with colleagues.

Converting and attaching a file in Microsoft Outlook

Acrobat adds several Adobe PDF buttons to Microsoft Outlook that allow you to convert files or folder contents to Adobe PDF and attach the converted file or files to an email without leaving the Outlook application. Additionally, when you open a New Mail Message or New Discussion window, You'll see the Attach as Adobe PDF and Attach as Secured Adobe PDF buttons. (You'll only see the Attach as Secured Adobe PDF button if you've configured an Adobe Policy Server in the Acrobat Security Settings window.)

1 Open Microsoft Outlook, and click the New button (or choose New > Mail Message) to open a new mail message.

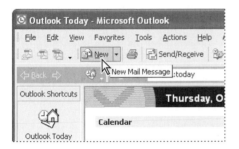

Click the New button to open a new mail message.

2 On the toolbar of the new mail message, click the Attach as Adobe PDF button to open the Choose File to Attach as Adobe PDF dialog box.

3 Choose the Memo.txt file in the Lesson03\Win folder, and click Open.

Note: If the file type cannot be converted to an Adobe PDF file, you will be asked if you want to attach the unconverted file. For a list of supported file types, click the arrow next to the Files of Type box.

4 In the Save Adobe PDF File As dialog box, name the file **Memo.pdf** and save it in the Lesson03\Win folder.

A message box shows the progress of the conversion, and depending on file type, the authoring application may launch in the background and close automatically when the conversion is complete.

The source file is converted to Adobe PDF, saved in the designated location on your system, and a copy of the PDF file is attached to the new mail message window in Microsoft Outlook. All you have to do is provide recipient information, write the text of your email message, and click Send.

5 When you're finished, exit Microsoft Outlook.

You can use the Attach as Secured Adobe PDF button to protect your PDF attachment if you have configured an Adobe Policy Server in the Acrobat Security Setting dialog box.

If you want to try using the Convert Selected Messages to Adobe PDF, Convert Selected Folder to Adobe PDF, and Convert and Append Selected Messages to an Existing Adobe PDF, see "Exploring on your own: Converting emails and email folders in Microsoft Outlook" at the end of this lesson.

Converting web pages from Internet Explorer

Acrobat adds a button and a menu to the toolbar of Internet Explorer 5.0.1 or later that allow you to convert the currently displayed web page to an Adobe PDF file or convert and print it in one easy operation. When you print a web page that you have converted to an Adobe PDF file, the page is reformatted to a standard printer page size and logical page breaks are added. You can be sure that your print copy will have all the information on the web page that you see onscreen.

For more information on converting web pages from within Internet Explorer, see Lesson 5, "Creating Adobe PDF from Web Pages."

Converting other Microsoft files in Acrobat Standard and Professional:

You can convert a variety of Microsoft files using the same method as described in this lesson for Microsoft Office files.

• *You convert Microsoft Access files to Adobe PDF files in the same way as you convert Office files to Adobe PDF files.*

• *You can convert Publisher files, retaining crop marks, bleed marks, hyperlinks, bookmarks, spot colors, transparencies, and CMYK color conversion information.*

• *You can convert one or more pages in a Visio file to an Adobe PDF file quickly and easily from within Visio. The resulting Adobe PDF files preserve page sizes and support layers, searchable text, custom properties, hyperlinks, bookmarks, and comments. You can preserve all or just some layers from the Visio file, or you can flatten all layers. All shapes in the Visio drawing are converted, regardless of their protection or behavior, and shape custom properties can be converted to PDF object data.*

In Acrobat Professional:

• *You can convert Microsoft Project files to Adobe PDF files in the same way as you convert Office files to Adobe PDF files, except in Project, you can convert only the currently selected view.*

Exploring on your own: Exporting tables from PDF files

You can easily copy and paste tables from a tagged PDF file into spreadsheet applications such as Excel. Earlier in this lesson ("Converting an Excel document and starting a review"), you converted an Excel workbook into a PDF file. You'll use that file again to see how easy it is to copy and paste tables from PDF files back into spreadsheet applications.

1 Navigate to the Lesson03\Win folder, and double-click the Proj_Export.pdf file to open it in Acrobat.

2 On the Acrobat toolbar, click the Select tool (⌶).

3 Drag from the top left of the table to the bottom right, selecting all the text in the table, or click in the table. Notice that the cursor changes to indicate a table selection (⊟).

4 Move the cursor over the Select icon that appears on the selected table, and choose the Open Table in Spreadsheet command from the context menu.

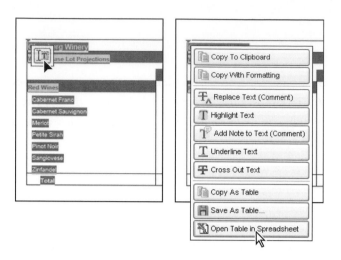

Acrobat automatically launches Excel and copies and pastes the table into a new spreadsheet.

5 When you are finished close the new Excel spreadsheet and exit Excel. Then close Projections1.pdf.

Exploring on your own: Converting and combining multiple Office files

As you saw in this lesson, you can convert Office files to Adobe PDF from within the Office application that you used to author the files. However, if you have several Office files—for example, a Word file, a PowerPoint file, and an Excel file—you can also convert and consolidate the files in one easy step from within Acrobat.

1 In Acrobat, choose File > Create PDF > From Multiple Files.

2 In the dialog box, click the Browse button under Add Files, and navigate to the Lesson03\Win folder.

3 Make sure that All Supported Formats is selected for Files of Type, and then Ctrl-click to select the files, Our_Wines.doc, Projections.xls, and Welcome.ppt. Click Add.

You can rearrange the files in the Files to Combine panel in the Create PDF from Multiple Documents dialog box. For this exercise though, you'll simply convert the files. You'll learn more about the Create PDF From Multiple Files command in Lesson 4, "Converting Other File Types to Adobe PDF."

4 Click OK.

Acrobat converts the files to Adobe PDF and consolidates them into one file. You have more control over the conversion process if you create individual PDF files and consolidate them separately, but if you have a number of similar and simple files, creating a PDF file from multiple source files in this one easy step is convenient.

5 Click Save to save the consolidated and converted file.

Acrobat then opens the consolidated PDF file. Notice that only one page of the Excel spreadsheet is converted.

6 When you have reviewed the file, close it without saving your work and exit Acrobat.

Exploring on your own: Converting emails and email folders in Microsoft Outlook

If you use Microsoft Outlook as your email program, you can convert individual emails, selected emails, or folders of emails into easily archivable and searchable PDF files. If you receive more messages that belong in a converted folder or an email thread, you can convert these messages and attach them to the existing PDF file for the email folder or thread.

1 In Microsoft Outlook, select a folder and then click the Convert Selected Folder to PDF button.

2 In the Save Adobe PDF File As dialog box, choose a name and location for the PDF file that you are about to create, and then click Save.

A progress box shows the conversion and the file opens in Acrobat.

You can use the bookmarks in the bookmarks tab to quickly locate a specific email, or you can use the Acrobat Search or Find feature.

3 After you have explored this feature, exit both Microsoft Outlook and Acrobat.

Review questions

1 How can you be sure that Word styles and headings are converted to Acrobat bookmarks when you convert Word documents to Adobe PDF using PDFMaker?

2 Can you convert an entire Excel workbook to Adobe PDF?

3 How can you add security to a PDF file that you create from a Microsoft Office application?

Review answers

1 If you want Word headings and styles to be converted to bookmarks in Acrobat, you must be sure that the headings and styles are identified for conversion in the Acrobat PDFMaker dialog box. In Microsoft Word, choose Adobe PDF > Change Conversion Settings, and click the Bookmarks tab. Make sure that the required headings and styles are checked.

2 Yes. Before you convert your Excel file to Adobe PDF, choose Adobe PDF > Convert Entire Workbook on the Excel toolbar. The option is selected when it has a check mark next to it.

3 You can add security in the Acrobat PDFMaker dialog box. Before you convert your Microsoft Office file to Adobe PDF, in your Microsoft Office application, choose Adobe PDF > Change Conversion Settings. Set the required security on the Security tab.

3m | Converting Microsoft Office Files (Mac OS)

Acrobat is designed to work efficiently with your Microsoft Office applications. You can create Adobe PDF files and email them without ever leaving your Microsoft application. Friends and colleagues can open your documents reliably, regardless of what platform they work on.

This lesson is designed for Mac OS users who have Microsoft Office applications—Microsoft Word, Microsoft PowerPoint, and Microsoft Excel—installed on their computer. You cannot complete this lesson if you do not have any or all of these Microsoft applications installed. If you do not use Microsoft Office applications, you should skip this lesson and move on to Lesson 4, "Converting Other File Types to Adobe PDF."

In this lesson, you'll learn how to do the following:

- Convert a Microsoft Word file to Adobe PDF.

- Change the conversion settings in Acrobat Distiller.

- Add password protection to your Adobe PDF files.

- Convert a Microsoft PowerPoint file and attach it to an email message.

This lesson will take about 30 minutes to complete.

If needed, remove the previous lesson folder from your hard drive, and copy the Lesson03:Mac folder onto it.

Note: *Only Microsoft Office 2004 (SR-1) is supported.*

About PDFMaker

PDFMaker, which is installed automatically when you install Acrobat, is used to create Adobe PDF files from within Microsoft Office applications. Convert to Adobe PDF buttons are added automatically to the toolbar in the Microsoft Office applications so that you can easily convert your files to Adobe PDF and convert and email your files without leaving your Microsoft application. For current information on which Microsoft applications and which versions of the Microsoft applications are supported, visit the Adobe website (www.adobe.com).

Acrobat
adds two buttons.

Acrobat installs essentially the same buttons for creating PDF files and creating and emailing PDF files in Word, PowerPoint, and Excel. You should be able to complete all sections in this lesson, even if you have only one Microsoft Office application, such as Word. Just follow the steps in each section, avoiding any application-specific steps, and use the lesson file for the application that you have. For example, if you only have Word, you can use the Word file in the Lesson folder to do the exercise in the "Converting and emailing a PowerPoint presentation". You'll just open Word instead of PowerPoint.

Converting a Microsoft Word file to Adobe PDF

Word is a popular authoring program that makes it easy to create a variety of documents. When you convert your Word file to Adobe PDF, your Adobe PDF file will look just like your Word file and retain the same functionality, but it will be equally accessible to readers on all platforms, regardless of whether or not they have the Word application.

About the Microsoft Word file

First you'll open the Word file that you'll convert to Adobe PDF.

1 Start Microsoft Word.

2 Choose File > Open. Select the file Our_Wines.doc, located in the Lesson03:Mac folder, and click Open. Then choose File > Save As, rename the file **Our_Wines1.doc**, and save it in the Lesson03:Mac folder.

Changing your conversion settings in Distiller

On Mac OS, PDFMaker uses the Distiller Adobe PDF Settings when converting Office files to Adobe PDF. In this part of the lesson, you'll use one of the predefined settings to create your PDF file, but you can also create custom settings.

Note: When you convert your files to Adobe PDF using the Convert to Adobe PDF and Convert to Adobe PDF and Email buttons, the printer settings or page setup that you have selected in your Microsoft application are used in conjunction with the Distiller Adobe PDF Settings. Thus, if you choose Handouts in the Print dialog box in Microsoft PowerPoint, the resulting PDF file is based on the Handouts version of the presentation.

First you'll open Distiller and look at the conversion settings.

1 Start Acrobat, and choose Advanced > Acrobat Distiller.

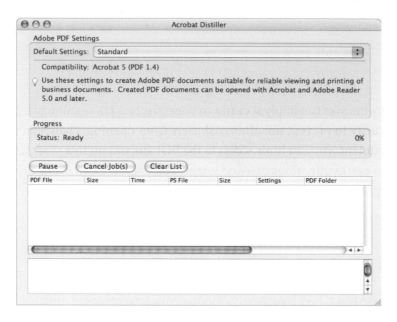

2 In the Acrobat Distiller dialog box, click the arrow to open the Default Settings pop-up menu.

You have several predefined settings to select from. For most users, these predefined settings are sufficient. If you need to customize the conversion settings you can use the Settings > Edit Adobe PDF Settings command in Distiller to access the Adobe PDF Settings dialog box. Lesson 6, "Customizing Quality and File Size," describes how to customize the Adobe PDF settings. Any customized settings that you have created are also listed in this menu.

For information on the PDF/A and PDF/X settings, see Lesson 15, "Using Adobe Acrobat for Professional Publishing."

3 From the Default Settings menu, click Press Quality, and notice that the description under Compatibility changes.

If you have time, click each of the predefined Adobe PDF Settings and read the descriptions.

Later in the lesson, you'll use a different set of conversion settings to create a smaller file that is more suitable to be emailed as an attachment. For this part of the lesson though, you'll revert to the default settings for the conversion—the Standard set.

4 From the Default Settings pop-up menu, choose Standard.

You should check your Distiller conversion settings often. The settings do not revert to the default settings automatically.

Adding security to your Adobe PDF file

There are several ways you can apply security to your Adobe PDF documents. You can add password security to prevent unauthorized users from opening, changing, or even printing your document, you can limit access to the PDF document to a predefined list of users, and you can certify the status of a document. You'll learn more about this in Lesson 11, "Adding Signatures and Security."

In this lesson, you'll add password security to your document to prevent unauthorized users from opening the document.

1 In Distiller, choose Settings > Security.

Set security options for your Adobe PDF document.

You'll see that no security is specified for opening, editing, or printing the Adobe PDF document that you will create. Since this is a copy for internal review only, you'll require that a password be used to open the document so that it isn't released to the public prematurely.

2 Click in the Require a Password to Open the Document box. The option is selected when the box contains a checkmark.

Now you'll set the password that opens the document.

3 In the Document Open Password text box, type in your password. We entered **wine123**. Be sure not to forget your password. You'll need to share this password with your colleagues, otherwise they won't be able to open your document. Passwords are case-sensitive, so if you use capital letters, be sure to remember that.

You could restrict the printing and editing of the document, but since this document is going to be circulated for inhouse review, you won't bother adding that level of security. You can learn more about restricting printing and editing in Lesson 11, "Adding Signatures and Security."

4 Click OK to apply your security settings.

Before you can finish the process, you have to re-enter the password that you just set.

5 Re-enter your password. We entered **wine123.** Click OK to clear the confirmation dialog box.

6 Choose Distiller > Quit Acrobat Distiller to quit Distiller.

💡 *You should remove your Distiller security setting as soon as you no longer need it to be applied. The security settings do not revert automatically to the default of no security.*

Now that you've set the conversion settings and the security settings, you're ready to convert your Word file to Adobe PDF.

About document security

When creating Adobe PDF documents, authors can use the following methods to enhance document security:

- *Password security. You can add passwords and set security options to restrict opening, editing, and printing PDF documents.*

- *Certification security. Encrypt a document so that only a specified set of users have access to the documents.*

- *Adobe Policy Server. Apply server-based security policies to PDF documents. Server-based security policies are especially useful if you want others to have access to PDF documents only for a limited time.*

- *Document certification. When an author digital signature is added, editing changes are restricted and detected.*

Tip: *If you often use the same security settings for a set of PDF documents, consider creating a security policy to simplify your workflow.*

—From the Complete Acrobat 7.0 Help.

Converting your Word file

1 In Word, simply click the Convert to Adobe PDF button (📄) on the Word toolbar.

2 In the Save dialog box, make sure that the PDF file will be named **Our_Wines1.pdf** and saved in the Lesson03:Mac folder. Click Save.

By default, your PDF file is saved in the same directory as the source file.

The Acrobat PDFMaker dialog box shows the status of the conversion.

3 When the conversion is complete, click the View File button.

Acrobat launches automatically, but because you have applied password protection, you have to enter the password before Acrobat will open the file.

4 In the Enter Password text box, enter the password that you entered in Step 3, "Adding security to your Adobe PDF file" earlier in this lesson. We entered **wine123**. And then click OK.

Your Adobe PDF file opens in Acrobat.

That's all there is to creating an Adobe PDF file from your Microsoft Office file.

5 When you're finished reviewing your PDF file, choose File > Close to close your work.

Note: If you aren't going to do any more of this lesson, be sure to reset your security settings in Distiller, otherwise all the PDF files you create will be password-protected.

6 Choose Acrobat > Quit Acrobat.

7 Choose Word > Quit Word to quit Microsoft Word.

Converting and emailing a PowerPoint presentation

PowerPoint presentations are an effective way to deliver your message, but not every place that you visit has a system available with Microsoft PowerPoint installed on it, nor does every person that you'd like to share your presentation with have this software. Converting your PowerPoint presentation to Adobe PDF allows you to show the presentation on any system that has the free Adobe Reader software installed. Similarly, you can email a PDF version of your presentation to anyone who has Adobe Reader. They'll see your presentation as you created it. And the PDF file is almost always substantially smaller than the source file.

In this section of the lesson, you'll convert a PowerPoint presentation to Adobe PDF and email it without ever leaving your PowerPoint application.

If you don't have PowerPoint installed on your system, you can use the Convert to Adobe PDF and Email button in Word to convert and email the Our_Wines.doc file. Open Our_Wines.doc in Word, skip the "About the PowerPoint file" section, and go directly to the section on checking the conversion settings and security settings in Distiller.

About the PowerPoint file

1 Start Microsoft PowerPoint.

2 Choose File > Open. Select the file Welcome.ppt, located in the Lesson03:Mac folder, and click Open. Then choose File > Save As, rename the file **Welcome1.ppt**, and save it in the Lesson03:Mac folder.

First you'll review the PowerPoint file.

3 Choose View > Slide Show.

4 Press Return to move to the second page.

Notice the fly-in bullets and the locators on the map on the second page. All these elements will appear in the Adobe PDF file that you create. (The fly-in animation is not preserved, but all the information is present.)

5 Press the Esc key to return to the normal PowerPoint view.

Checking your conversion settings and security settings in Distiller

You'll check the default Adobe PDF settings first to make sure they are appropriate for your needs.

1 Start Acrobat, and choose Advanced > Acrobat Distiller.

Because you're going to email the file to various people, you want the file to be as small as possible.

2 Click the arrow next to the Default Settings menu, and choose Smallest File Size.

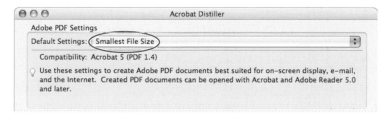

Choose the predefined conversion setting that gives the smallest file size.

For information on customizing the conversion settings, see Lesson 6, "Customizing Quality and File Size."

Now you'll remove the security settings that you applied for the conversion of the Word document in the prior section.

3 In Distiller, choose Settings > Security.

4 Click in the Require a Password to Open the Document box. The option is deselected when the box is empty.

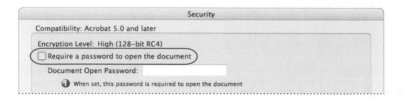

5 Click OK to remove the previously used security settings.

6 Choose Distiller > Quit Acrobat Distiller to quit Distiller.

You should check your Distiller conversion settings periodically. The settings do not revert to the default settings automatically.

Converting and emailing the presentation

Now you're ready to convert your PowerPoint presentation to Adobe PDF and email it in one easy step.

Note: The Adobe PDF buttons appear at the far right and below the PowerPoint toolbar. You may need to move any palettes that you have open in order to see them. (In Word, the Adobe PDF buttons are at the bottom left of the toolbar.)

1 On the PowerPoint toolbar, click the Convert to Adobe PDF and Email button (🔳).

First you'll be prompted to save the file.

2 Click Save, and save the file as Welcome1.pdf in the Lesson03:Mac folder.

The conversion to Adobe PDF is shown in a progress window.

Your default email application is opened automatically, and your Adobe PDF document is attached. All you have to do is fill out recipient information and type a message.

3 In the newly opened email message window, type in recipient information, a subject line, and a message if you wish. We suggest that you send the message to yourself as a test.

4 When you're ready to send the message, click Send or Send Message.

That's all there is to it. You've created a PDF version of your PowerPoint presentation and emailed it without ever leaving PowerPoint. The PDF version of your presentation is also saved on your hard drive. Now you'll check your PDF file.

5 If you emailed the PDF file to yourself, open your email application and open the PDF attachment. If you didn't email the PDF file to yourself, click the View File button in the Acrobat PDFMaker status box to open the file or double-click the Welcome1.pdf file in the Lesson03:Mac folder.

6 Click the Next Page button (▶) on the Acrobat status bar to move to the next page of the presentation.

Notice that although the animation of the fly-in bullets is lost, all the text is preserved.

In a later lesson, you'll learn how to create a PDF file that opens in full-screen view so that your PDF files look just like PowerPoint presentations. (See Lesson 12, "Creating Multimedia Presentations.")

7 When you're finished reviewing the Welcome1.pdf file, close the file and quit Acrobat.

8 In PowerPoint, choose PowerPoint > Quit PowerPoint.

9 If necessary, close your email application.

Tips on converting Excel files

In the prior section, you saw how easy it is to create a PDF file from a Microsoft Office application and email it to friends or colleagues without ever leaving your Microsoft Office application. You can equally easily convert Excel files to Adobe PDF or convert and email them without leaving Excel.

You cannot convert password-protected Excel files using this method.

About the Excel file

1 Start Microsoft Excel.

2 Choose File > Open. Select the file Projections.xls, located in the Lesson03:Mac folder, and click Open. Then choose File > Save As, rename the file **Projections1.xls**, and save it in the Lesson03:Mac folder.

Now you'll review the Excel file. Notice that the first sheet has case-lot projections for red-wine sales.

3 Click the Sheet 2 tab at the bottom of the Excel spreadsheet. The second sheet has case-lot projections for white wines. When you create your PDF file, you'll need to convert both these sheets.

Converting the entire workbook

If you convert an Excel file to Adobe PDF by simply clicking the Convert to Adobe PDF button (📄) on the Excel toolbar, you'll convert only the active worksheet. If you want to convert all the worksheets in a book, you must convert each sheet individually and then use the Create PDF From Multiple Files command to consolidate the PDF files of the individual sheets. You will need to give each sheet a unique name as you convert the Excel spreadsheets to Adobe PDF.

Note: Your Excel worksheet will be automatically sized for your printer page size. You don't need to worry about defining a custom page size.

Checking the conversion settings

You'll use the same settings to convert Excel files to Adobe PDF as you used to convert PowerPoint files. If you need help, follow the steps in "Checking your conversion settings and security settings in Distiller" on page 111 to verify that Smallest File Size is selected for the Adobe PDF Setting and that no security will be applied to the document.

Creating an Adobe PDF file

You'll convert your Excel file to Adobe PDF in the same way as you converted the Word file to Adobe PDF.

1 Click the Sheet 1 tab at the bottom of the Excel window to return to the first page of the workbook.

2 Click the Convert to Adobe PDF button (⬚) on the Excel toolbar.

3 Name and save your PDF file. We named Sheet 1, **Projections1.pdf**, and saved it in the Lesson03:Mac folder.

4 When the conversion is complete, click the View File button in the Acrobat PDFMaker status box to view your PDF file.

5 Repeat steps 1 through 4 for Sheet 2, naming the PDF file **Projections2.pdf**, and saving it in the Lesson03:Mac folder.

6 When you are finished, quit Excel and Distiller (if necessary). Leave the two PDF files open.

Consolidating PDF files

Now you'll consolidate the two PDF files, Projections1.pdf and Projections2.pdf, into one PDF file.

1 In Acrobat, choose File > Create PDF > From Multiple Files.

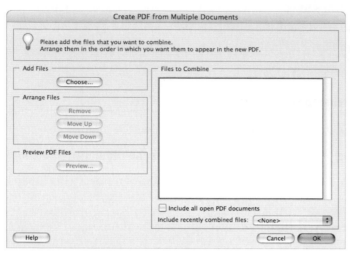

You can consolidate PDF files in Acrobat.

The Create PDF From Multiple Documents dialog box is where you assemble PDF documents that you want to consolidate. You can also assemble documents that you want to convert to Adobe PDF and consolidate them in one step in this dialog box. (See Lesson 4, "Converting Other File Types to Adobe PDF.")

2 Click the Include All Open PDF Documents option at the bottom of the Files to Combine window.

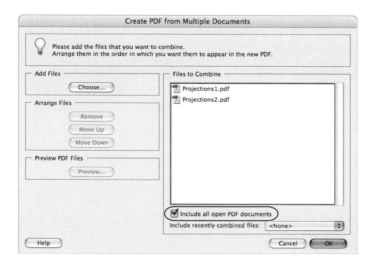

The Files to Combine window should now display both the file Projections2.pdf and the file Projections1.pdf.

It doesn't matter in what order the files are in, because you can rearrange them.

3 If the files are not in the correct order (Projections1.pdf first and Projections2.pdf second), select the Projections1.pdf file and click the Move Up button once.

Now you're ready to create the consolidated Adobe PDF file.

4 Click OK to consolidate the listed files into one Adobe PDF file.

5 In the Save As dialog box, type in **Projections.pdf** as the file name, and choose the Lesson 3 folder as the target directory. Click Save to save your work.

6 Use the Next Page (▶) and Previous Page (◀) buttons to page through your consolidated document.

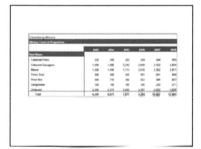
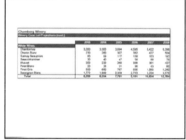

Both pages of the spreadsheet are converted and combined into one PDF document.

7 When you are finished, choose Acrobat > Quit Acrobat. All your saved PDF files are closed automatically.

Review questions

1 Where do you select the Adobe PDF Settings used to convert Microsoft Office files to Adobe PDF on Mac OS?

2 How do you add security to a file created using PDFMaker on Mac OS?

3 Can you convert an entire Excel workbook to Adobe PDF?

Review answers

1 PDFMaker on Mac OS uses the Adobe PDF Settings from Distiller. You must open Distiller and change the Default Settings in Distiller to change the conversion settings used by PDFMaker. The Default Settings menu lists the predefined Adobe PDF Settings as well as any custom settings that you may have defined.

2 You change the security settings for Adobe PDF files in the Security dialog box of Distiller. In Distiller, choose Settings > Security to limit access to a file and to restrict printing and editing.

3 No. But you can convert each worksheet to an Adobe PDF file and then consolidate the PDF files using the Create PDF From Multiple Files command in Acrobat.

4 Converting Files to Adobe PDF

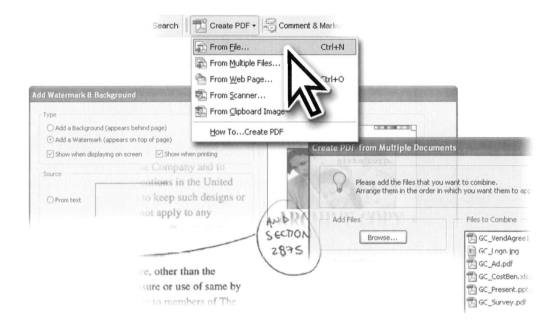

You can convert a variety of file formats to Adobe PDF quickly and easily. You can even assemble files of different types, including Adobe PDF files, and consolidate and convert them to one Adobe PDF file in a single action. Once you've created your PDF file, you can add custom headers and footers to the pages and add watermarks or backgrounds. Creating and customizing Adobe PDF files has never been easier.

In this lesson, you'll learn how to do the following:

- Convert a TIFF file to Adobe PDF using the Create PDF command.

- Consolidate PDF files into one Adobe PDF file using the Create PDF From Multiple Files command.

- Add headers and footers to a PDF document.

- Add a background to a PDF document.

- Search a PDF file.

- Convert a file to Adobe PDF using the authoring application's Print command.

- Create a PDF file from the desktop using the Convert to Adobe PDF command (Windows) in the context menu.

This lesson will take about 60 minutes to complete.

If needed, remove the previous lesson folder from your hard drive, and copy the Lesson04 folder onto it.

Note: Windows 2000 users may need to unlock the lesson files before using them. For information, see "Copying the Classroom in a Book files" on page 4.

About creating Adobe PDF files

You can convert a variety of file formats to Adobe PDF, preserving all the fonts, formatting, graphics, and color of the source file, regardless of the application and platform used to create it. In addition to creating Adobe PDF files from virtually any software application, you can also create PDF files by downloading and converting web pages and by scanning and capturing paper documents.

The prior lesson, Lesson 3, "Converting Microsoft Office Files," describes how to create Adobe PDF files directly from Microsoft Office files. This lesson covers several ways of creating Adobe PDF files from image files and from other types of application files. Lesson 5, "Creating Adobe PDF from Web Pages," describes how to create Adobe PDF files from web pages. Lesson 15, "Using Adobe Acrobat for Professional Publishing," covers the use of Distiller to create press-quality PDF files. Converting paper documents to Adobe PDF by scanning is not covered in this book.

Increasingly the content of Adobe PDF files is being reused when the security settings applied by the creator of the document allow reuse of the content. Content can be extracted for use in another authoring application or the content can be reflowed for use with handheld devices or screen readers. The success with which content can be repurposed or reused depends very much on the structural information contained in the PDF file. The more structural information a PDF document contains the more opportunities you have for successfully reusing the content and the more reliably a document can be used with screen readers. (See Lesson 9, "Making Documents Accessible and Flexible," and "Creating Accessible Adobe PDF Documents" in the Complete Acrobat 7.0 Help.)

Creating an Adobe PDF file using the Create PDF command

You can convert a variety of different file formats to Adobe PDF using the Create PDF command in Acrobat.

In this section of the lesson, you'll convert a single TIFF file to an Adobe PDF file. You can use this method to convert a variety of both image and non-image file types to Adobe PDF.

1 Open Acrobat.

2 Click the Create PDF button on the Acrobat toolbar, and choose From File.

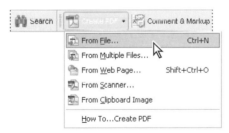

The Create PDF button gives you easy access to several commands for creating Adobe PDF files.

3 In the Open dialog box, click the arrow to open the Files of Type (Windows) or Show (Mac OS) pop-up menu, and choose TIFF for the file type. (The pop-up menu lists all the file types that can be converted using this method.)

4 Click the Settings button to open the Adobe PDF Settings dialog box.

This is where you set the compression that will be applied to color, grayscale, and monochrome images, and where you select the color management options used when the file is converted to Adobe PDF. For more information on these settings, see Lesson 6, "Customizing Quality and File Size."

5 Click Cancel to leave the options unchanged for now.

Resolution is determined automatically.

6 In the Open dialog box, navigate to the Lesson04 folder, select the file GC_VendAgree.tif, and click Open.

7 If necessary, click OK to close the Adobe Picture Tasks dialog box.

You'll learn more about the Picture Tasks button in Lesson 12, "Creating Multimedia Presentations."

Using Picture Tasks features

The Picture Tasks plug-in is specifically designed to allow you to extract JPEG formatted pictures sent to you in an Adobe PDF file that was created with Adobe Photoshop Album, Adobe Photoshop Elements 2.0, or Adobe Acrobat using JPEG source files. With Picture Tasks, you can export and save the pictures to your local machine, and edit them using Photoshop or Photoshop Elements. You can also print them locally using standard photo print sizes and layouts. In Acrobat for Windows, you can share pictures on the Internet or send them to an online service provider to have the prints directly mailed to you.

Note: *Picture Tasks does not support JPEG-formatted PDF files created from other applications, or Adobe PDF files with ZIP compression created using Photoshop Elements 2.0.*

—From the Complete Acrobat 7.0 Help.

Acrobat converts the TIFF file to Adobe PDF and opens the PDF file automatically.

Notice the hand-written note "And Section 2875" that the signer of the agreement has added is preserved in the Adobe PDF file.

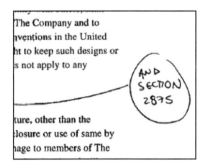

8 Choose File > Save As, name the file **GCVend_Agree1.pdf**, and save it in the Lesson04 folder.

💡 *On Windows, you can also create and consolidate Adobe PDF files using the Convert to Adobe PDF command and the Combine in Adobe Acrobat command in the context menu. For more information, see "Exploring on your own: Creating Adobe PDF from the context menu (Windows)" later in this lesson.*

Converting and combining different types of files

In the prior section, you converted a TIFF file to Adobe PDF using the Create PDF command. As you saw from the listed file types in the Open dialog box, you can use this approach to convert a variety of file formats to Adobe PDF. You can also convert a variety of file formats to Adobe PDF and consolidate them into one Adobe PDF file in one simple operation.

In this part of the lesson, you'll use the Create PDF From Multiple Files command to assemble several documents related to a network upgrade project for the Global Corp. The files that you'll consolidate include PDF files and JPEG image files.

In the past, if you needed to archive project documents such as these, you'd need to generate paper copies that you could file, or you'd need to be sure that you always had the necessary software to open and view your archived electronic files. Similarly, if you had wanted to circulate the project documents for review, each of your colleagues would have had to have the necessary software to open and view the files, or you'd have had to create and distribute paper copies. With Adobe PDF you don't have these problems. When you convert your application files to Adobe PDF, they can be opened on any platform using the free Adobe Reader.

Assembling the files

1 In Acrobat, click the Create PDF button on the toolbar, and choose From Multiple Files.

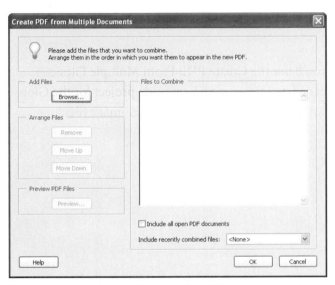

You can convert and consolidate a variety of file types without leaving Acrobat.

The Create PDF From Multiple Documents dialog box is where you assemble PDF documents that you want to consolidate or where you assemble the documents that you want to convert to Adobe PDF and consolidate.

2 Click in the empty box to select the Include All Open PDF Documents option. (The option is on if the box is checked.) After you turn this option on, the file GCVend_Agree1.pdf is listed in the Files to Combine panel because the document is open.

Now you'll add the other project documents to the dialog box.

3 Click the Browse (Windows) or Choose (Mac OS) button under Add Files.

4 In the Open dialog box, click the arrow next to the Files of Type (Windows) or Show (Mac OS) text box to show the pop-up menu. This menu lists the types of files that you can convert and consolidate using this dialog box. Make sure that All Supported Formats is selected.

Note: *The types of files that you can convert varies depending on whether you are working on Windows or Mac OS.*

5 Still in the Open dialog box, navigate to the Lesson04 folder and select the file GC_Logo.jpg, and click Add to add the file to the Files to Combine list in the Create PDF From Multiple Documents dialog box.

6 Click Browse or Choose again, and add the following files:

- GC_CostBen.xls.pdf

- GC_Ad.pdf

- GC_Survey.pdf

- GC_Present.ppt.pdf

You can Ctrl-click (Windows) or Command-click (Mac OS) to select multiple files to include in the files name box. Click Add to include the files in Files to Combine window.

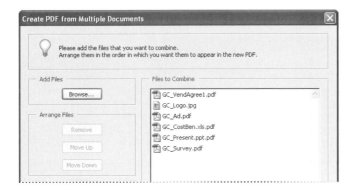

It doesn't matter in what order you added these files, because now you'll rearrange them. But first you'll remove the GCVend_Agree1.pdf file because that version of the vendor agreement still needs to be corrected.

7 In the Create PDF From Multiple Documents dialog box, select the file GCVend_Agree1.pdf, and click the Remove button to remove the file from the list.

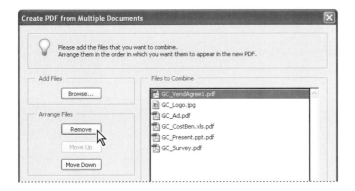

8 Select each of the remaining files in turn, and use the Move Up and Move Down button to arrange the files in the following order:

- GC_Ad.pdf

- GC_Present.ppt.pdf

- GC_Survey.pdf

- GC_CostBen.xls.pdf

- GC_Logo.jpg

Note: You can also drag files up and down in the list.

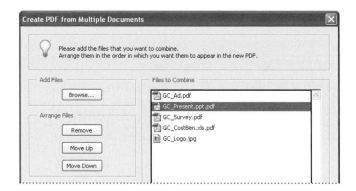

Now you're ready to create the Adobe PDF file.

If you're unsure that you've selected the correct files, you can use the Preview button to verify the contents of any PDF file. Simply select the file in the Files to Combine panel and click Preview. You can only preview PDF files.

Converting and consolidating the files

1 Click OK to convert and consolidate the listed files into one Adobe PDF file.

A dialog box shows the progression of the conversion and consolidation process. Depending on the files you convert and your operating system, some of the authoring programs may open and close automatically.

2 In the Save As dialog box, rename the file **GC_Presentation.pdf**. Click Save, and save your work in the Lesson04 folder.

The consolidated Adobe PDF file, originally called Binder1.pdf and renamed GC_Presentation.pdf, opens automatically.

3 Use the Next Page (▶) and Previous Page (◀) buttons to page through your consolidated documents.

Without leaving Acrobat, you have converted a JPEG file to Adobe PDF and combined it with several other PDF files.

When you convert files to Adobe PDF using the Create PDF From Multiple Files command, Acrobat uses the conversion settings from the Convert to Adobe PDF preferences. You can edit these conversion settings in the Convert to PDF preferences dialog box. Not all the conversion settings for all file types are editable.

Now you'll add project-related text, page numbers, and a background image to each page to identify the pages as being part of one project, but first you'll close the vendor agreement file.

4 Choose Window and select the GC_VendAgree1.pdf file to make the file active. Choose File > Close to close the vendor agreement file.

Adding header text and page numbers

1 Click the First Page button (◀) to go to the first page of the consolidated document.

2 Choose Document > Add Headers & Footers to open the dialog box that lets you add page numbers and text to each of your PDF pages.

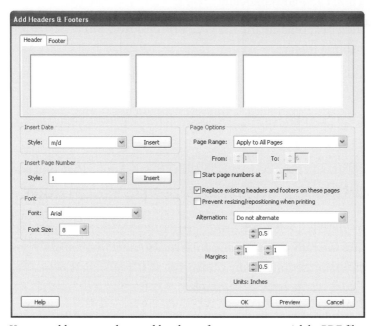

You can add page numbers and header or footer text to any Adobe PDF file.

3 In the Add Headers & Footers dialog box, click the Footer tab to bring it to the front. You'll add a page number to the bottom of each page.

4 Under Insert Page Number, click the down arrow next to the Style text box to open the pop-up menu and review your choices. We used the default value **1**. Then click the Insert button.

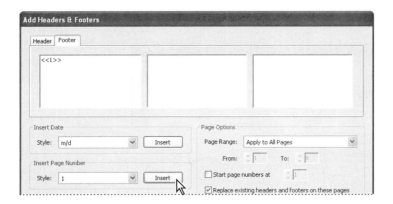

By default, the page number is added to the bottom left of the page (the left panel in the dialog box). You can change the position of the page number by using Margins settings or by moving the <<1>> notation from the left window to the center or right window.

5 Drag to highlight the <<1>> notation, and choose Ctrl-X (Windows) or Command-X (Mac OS). Click in the center window to create an insertion point, and choose Ctrl-V (Windows) or Command-V (Mac OS) to paste the page notation in the desired window.

You can also highlight the footer entry and drag it from window to window.

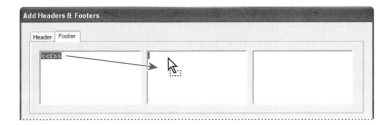

6 Click the Preview button at the bottom of the dialog box to preview your page numbering style. When you're finished, click OK to close the Preview pane.

You can experiment with a variety of options in this dialog box, including changing the margin settings and changing the font and font size, adding page numbers to every page or to alternate pages, and starting the page numbers at a number other than 1. In each case, you can preview your settings.

We chose to apply a page number to every page, at the bottom center of each page using the default margin settings and the default font and type size settings.

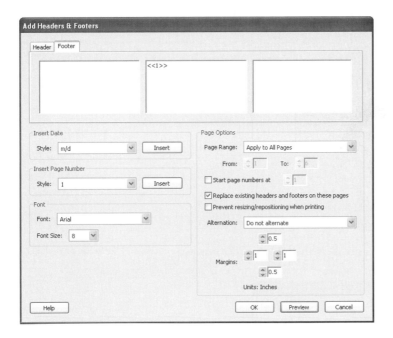

Now you'll add a header to identify the project that the documents relate to.

7 In the Add Headers & Footers dialog box, click the Header tab. (If you closed the Add Headers & Footers dialog box, choose Document > Add Headers & Footers to reopen the dialog box.)

8 Click in the center window to create an insertion point, and type in the text you want to use as a header. We typed in **Red Dot Project**. Be sure to click outside the text to deselect it.

Now you'll add a date.

9 In the Insert Date area, click the down arrow next to the Style text box to open the menu. Select a style for the date. We used mm/dd/yy. Click the Insert button.

The date is adjacent to the header, but you want it to be at the top left of the pages, so you'll realign it now.

10 Drag to highlight the date, and then drag the highlighted date to the left panel. (On Mac OS, you may need to delete the date from the center panel.)

11 Click Preview to preview the header information.

The header is a little low on the page, so now you'll adjust the margins to move the added text higher on the page.

12 Click OK to close the Preview and return to the Add Headers & Footers dialog box.

13 In the Page Options area, select the top value for Margins, and replace 0.5 with 0.25. The units are in inches. For information on changing the page units, see Lesson 7, "Modifying PDF Files."

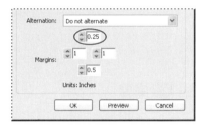

Again, you can choose whether to add the header information to all or selected pages. For this project, you'll add the information to all pages (the default value).

14 When you are satisfied with your header and footer information, click OK to add both your header information and footer information to each page.

15 Use the Next Page (▶) and Previous Page (◀) buttons to page through the document and view your work.

As you page through the document, you notice that the header and footer do not look good on page 6, the last page of the combined document. You'll remove the header and footer from this page, but first you'll save your work.

16 Choose File > Save.

Editing headers and footers

First you'll remove all the headers and footers.

1 If necessary, click the First Page button (◀|) to go to the first page of the PDF file.

2 Choose Edit > Undo Headers/Footers.

Note: If you closed the Add Headers & Footers dialog box between adding the footer information and adding the header information, you may have to do Step 2 twice.

All the header and footer information is removed from all pages.

3 Choose Document > Add Headers & Footers.

Notice that your header and footer information is preserved. Now you'll reapply the information, but only to the first five pages.

4 Click the Header tab, and click the down arrow to open the Page Range menu. Choose Apply to Page Range.

5 Leave the 1 in the From text box, but click the down arrow of the To text box to change the value from 6 to 5.

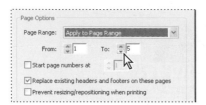

6 Click the Footer tab and verify that the page range for the footer has been changed also.

7 Click OK to apply the changes.

8 Use the Next Page (▶) and Previous Page (◀) buttons to page through the document to make sure your changes have been made. When you're sure the changes are satisfactory, choose File > Save to save your work.

Adding a watermark image

Now that you've consolidated the project files, you want to be sure that anyone who opens and reviews this PDF file understands that this is the archive copy of the project documentation. To do this, you'll add a watermark image to each page.

1 Choose Document > Add Watermark & Background.

2 For Type, select the option Add a Watermark. Verify that the options Show When Displaying On Screen and Show When Printing are selected.

Now you'll locate the file that contains the watermark image. The file in which you keep this watermark image may contain multiple images, but each image must be on a separate page.

3 For Source, select From File, and then click Browse (Windows) or Choose (Mac OS).

4 In the Open dialog box, select WaterImage.pdf in the Lesson04 folder, and click Open.

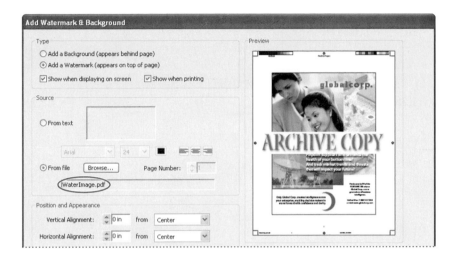

The Preview pane shows the composite effect.

Now you'll rotate the watermark image and set the opacity.

5 For Position and Appearance, make sure that Center is selected for Vertical Alignment and for Horizontal Alignment. This centers the image on the page.

6 For Rotation, enter the degree of rotation for the image, and press Enter or Return. We entered 45 degrees. You can type in a value or use the up and down arrows to change the value. Then drag the opacity slider to 40% or replace 100% with 40% in the text box. This sets the opacity of the watermark image.

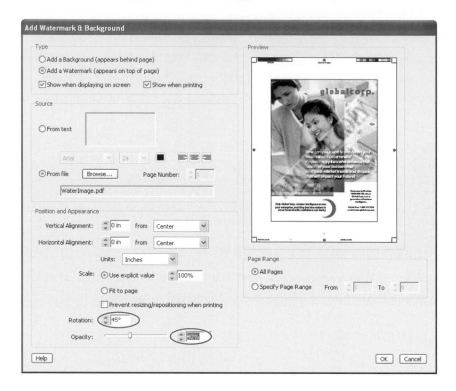

7 For Page Range, make sure that the option All Pages is selected.

8 When you're satisfied with the appearance, as shown in the preview panel of the dialog box, click OK.

Again, because page 6 is an odd-sized page, the watermark is too large to fit on the page. You could remove the watermark as you did with the headers and footers in the previous section, re-add the water mark to the first five pages, and then use the Fit to Page option in the Add Watermark & Background dialog box to resize the watermark for page 6. For this lesson, though, you'll leave it as is.

9 Use the Next Page (▶) and Previous Page (◀) buttons to browse through the file.

10 Choose File > Save, and save the GC_Presentation.pdf file when you are finished reviewing your work. Minimize the window.

Using the Print command to create Adobe PDF files

As you just saw, you can easily create Adobe PDF files using the Acrobat Create PDF command and the Create PDF From Multiple Files command. Additionally as you saw in Lesson 3, Microsoft applications such as Word, PowerPoint, and Excel, include Convert to Adobe PDF buttons that allow you to convert a Microsoft file to Adobe PDF quickly and easily without leaving your authoring program. Other authoring applications, such as Adobe InDesign®, Adobe Photoshop®, and Adobe PageMaker®, have special commands such as the Export command and the Save As command that allow you to convert a file to Adobe PDF. To make full use of these commands, you should consult the documentation that came with your application.

While not all file types are supported by the Create PDF command or the Create PDF From Multiple Files command and while not all authoring applications have special buttons or commands for converting files to Adobe PDF, you can still create an Adobe PDF file from almost any application file by using the application's Print command in conjunction with the Adobe PDF printer.

Note: *The Adobe PDF printer isn't a physical printer like the one sitting in your office or on your desk. Rather, it is a simulated printer that converts your file to Adobe PDF instead of printing it to paper. The printer name is Adobe PDF (Windows) or Adobe PDF 7.0 (Mac OS).*

Finding your Adobe PDF printer

On both Windows and Mac OS, the Adobe PDF printer is installed and added to your list of printers automatically when you install Acrobat.

1 To verify that the Adobe PDF printer is installed, do one of the following:

- On Windows 2000, click the Start menu, and choose Settings> Printers.

- On Windows XP, click the Start menu, and choose Printers and Faxes.

- On Mac OS, navigate to Applications:Utilities:Printer Setup Utility.

You'll see the Adobe PDF printer (or Adobe PDF 7.0 printer) listed with the other printers present on your system.

2 Close the dialog box when you're finished.

Printing to the Adobe PDF printer

In this part of the lesson, you'll convert a text file to Adobe PDF using the File > Print command in conjunction with your Adobe PDF printer. You can use this technique from almost any application, including the Microsoft and Adobe applications that have built-in Convert to Adobe PDF buttons and Export or Save as Adobe PDF commands.

Navigate to the Lesson04 folder, and double-click the Memo.txt file.

The text file should open in NotePad (or equivalent) on Windows and in TextEdit (or equivalent) on Mac OS. Follow the steps for your platform, Windows or Mac OS, to convert the file to Adobe PDF.

On Windows:

Note: Steps may vary depending on whether you are using Windows 2000 or XP. These steps assume that you are using Windows XP Pro.

1 In your text editing program, choose File > Page Setup.

2 In the Page Setup dialog box, click the Printer button.

3 Click the arrow next to the Name text box to open the list of available printers. Select Adobe PDF, click OK, and click OK again to return to the memo.

If you want to change the settings used in the conversion of the text file to Adobe PDF, you would do so by clicking the Properties button in the Page Setup dialog box. Lesson 6, "Customizing Quality and File Size" describes how to change these Adobe PDF Settings. For this lesson, you'll use the default values.

4 Choose File > Print, make sure that the Adobe PDF printer is selected, and click Print.

5 Click Save in the Save PDF File As dialog box. You can name the PDF file and choose where it is saved in this Save dialog box. For this lesson, save the file using the default name (Memo.pdf) in the default location (My Documents).

A dialog box shows the progression of the conversion.

6 If the PDF file doesn't open automatically, navigate to your My Documents directory, and double-click the Memo.pdf file to open it in Acrobat. When you have reviewed the file, close it and exit NotePad (or equivalent).

On Mac OS:

1 Choose File > Print, and make sure that the Adobe PDF 7.0 printer is selected.

If you want to change the settings used in the conversion of the text file to Adobe PDF, you would do so by choosing PDF Options from the pop-up menu below Presets. Lesson 6, "Customizing Quality and File Size" describes how to change the Adobe PDF Settings. For this lesson, you'll use the default values.

2 Click Print.

3 In the Save to File dialog box, you can rename the PDF file and choose where to save it. For this lesson, save the file as **Memo.pdf** in the Lesson04 folder.

4 Click Save.

A dialog box shows the progression of the conversion.

5 If the PDF file doesn't open automatically, navigate to the Lesson04 folder, and double-click the Memo.pdf file to open it in Acrobat. When you have reviewed the file, close it and quit the TextEdit (or equivalent) application.

You have just converted a simple text document to an Adobe PDF document using the authoring application's Print command.

Searching a PDF file

You can easily search any PDF file that you have open in Acrobat using the Search PDF pane, and if you have an active Internet connection, you can also search the web for Adobe PDF files that meet your search criteria.

In this lesson, you'll search the document that you assembled earlier for a word that may need to be replaced. After reviewing the project document that you assembled, your marketing department decided to replace the term "program" with "application" when the word program is used to refer to a software product. You'll search the GC_Presentation.pdf file to see how often the word is used.

1 Click the GC_Presentation.pdf at the bottom of your screen to maximize the document window for the consolidated file.

Windows   *Mac OS*

2 Click the Search button (🔍) on the Acrobat toolbar to open the Search PDF pane to the right of the document window.

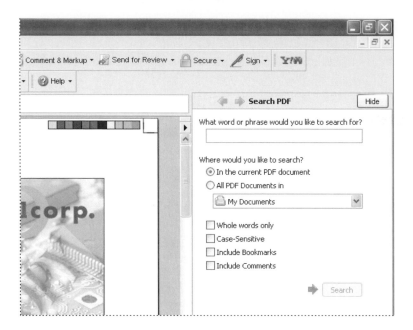

From this Search PDF pane, you can search the active document, or you can search all documents in a specified folder or location. You can refine your search by using the search criteria options. You can also extend your search to the Internet.

First, you'll search the current PDF document for the one word, "program."

3 Click the option Find a Word in the Current Document at the bottom of the Search pane.

The Find toolbar opens in the document pane.

4 Enter **program** in the text box, and click the Next button.

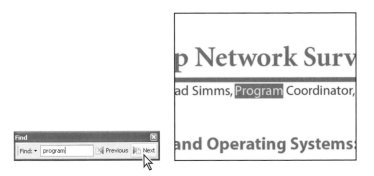

Acrobat searches your document, highlighting the first occurrence of the word **program**.

5 Click the Next button again to move to the next occurrence of **program**.

While this Find mechanism is effective, you can imagine how time consuming it might be to search a long document for a regularly used word. A more efficient search mechanism is offered by the Search button.

On the Find toolbar, click the arrow next to the Find button to see additional options for refining the Find command.

6 Click the Close button on the Find toolbar to hide the toolbar.

7 At the top of the Search PDF pane, enter **program** in the text box labeled "What word or phrase would you like to search for?" You can enter a word, several words, or a word fragment.

8 For Where Would You Like to Search, make sure that In the Current PDF Document is checked. Leave all the other options unchecked, and then click Search.

The search results are listed in the Results window. The icon next to the search result indicates that the word occurs in the document. (In a moment, you'll extend your search to include bookmarks and you'll see these search results denoted with different icons.)

Additional search criteria are available if you click the Use Advanced Search Options link at the bottom of the Search PDF pane. You can restore the limited search criteria by clicking the Use Basic Search Options link at the bottom of the Search PDF pane.

If you were looking for information on a topic, you can see that having the search word presented in context would help you quickly find the more important occurrences.

9 Click on each occurrence of the search term to go to that word in the document pane.

You can also extend your search to include bookmarks and comments.

10 Click the New Search button in the Search PDF pane.

11 Type **Global Corp.** in the search text box.

12 Click the Include Bookmarks option so that the box contains a check mark.

13 Click the Search button.

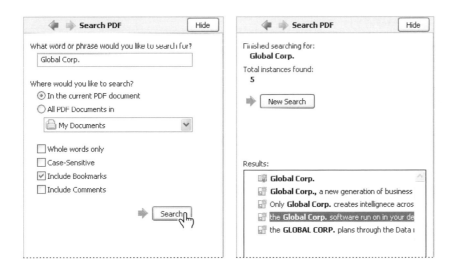

Notice that the first occurrence of Global Corp. is preceded by a different icon (🗐). This icon indicates that the search term is found in a bookmark.

14 Click the search result marked with the bookmark icon. The Bookmarks tab opens automatically, and the bookmark label containing the search term is highlighted.

15 When you are finished, choose File > Close, and close the GC_Presentation.pdf file.

16 Choose File > Exit (Windows) or Acrobat > Quit Acrobat (Mac OS) to exit or quit Acrobat.

💡 *Click the Search the Internet Using Yahoo button (   ) on the Acrobat toolbar to extend your search to the internet.*

Exploring on your own: Dragging and dropping files

In this lesson, you've looked at several ways to create Adobe PDF files. You can also create Adobe PDF files from a variety of image, HTML and plain text files by simply dragging the file onto the Acrobat icon or (in Windows) by dragging the file into the document pane in Acrobat.

Experiment with dragging the Orchids.jpg file and the Domino_Dog.jpg files onto the Acrobat icon on your desktop. Close any open PDF files when you are finished.

Exploring on your own: Creating Adobe PDF from the context menu (Windows)

On Windows, you can also create and consolidate Adobe PDF files using the context menu.

Using the Convert to Adobe PDF command

1 Navigate to the Lesson04 folder, and right-click on the file Memo.txt.

2 From the context menu, choose Convert to Adobe PDF.

Text files are converted to Adobe PDF using Web Capture and opened in Acrobat. Different conversion methods are used for other file types, but the conversion method is always determined automatically by Acrobat.

3 Choose File > Save. Name the file and choose where to save it in the Save As dialog box.

When you are finished, close any open Adobe PDF files and exit Acrobat.

Using the Combine in Adobe Acrobat command

1 Navigate to the Lesson04 folder, and select the file GC_Logo.jpg.

2 Ctrl-click to add more files to the selection. We added GC_VendAgree.tif.

3 Right-click, and from the context menu, choose Combine in Adobe Acrobat.

Acrobat opens and displays the Create PDF From Multiple Files, with the target files listed in the Files to Combine list. You can add to the list of files, rearrange files, delete files, and convert and consolidate files as described in "Converting and combining different types of files" in this lesson.

When you are finished, close any open PDF files and exit Acrobat.

Review questions

1 How can you find out which file types can be converted to Adobe PDF using the Create PDF From File or Create PDF From Multiple Files commands?

2 If you're working with a file type that isn't supported by the Create PDF From File or From Multiple Files command, how can you create a PDF file?

3 How can you add a "confidential" image or text to some or all pages in an Adobe PDF file?

4 After you have added a header or footer to an Adobe PDF document, can you change the header or footer?

Review answers

1 Do one of the following:

• Choose File > Create PDF > From File. Open the Files of Type (Windows) or Show (Mac OS) menu in the Open dialog box to view the supported file types.

• Choose File > Create PDF > From Multiple Files. Click the Browse or Choose button, and open the Files of Type (Windows) or Show (Mac OS) menu in the Open dialog box to view the supported file types.

2 Simply "print" your file using the Adobe PDF printer. In your authoring application, choose File > Print, and choose the Adobe PDF printer in the Print or Page Setup dialog box. When you click the Print button, Acrobat creates an Adobe PDF file rather than sending your file to a desktop printer.

3 First you need to create the image or text that you want to add to each page. Then you can add this image or text file as a background or watermark using the Document > Add Watermark & Background command.

4 Yes. You can undo any header or footer operation using the Edit > Undo Headers/Footers command.

Lesson 5

5 Creating Adobe PDF from Web Pages

Acrobat lets you create editable and searchable files by converting web pages to Adobe PDF. You can use the resulting PDF files for a variety of archival, presentation, and distribution needs. On Windows, you can convert web pages directly from Internet Explorer.

In this lesson, you'll learn how to do the following:

• Convert a web page to Adobe PDF. This process uses PDFMaker.

• Download and convert weblinks from a PDF version of a web page.

• Build a PDF file of favorite web pages.

• Update or refresh your PDF version of a website or collection of converted web pages.

• Convert web pages to Adobe PDF and print them directly from Internet Explorer (Windows).

This lesson will take about 45 minutes to 1 hour to complete.

Copy the Lesson05 folder to your desktop, or create a Lesson05 folder on your desktop. This is where you'll save your converted web pages.

Note: *Windows 2000 users may need to unlock the lesson files before using them. For information, see "Copying the Classroom in a Book files" on page 4.*

Converting web pages to Adobe PDF

You can use Acrobat to download or "capture" pages from the World Wide Web and convert them to Adobe PDF. You can define a page layout, set display options for fonts and other visual elements, and create bookmarks for web pages that you convert to Adobe PDF.

Because converted web pages are in Adobe PDF, you can easily save them, print them, email them to others, or archive them for your own future use and review. Acrobat gives you the power to convert remote, minimally formatted files into local, fully formatted PDF documents that you can access at any time.

The ability to convert web pages to Adobe PDF is especially useful for people who make presentations that include web pages and for those who travel a lot. If you need to include a website in a presentation, you can convert the required portions of the website to PDF so that you have no concern about web access during your presentation. If you have downloaded and converted all the linked pages, links will behave in the same way as if you were on the actual website. Similarly, if you travel extensively, you can create one PDF file that contains all of your most visited websites. Whenever you have convenient web access, you can refresh all pages on the site in one simple action. You can then browse your updated PDF version of the websites at your leisure.

Connecting to the web

Before you can download and convert web pages to Adobe PDF, you must be able to access the World Wide Web. If you need help with setting up an Internet connection, talk to your Internet Service Provider (ISP).

When you have a connection to the Internet, you can set your Acrobat preferences for handling Adobe PDF files.

1 Start Acrobat.

2 In Acrobat, choose Edit > Preferences (Windows) or Acrobat > Preferences (Mac OS), and select Internet in the left pane of the Preferences dialog box.

3 In the Preferences dialog box, if you are working on Mac OS, make sure that the option for checking your browser settings when starting Acrobat is checked. Having this option checked, ensures that your settings are checked automatically whenever you launch Acrobat. Acrobat 7.0 works automatically with Safari (Mac OS) to make viewing Adobe PDF documents on the web easy. The first time you open Acrobat, your system automatically is configured to use Acrobat to open PDF files in your browser.

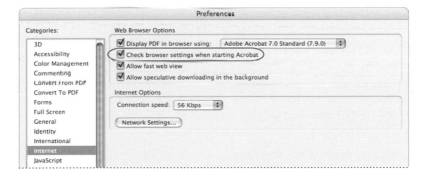

4 Click the Internet Settings button (Windows) or Network Settings button (Mac OS) to check your network settings. On Windows, your settings are on the Connections tab. (If you need help with your internet settings, consult your IT professional.)

5 Click OK in the Preferences dialog box to apply any changes you have made Click Cancel to exit the dialog box without making any changes.

Setting web browser options

By default, several Internet preference options that control how Acrobat interacts with your web browser are automatically set to be on.

• Display PDF in Browser displays any PDF document opened from the web inside the browser window. If this option is not selected, PDF documents open in a separate Acrobat window.

• Check Browser Settings When Starting Acrobat checks your default browser settings for compatibility with the application each time the application is launched (Mac OS).

• Allow Fast Web View downloads PDF documents for viewing on the web one page at a time. If this option is not selected, the entire PDF file downloads before it is displayed. If you want the entire PDF document to continue downloading in the background while you view the first page of requested information, also select Allow Speculative Downloading in the Background.

• Allow Speculative Downloading in the Background allows a PDF document to continue downloading from the web, even after the first requested page displays. Downloading in the background stops when any other task, such as paging through the document, is initiated in Acrobat.

Setting options for converting web pages

You should set the options that control the structure and appearance of your converted web pages before you download and convert the pages.

1 In Acrobat, choose File > Create PDF > From Web Page.

2 Click Settings.

3 In the dialog box, click the General tab.

4 Under File Type Settings, in the File Description column, select HTML and click Settings.

5 Click the General tab and look at the options available.

You can select colors for text, page backgrounds, links, and Alt text (the text that replaces an image on a web page when the image is unavailable). You can also select background display options. For this lesson, you'll leave these options unchanged and proceed to select font and encoding options.

6 Click the Fonts and Encodings tab.

You see that Times-Roman is used for body text, Helvetica for headings, and Courier for pre-formatted text. You'll change these defaults.

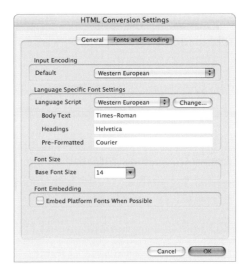

7 Click the Change button under Language Specific Font Settings.

This opens the Select Fonts dialog box that allows you to reset the fonts used for body, heading and pre-formatted text in converted web pages.

8 Under Font for Body Text, choose a font from the pop-up menu. (We chose **Helvetica**.)

9 Under Font for Headings, choose a thick sans serif font from the menu. (We chose **Arial Black**.)

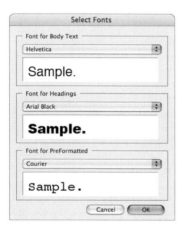

10 Click OK to accept the new font settings.

11 For the Base Font Size menu, choose a size for the body text. We used **14**. Heading text will be proportionately larger, as determined by the HTML coding.

Be sure to leave the Embed Platform Fonts When Possible option unchecked (blank). The embedding platform fonts option stores the font used on the pages in the PDF file so that the text always appears in the original fonts. Embedding fonts in this way increases the size of the file.

12 Click OK to return to the General tab of the Web Page Conversion Settings dialog box.

13 On the General tab, under PDF Settings, make sure that the following options are selected (options are selected when they are checked):

• Create Bookmarks to create a tagged bookmark for each downloaded web page, using the page's HTML title tag as the bookmark name. Tagged bookmarks help you organize and navigate your converted pages.

• Create PDF Tags to store structure in the PDF file that corresponds to the HTML structure of the original web pages.

- Place Headers and Footers on New Pages to place a header with the web page's title and place a footer with the page's URL, page number in the downloaded set, and the date and time of download.

- Save Refresh Commands to save a list of all URLs in the PDF file for the purpose of refreshing pages.

14 Click the Page Layout tab.

On Windows, a sample page with the current settings applied appears in the dialog box. You can choose from standard page sizes in the Page Size menu, or you can define a custom page size. You can also define margins and choose page orientation.

15 Under Margins, enter **0.25** for Left and Right, Top and Bottom.

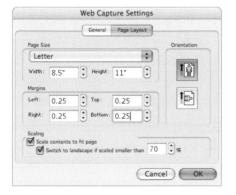

16 Click OK to accept the settings and return to the Create PDF from Web Page dialog box.

After you have some experience converting web pages to Adobe PDF, you can experiment with the conversion settings to customize the look and feel of your converted web pages.

About pages on websites

Keep in mind that a website can have more than one level of pages. The opening page is the top level of the site, and any links on that page go to other pages at a second level. Links on second-level pages go to pages at a third level, and so on. In addition, links may go to external sites (for example, a link at a website on tourism may connect to a website for a travel agency). Most websites can be represented as a tree diagram that becomes broader as you move down the levels.

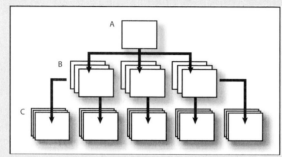

Important: *You need to be aware of the number and complexity of pages you may encounter when downloading more than one level of a website at a time. It is possible to select a complex site that will take a very long time to download. Use the Get Entire Site option with great caution. In addition, downloading pages over a modem connection will usually take much longer than downloading them over a high-speed connection.*

Web site tree diagram
A. First level B. Second level C. Third level

Creating an Adobe PDF file from a web page

Note: Because web pages are updated on a regular basis, when you visit the web pages described in this lesson, the content of the pages may have changed. Even though we have tried to use links that we think will be relatively stable, you may have to use links other than those described in this section. However, you should be able to apply the steps in this lesson to virtually any links on any website. If you are working inside a corporate firewall, for example, you might find it easier to do this lesson substituting an internal site for the Adobe Press site or the Peachpit site.

Now you'll enter a URL in the Create PDF from Web Page dialog box and convert some web pages.

1 If the Create PDF from Web Page dialog box is not open, choose File > Create PDF > From Web Page.

2 For URL, enter the address of the website you'd like to convert. (We used the Adobe Press website at http://www.adobepress.com.)

You control the number of converted pages by specifying the levels of site hierarchy you wish to convert, starting from your entered URL. For example, the top level consists of the page corresponding to the specified URL; the second level consists of pages linked from the top-level page, and so on.

3 Make sure that the Get Only option is selected, and that 1 is selected for the number of levels.

4 Select Stay on Same Path to convert only pages that are subordinate to the URL you entered.

5 Select Stay On Same Server to download only pages on the same server as the URL you entered.

6 Click Create. The Download Status dialog box displays the status of the download in progress. When downloading and conversion are complete, the converted website appears in the Acrobat document window, with bookmarks in the Bookmarks panel. Tagged bookmark icons differ from the icons for regular bookmarks.

If any linked material is not downloadable you will get an error message. Click OK to clear any error message.

7 Click the Fit Page button (⬍) on the Acrobat toolbar and the Single Page button (▢) on the Acrobat status bar to fit the view of the converted web page to your screen.

8 Use the Next Page button (▶) and the Previous Page button (◀) to review the several PDF pages. The single home page of the AdobePress.com website has been converted into several web pages to preserve the integrity of the page content.

9 Choose File > Save As, name the file Web.pdf and save it in the Lesson 11 folder.

Note: On Windows, if you're downloading more than one level of pages, the Download Status dialog box moves to the background after the first level is downloaded. The globe in the Create PDF from Web Page button in the toolbar continues spinning to show that pages are being downloaded. Choose Advanced > Web Capture > Bring Status Dialogs to Foreground to see the dialog box again. (On Mac OS, the Download Status dialog box stays in the foreground.)

The converted website is navigable and editable just like any other PDF document. Acrobat formats the pages to reflect your page-layout conversion settings, as well as the look of the original website.

Downloading and converting links in a converted web page

When you click a weblink in the Adobe PDF version of the web page and when the weblink links to an unconverted page, Acrobat downloads and converts that page to Adobe PDF. In order to convert linked pages to Adobe PDF, you must have the Web Capture preferences set to open weblinks in Acrobat (the default setting) rather than in your default browser. You'll check the setting now.

1 In Acrobat, choose Edit > Preferences (Windows) or Acrobat > Preferences (Mac OS), and select Web Capture in the left pane of the Preferences dialog box.

2 For Open Weblinks, make sure that In Acrobat is selected. Then click OK.

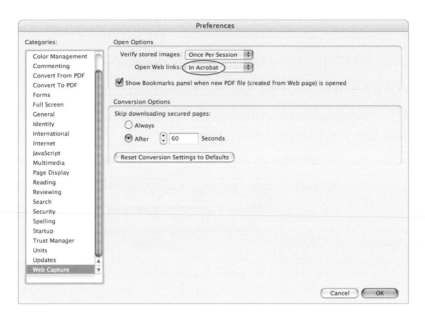

3 Navigate through the converted website until you find a weblink to an unconverted page (we used the "Events & Promotions" link), and click the link. (The pointer changes to a pointing finger with a plus sign when positioned over a weblink, and the URL of the link is displayed.)

Note: *If the Specify Weblink Behavior dialog box appears, make sure that Open Weblink in Acrobat is selected, and click OK.*

The Download Status dialog box again displays the status of the download. When the download and conversion are complete, the linked page appears in the Acrobat window. A bookmark for the page is added to the Bookmarks list.

Choose File > Save As, rename the file **Web1.pdf**, and save it in the Lesson05 folder.

4 Click the Previous View button () to return to the first page of the converted Adobe Press page.

You also think you might like to see what's involved in registering as a member.

5 Click the "registered" link under the "Join the Adobe Press Club!" heading.

The Download Status dialog box again displays the status of the download, and another bookmark for the page is added to the Bookmarks list.

Deleting converted web pages

After reading the membership information, you decide not to register at this moment. Rather than keep the unwanted form in your file, you'll delete the unwanted page.

1 In the Bookmarks panel, click the bookmark Login to view the related page.

This is the page you'll delete.

2 Right-click (Windows) or Control-click (Mac OS) the bookmark, and choose Delete Page(s) from the context menu. Click Yes in the alert box.

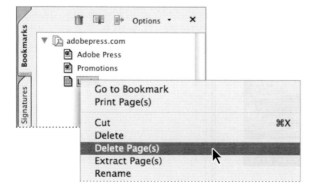

3 The page is deleted.

Each bookmark represents one HTML page, so when you delete a page using the bookmark, you delete all the Adobe PDF pages that correspond to that bookmark.

Note: If you click Delete in the context menu, you delete the bookmark only.

Now you'll use the Bookmarks panel to navigate to another converted page.

4 Click the Adobe Press bookmark in the Bookmarks panel to return to the first page of your PDF file.

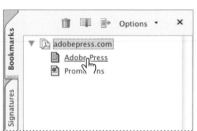 

Clicking a bookmark...   *... takes you to the corresponding page.*

Updating converted web pages

Because you selected the Save Refresh Commands option when you first converted the web pages to Adobe PDF, you can refresh or update all pages from one or multiple sites from one Acrobat dialog box.

You can refresh web pages in a PDF document to retrieve the most up-to-date version from the website. Whenever you use the Refresh command, you download the entire website or link again and build a new PDF file. Any pages where components have changed—for example, text, weblinks, embedded filenames, and formatting—are listed as bookmarks in the Bookmarks panel under the New and Changed Pages bookmark. Any new pages that have been added to the site are also downloaded.

Note: The Refresh command may not update converted web pages that contain forms data. In this case, you will get an error message identifying the pages.

1 With an internet connection open, choose Advanced > Web Capture > Refresh Pages.

2 Select Create Bookmarks for New and Changed Pages.

You specify whether Acrobat looks only for text changes or all changes, including text, images, weblinks, embedded files, etc. (We used Compare All Page Components to Detect Changed Pages.)

3 Click Edit Refresh Commands List.

This window displays the URLs of all the websites that have been converted to Adobe PDF in this file. You can deselect any URLs for pages that you don't want to refresh. (Click Clear All and then reselect the URLs that you want to refresh.)

4 Click OK to accept the default selection, and click Refresh to update your converted PDF pages.

Note: *If you have difficulty here, you may need to open your browser and repeat the above steps from step 1 on.*

Earlier in the lesson, you deleted a page from the PDF file of the converted website. Notice that the page you deleted in the earlier version is present in the refreshed file and is also listed in the Bookmarks panel under the New and Changed Pages bookmark. Any reorganization or deletion of pages in the PDF file is lost when you refresh, though you could have excluded the deleted page in step 3 above. (You have two sets of bookmarks because you elected to create bookmarks for new and changed pages earlier.)

5 Click the Window command on the Acrobat menu bar, and notice that you have two windows open. Because you want to keep the Web1.pdf file, you'll save the new file under a different name.

6 Choose File > Save As, and save the new file as **Web2.pdf**. Close the Web2.pdf file.

Building an Adobe PDF file of favorite web pages

You've created a PDF file containing web pages from the Adobe Press website. In addition to surfing this site, suppose you would also like to check the Adobe home page.

In this section, you'll start to build an Adobe PDF file of your favorite web pages by appending the Adobe home page to the Adobe Press PDF pages that you have already created.

1 With the Web1.pdf file open, choose Advanced > Web Capture > Append Web Page.

2 In the Add to PDF from Web Page dialog box, enter the URL for your favorite Web site. (We used **http://www.adobe.com**.)

3 For Get Only, select 1. Select the Stay on Same Path option and the Stay on Same Server option.

4 Click Create.

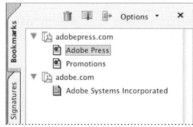

Acrobat appends a PDF version of the Adobe home page to the Adobe Press pages. You can download any linked pages on this site as described in "Downloading and converting links in a converted web page" in this lesson.

You can repeat this process to build up a file of your favorite websites that you can keep on your system, share with friends, and refresh at your convenience.

5 When you are finished, choose Window > Close All to close any open files. If you are working on Mac OS, this concludes the lesson.

Converting web pages in Internet Explorer (Windows)

If you've ever had the frustrating experience of printing a web page from your browser only to discover text missing at the end of each line, you'll love the Acrobat feature that allows you to create and print Adobe PDF without ever leaving your browser.

On Windows, Acrobat adds a button with a drop-down menu to the toolbar of Internet Explorer (version 5.01 and later), which allows you to convert the currently displayed web page to an Adobe PDF file or convert and print it, email it, or send it for review in one easy operation. When you print a web page that you have converted to an Adobe PDF file, the page is reformatted to a standard page size and logical page breaks are added.

*Button on PDF toolbar
provides easy conversion and
print options.*

First you'll set the preferences used to create Adobe PDF pages from your web pages.

Setting the conversion preferences

You set preferences from the drop-down menu that Acrobat adds to the Internet Explorer toolbar. Note that the preferences that you set using the Internet Explorer Adobe PDF toolbar determine only whether converted files are opened in Acrobat automatically, and whether you are prompted to confirm the deletion of files or addition of pages to an existing PDF file. The Acrobat web page conversion settings (see "Setting options for converting web pages" in this lesson), which are available only from Acrobat itself, let you set more advanced settings such as creating bookmarks and tags. After you've set the Acrobat web page conversion settings, you need to use the Create PDF from Web Page feature in Acrobat at least once before the settings take effect in Internet Explorer web page conversions.

1 Open Internet Explorer, and navigate to a favorite web page. We opened the Peachpit Press home page at http://www.peachpit.com.

2 In Internet Explorer, click the arrow next to the Convert Current Web Page to an Adobe PDF File button ( ), and choose Preferences from the menu. (The button is at the right end of the toolbar.)

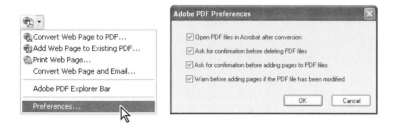

💡 *If you don't see the button in Internet Explorer, choose View > Toolbars > Adobe PDF.*

3 For this part of the lesson, you'll use the default values for the preferences. After you've reviewed the options, click Cancel to close the dialog box without making any changes.

Opening the Adobe PDF pane

Acrobat also adds an Adobe PDF pane to Internet Explorer where you can manage your converted web pages. Folders and PDF files are organized under the root directory Desktop. You can create, rename, and delete folders in this pane, as well as rename and delete files. Only PDF files and folders containing PDF files are listed.

Note: The files and folders displayed in the Adobe PDF pane are the same files and folders on your system. Because only PDF files are displayed in the Adobe PDF pane, if you attempt to delete a folder that contains files other than PDF files (files that will not be visible in the Adobe PDF pane), you will be asked to confirm the deletion.

1 In Internet Explorer, click the arrow next to the Convert Current Web Page to an Adobe PDF File button ( ), and choose Adobe PDF Explorer Bar from the menu.

Before you convert the Peachpit web page to Adobe PDF, you'll create a folder at the desktop level in which to save the file.

2 Select the Desktop icon in the Adobe PDF pane, and click the New Folder button (📁) at the top of the Adobe PDF pane.

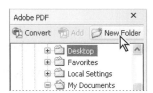

The new folder is automatically called New Folder.

💡 *If you want to add a new folder under an existing folder, select the folder in the Adobe PDF pane and click the New Folder button, or right-click the folder and choose New Folder.*

Now you'll rename the folder you created.

3 If necessary, click in the New Folder text label to select the text, and type in your new label. We typed in **Peachpit**.

Now you'll convert the Peachpit home page to Adobe PDF and save it in the folder that you just created.

Converting web pages to Adobe PDF

1 In the Adobe PDF pane, select the Peachpit folder that you just created.

2 Click the Convert button (📥) at the top of the Adobe PDF pane.

3 In the Convert Web Page to Adobe PDF dialog box, your Peachpit folder should be selected automatically. You just need to rename the PDF file if necessary. We typed in the name **PeachpitHome.pdf**.

4 Check the Open in Acrobat when Complete option, and then click Save.

The default filename used by Acrobat is the text used in the HTML tag <TITLE>. Any invalid characters in the web page filename are converted to an underscore when the file is downloaded and saved.

You can convert a web page to Adobe PDF and email it using the Convert Web Page and Email command in the Convert Current Web Page to an Adobe PDF File pop-up menu. (For more information, see Setting up an email-based review in the Complete Acrobat 7.0 Help.)

Converting linked pages

You can convert linked pages to Adobe PDF and add them to your current PDF file, just as you did in "Downloading and converting links in a converted web page" in this lesson.

Remember that in order to convert linked pages to Adobe PDF, you must set Web Capture preferences to open weblinks in Acrobat rather than in your default browser.

In this section, you'll convert and add the Adobe Press pages to your PDF version of the Peachpit home page.

1 In Acrobat, click the Peachpit Family link at the top of the page. The Download Status dialog box shows the progress of the conversion.

2 Click the Adobe Press link.

The PDF pages are automatically added to the end of the current file.

3 Choose File > Save to save your work, and then close any open files.

Now you'll see how converting a web page to PDF before printing it avoids unpleasant surprises. First you'll try printing a web page.

Printing web pages

1 In Internet Explorer, navigate to the Federal Emergency Management home page at http://www.fema.gov/.

2 If you have a printer connected to your system, click the Print button (🖨) on the Internet Explorer toolbar. Alternatively, choose File > Print Preview.

Your printed copy or print preview of the web page will probably be missing a word or so at the end of each line of text. In this next section, you'll convert the web page to Adobe PDF and print it without leaving Internet Explorer. With an Adobe PDF version of the page, you'll see *all* the text. Acrobat automatically resizes the web page to standard printer page sizes to avoid disappointing print results.

3 In Internet Explorer, click the arrow next to the Convert Current Web Page to an Adobe PDF file button (📄), and choose Print Web Page from the menu.

The progress of the conversion is shown in the Conversion to PDF Progress dialog box. When the conversion is complete, the Print dialog box for your default system printer opens automatically.

4 In the Print dialog box, select any required print options and click Print.

Take a look at the printed copy and notice that all the text is included and readable. Converting web pages to Adobe PDF before printing is an easy way to avoid unpleasant print results.

5 Close Internet Explorer, Acrobat, and close any open PDF files.

Review questions

1 How do you control the number of web pages converted by Acrobat?

2 How do you convert destinations of weblinks to PDF automatically?

3 How do you update your PDF file to show the latest version of a converted website?

Review answers

1 You can control the number of converted web pages by specifying the following options:

• The Levels option lets you specify how many levels in the site hierarchy you want to convert.

• The Stay on Same Path option lets you download only pages that are subordinate to the specified URL.

• The Stay on Same Server option lets you download only pages that are stored on the same server as the specified URL.

2 To convert the destination of a weblink to PDF, first choose Edit > Preferences (Windows) or Acrobat > Preferences (Mac OS), and then choose Web Capture in the left pane. Choose In Acrobat for the Open Weblinks option. After you have set this preference, clicking the weblink in the PDF file will convert the link's destination to PDF.

3 With an Internet connection open, choose Advanced > Web Capture > Refresh Pages to build a new PDF file using the same URLs and links. Select the Create Bookmarks for New and Changed Pages option if you want Acrobat to create bookmarks for pages that have been modified or added to the website since you last converted the website and its links. You also specify whether Acrobat looks only for text changes or for all changes. (You cannot refresh pages unless you selected the Save Refresh Commands option in the Web Page Conversion Settings dialog box to save a list of all URLs in the PDF file for the purpose of refreshing pages.)

6 Customizing Adobe PDF Output Quality

You control the output quality of your files by specifying appropriate Adobe PDF Settings for converting the files to PDF. In addition to the default Adobe PDF Settings designed to produce satisfactory results for the more common output needs, you can customize the Adobe PDF Settings to produce the best balance of file size and quality for your specific needs.

In this lesson, you'll learn how to do the following:

• Explore the different ways of changing the Adobe PDF settings used to convert files to Adobe PDF.

• Compare the quality and file size of Adobe PDF files converted with different Adobe PDF Settings.

• Customize compression, sampling, and image quality settings.

• Reduce the size of your final Adobe PDF file.

This lesson will take approximately 45 minutes to complete.

If needed, remove the previous lesson folder from your hard drive, and copy the Lesson06 folder onto it.

Note: Windows 2000 users may need to unlock the lesson files before using them. For information, see "Copying the Classroom in a Book files" on page 4.

Controlling Adobe PDF output quality

Acrobat produces Adobe PDF files that accurately preserve the look and content of the original document. When creating Adobe PDF files, Acrobat uses various methods to compress text and line art, and compress and downsample color, grayscale, and monochrome images. (Line art is described with a mathematical equation and is usually created with a drawing program such as Adobe Illustrator®. Images are described in pixels and are created with paint programs or from scanners. Monochrome images include most black-and-white illustrations made by paint programs and any images scanned with an image depth of 1 bit. Adobe Photoshop, for example, works with images.)

In this lesson, you'll learn how to choose Adobe PDF conversion settings to create an Adobe PDF file that best balances quality and size for your needs. First you'll look at the default settings that are available for converting your application files to Adobe PDF and where you can change these settings.

About the Adobe PDF Settings

The Adobe PDF Settings—the settings that control the conversion of files to Adobe PDF—can be accessed and set from a number of different places. You can access the Adobe PDF Settings from Distiller, from the Adobe PDF printer, from the Adobe PDF menu in Microsoft Office applications (Windows), from the Print dialog box in many authoring applications, and from the Start menu on Windows. Regardless of where you access the settings from, the Adobe PDF Settings dialog box and the options it contains are the same. (The dialog box for setting printing preferences may be named Adobe PDF Printing Preferences, Adobe PDF Printing Defaults, or Adobe PDF Document Properties, depending on how you access it.)

In this first part of the lesson, you'll look at where you change the predefined (or default) Adobe PDF Settings and where you define custom Adobe PDF Settings. Since some of the options vary by platform (Windows or Mac OS), you should skip the sections that don't apply to your platform.

In the later part of this lesson, you'll look at the results of using the different Adobe PDF Settings.

Changing the Adobe PDF Settings in Distiller

Distiller is available on both Windows and Mac OS.

1 Open Acrobat.

2 Choose Advanced > Acrobat Distiller to open Distiller.

You can choose one of the predefined Adobe PDF Settings from the Default Setting pop-up menu, or you can customize the settings.

3 To choose one of the predefined Adobe PDF Settings, click the arrow next to the Default Settings menu, and choose High Quality Print, Press Quality, Smallest File Size, or Standard. (For information on the PDF/A and PDF/X settings, see Lesson 15, "Using Adobe Acrobat for Professional Publishing" or see the Acrobat 7.0 online Help.)

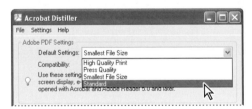

Choosing a default Adobe PDF Setting for converting files to Adobe PDF

These are the predefined Adobe PDF settings. A brief explanation of each setting is given in the information box below the Default Settings menu. For most beginning users of Acrobat, these predefined settings are sufficient. You'll examine the difference in quality and file size produced by the different settings later in this lesson.

Any customized Adobe PDF Settings that you may have created are also displayed in this menu.

4 We chose Smallest File Size.

5 To examine the Smallest File Size conversion settings or to customize the Adobe PDF Settings based on the selected default setting, choose Settings > Edit Adobe PDF Settings to open the Adobe PDF Settings dialog box.

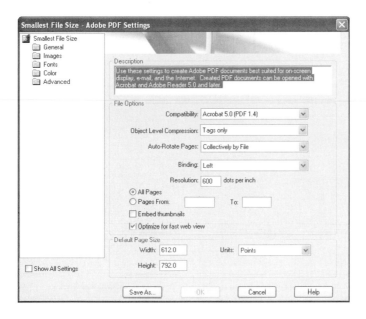

The settings on the various panels are those for the Smallest File Size Adobe PDF Settings. For information on customizing the options on these panels, see "Creating custom Adobe PDF Settings" in the Complete Acrobat 7.0 Help.

6 After you have reviewed the settings on the various panels, click Cancel to leave the settings unchanged, and exit or quit Distiller.

Later in this lesson you'll customize the settings on the Images panel of the Adobe PDF Settings dialog box.

If you are working in Mac OS, skip to "Changing the Adobe PDF Settings in the Adobe PDF printer" on page 183.

Changing the Adobe PDF Settings in PDFMaker (Windows)

On Windows, you can change the settings used to convert Microsoft Office documents to Adobe PDF without leaving your Microsoft Office application.

1 On Windows, open a Microsoft Office application, such as Word.

2 Click the Adobe PDF button on the Microsoft application menu bar, and choose Change Conversion Settings from the menu.

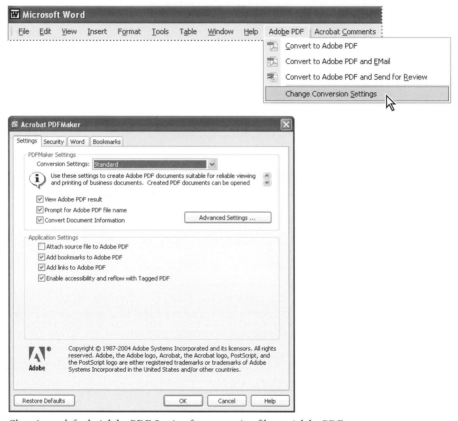

Choosing a default Adobe PDF Setting for converting files to Adobe PDF

You can choose one of the predefined Conversion Settings, or you can customize the settings.

3 To choose one of the predefined Conversion Settings, click the arrow next to the Conversion Settings menu, and choose a setting. A brief explanation of each setting is given in the information box below the Default Settings menu. Use the scroll bars to view the entire explanation if the text exceeds two lines. For most beginning users of Acrobat, these predefined settings are sufficient.Any customized Adobe PDF Settings that you may have created are also displayed in this menu.

For information on the PDF/A and PDF/X settings, see Lesson 15, "Using Adobe Acrobat for Professional Publishing" or the Acrobat 7.0 online Help.

For more information on setting the PDFMaker settings, see Lesson 3, "Converting Microsoft Office Files (Windows)."

4 We chose Smallest File Size.

5 To customize the Adobe PDF Settings, click the Advanced Settings button. Notice that the dialog box that opens has the same tabs and settings as the Adobe PDF Settings dialog box that you accessed using Distiller in the prior section of this lesson.

6 After you have reviewed the settings on the various tabs, click Cancel to leave the settings unchanged, and click Cancel to close the Acrobat PDFMaker dialog box.

7 Exit your Microsoft Office application. Note that any file that you subsequently convert using PDFMaker will use the setting selected in step 3 above until you change this setting again.

Changing the Adobe PDF Settings in the Adobe PDF printer

You can create a PDF file from just about any application that has a Print command by "printing" your file using the Adobe PDF printer. In this case, you simply use the File > Print command in your source application, and select Adobe PDF (or Adobe PDF 7.0) as your printer in your application's print dialog box. When you click the Print button, you create or "print" an Adobe PDF file rather than send a document to be printed on your printer. (Unless you change them, the settings used to convert your PDF file are the current Distiller settings.)

Note: *The Adobe PDF printer creates untagged PDF files. A tagged structure is required for reflowing content to a handheld device and is preferable for producing reliable results with a screen reader. (See Lesson 9, "Making Documents Accessible and Flexible.")*

On Windows:

1 Open an authoring application such as Adobe FrameMaker or Microsoft Word and create a new document and type in a few words of text.

2 Choose File > Print, and choose Adobe PDF from the printer menu.

Depending on your application, Click the Properties or Preferences button. (In some applications, you may need to click Setup in the Print dialog box to access the list of printers and the Properties or Preferences button.)

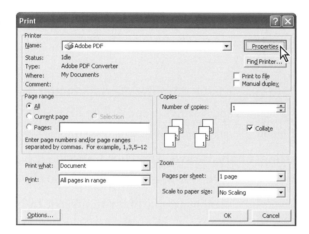

In the Adobe PDF Settings tab of the Adobe PDF Document Properties dialog box, choose one of the predefined Adobe PDF Settings from the Default Settings menu. Any customized Adobe PDF Settings that you may have created are also displayed in this menu.

3 To customize the conversion settings, click the Edit button next to the Default Settings menu.

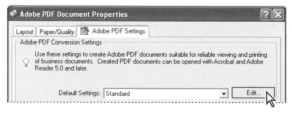

Customizing the Adobe PDF Settings

Notice that this Adobe PDF Settings dialog box has the same tabs and settings as the dialog box accessed from Distiller.

4 After you have reviewed the settings on the various tabs, click Cancel to leave the settings unchanged, and click Cancel to return to the Print or Print Setup dialog box.

If you wanted to convert the file you have open to Adobe PDF, you would click the Print button in the Print dialog box.

5 For this lesson, close the Print dialog box without printing.

6 Close the document without saving it and close your authoring application.

Changing the Adobe PDF Settings from the Print dialog box, changes the settings for that application only. To change the Adobe PDF Settings for all applications, change the settings from the Printers or Printers and Faxes Control Panel. For more information, see "Setting Adobe PDF printer properties" in the Complete Acrobat 7.0 Help.

On Mac OS:

1 Open an authoring application such as Microsoft Word or TextEdit and create a new document.

2 Choose File > Print, and choose Adobe PDF 7.0 from the Printer menu.

3 Select PDF Options from the pop-up menu (Copies & Pages) below the Presets menu to access the Adobe PDF Settings.

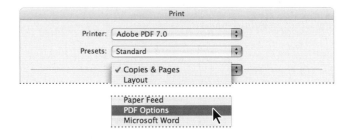

Choose PDF Options to change the PDF Settings.

4 Choose a setting from the Adobe PDF Settings menu. If you want to use a custom setting, you must first create the custom setting in Distiller. Any custom settings created in Distiller are available in the Adobe PDF Settings menu in this Print dialog box.

5 From the After PDF Creation menu, choose whether or not to launch Acrobat and display the PDF file.

6 Choose Cancel to close the Print dialog box without creating a PDF file. If you wanted to convert your open file to Adobe PDF, you would click the Print button in the Print dialog box.

7 Close your document and quit your authoring application.

💡 *Regardless of how you access the Adobe PDF Settings, you should check your settings periodically. Applications and utilities that create Adobe PDF use the last settings defined; the settings do not revert to the default values.*

Predefined Adobe PDF settings

You can choose a predefined settings file for creating Adobe PDF files. These settings are designed to balance file size with quality, depending on how the Adobe PDF file is to be used.

You can choose from the following sets of predefined Adobe PDF settings:

• *High Quality Print creates PDF files that have higher resolution than the Standard job option file. It downsamples color and grayscale images to 300 ppi and monochrome images to 1200 ppi, prints to a higher image resolution, and preserves the maximum amount of information about the original document. PDF files created with this settings file can be opened in Acrobat 5.0 and Acrobat Reader 5.0 and later.*

• *Press Quality creates PDF files for high-quality print production (for example, for digital printing or for separations to an imagesetter or platesetter), but does not create files that are PDF/X compliant. In this case, the quality of the content is the highest consideration. The objective is to maintain all the information in a PDF file that a commercial printer or prepress service provider needs in order to print the document correctly. This set of options downsamples color and grayscale images to 300 ppi and monochrome images to 1200 ppi, embeds subsets of fonts used in the document (if allowed), and prints a higher image resolution than the Standard settings. Print jobs with fonts that cannot be embedded will fail. These PDF files can be opened in Acrobat 5.0 and Acrobat Reader 5.0 and later.*

Note: *Before creating an Adobe PDF file to send to a commercial printer or prepress service provider, find out what the output resolution and other settings should be, or ask for a .joboptions file with the recommended settings. You may need to customize the Adobe PDF settings for a particular provider and then provide a .joboptions file of your own.*

• **Smallest File Size** *creates PDF files for displaying on the web or an intranet, or for distribution through an email system for onscreen viewing. This set of options uses compression, downsampling, and a relatively low image resolution. It converts all colors to sRGB, and does not embed fonts unless absolutely necessary. It also optimizes files for byte serving. These PDF files can be opened in Acrobat 5.0 and Acrobat Reader 5.0 and later.*

• **Standard** *creates PDF files to be printed to desktop printers or digital copiers, published on a CD, or sent to a client as a publishing proof. This set of options uses compression and downsampling to keep the file size down, but it also embeds subsets of all (allowed) fonts used in the file, converts all colors to sRGB, and prints to a medium resolution. Note that Windows font subsets are not embedded by default. PDF files created with this settings file can be opened in Acrobat 5.0 and Acrobat Reader 5.0 and later.*

—From the Complete Acrobat 7.0 Help

For information on the PDF/X and PDF/A settings, see Lesson 15, "Using Adobe Acrobat for Professional Publishing" or the Acrobat 7.0 online Help.

Using the default Adobe PDF Settings

In this section, you'll compare the image quality and file size of three different PDF files prepared by converting a sample PostScript° file to Adobe PDF three times, using a different predefined set of Adobe PDF Settings each time. To save time, we've created the PDF files for you.

1 In Acrobat, choose File > Open, and select the three Adobe PDF files—Color1.pdf, Color2.pdf, and Color3.pdf—in the PDF folder in the Lesson06 folder. (You can Ctrl-click or Command-click to select contiguous files.) Click Open.

Color1.pdf was created using the Standard Adobe PDF Settings, Color2.pdf was created using the High Quality Print Adobe PDF Settings, and Color3.pdf was created using the Smallest File Size Adobe PDF Settings.

2 Choose Window > Tile > Vertically to display all the files in the document pane. If needed, use the scroll bars to display the same area in each of the files.

At the default magnification, all three images look very similar.

Color1.pdf   *Color2.pdf*   *Color3.pdf*

3 Click in each image several times with the Zoom In tool (⊕) to display each image at 400% magnification. Scroll as needed so that you can see the same area in each of the files.

  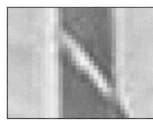

Color1.pdf   *Color2.pdf*   *Color3.pdf*

In comparison with the other images, Color3.pdf (the smallest file size) has a more jagged display quality. Since Color3.pdf is intended for onscreen viewing, for emailing, and especially for web use where download time is important, it does not require as high a display quality.

4 Select the Hand tool (✋).

5 With the Color3.pdf window active, choose File > Close, and close the Color3.pdf file without saving any changes.

6 Choose Window > Tile > Vertically to resize the remaining two images.

7 Select the Zoom In tool and click twice in each document pane to display Color1.pdf and Color2.pdf at 800% magnification. Scroll as needed to display the same area in the two files.

Color1.pdf (the Standard file) has the coarser display quality of the two. The Standard Adobe PDF Settings are chosen to balance image quality with a reasonable file size. The conversion settings are designed to produce a file that is suitable for printing to desktop printers or digital copiers, distributed on a CD, or used as a publishing proof. The display quality of Color2.pdf (the High Quality Print file) is much better. The image resolution is higher for superior print quality.

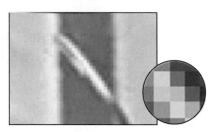
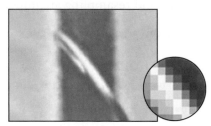

Color1.pdf   76KB   *Color2.pdf   960KB*

8 Select the Hand tool, and choose Window > Close All to close both files without saving them.

9 Click the Minimize button to minimize the Acrobat window.

In Acrobat Professional, you can use the Pan and Zoom Window tool or the Loupe tool to magnify an image area. For more information on these tools, see Lesson 13, "Using Acrobat's Engineering and Technical Features."

Now you'll compare the file sizes of the three Adobe PDF files.

10 On Windows, use Windows Explorer to open the Lesson06 folder, and note the sizes of the three files. On Mac OS, open the PDF folder in the Lesson06 folder, select the file Color1.pdf, and view the files in list view. (If necessary, choose File > Get Info to determine the file size on Mac OS.) Do the same for the Color2.pdf, and Color3.pdf files and note the comparative file sizes.

Color3.pdf has the lowest image quality and the smallest file size, while Color2.pdf has the highest image quality and the largest file size. Note that the significantly smaller Color1.pdf file does indeed balance image quality with small file size.

Note: File sizes may vary slightly depending on whether you are using a Windows or Mac OS system.

11 Close all open windows.

PDF creation often involves a trade-off between image quality and file compression. More compression means smaller file sizes but also coarser image quality, while finer image quality is achieved at the expense of larger file sizes.

About compression and resampling

Many factors affect file size and file quality, but when you're working with image-intensive files, compression and resampling are important.

You can choose from a variety of file compression methods designed to reduce the file space used by color, grayscale, and monochrome images in your document. Which method you choose depends on the kind of images you are compressing. The default Adobe PDF Settings use automatic (JPEG) compression for color and grayscale images and CCITT Group 4 compression for monochrome images.

In addition to choosing a compression method, you can resample bitmap images in your file to reduce the file size. A bitmap image consists of digital units called pixels, whose total number determines the file size. When you resample a bitmap image, the information represented by several pixels in the image is combined to make a single larger pixel. This process is also called downsampling because it reduces the number of pixels in the image. (When you downsample or decrease the number of pixels, information is deleted from the image.) The Adobe PDF Settings use bicubic downsampling ranging from 100 to 1200 pixels per inch.

Using custom compression settings

The default Adobe PDF Settings are designed to produce optimum results in most cases. However, you can customize the Adobe PDF Settings if you want to fine-tune the compression methods used. In this part of the lesson, you'll practice applying custom compression and resampling settings to a color PostScript file.

Note: Compression and resampling do not affect the quality of either text or line art.

Customizing the Adobe PDF Settings

By combining the appropriate compression and downsampling Adobe PDF Settings, you can greatly reduce the file size of a PDF document without losing noticeable detail in an image. You'll apply your custom settings to the original high-resolution PostScript file Color.ps.

1 Maximize the Acrobat window.

2 In Acrobat, choose Advanced > Acrobat Distiller.

First you'll change the Distiller preferences.

3 On Windows, choose File > Preferences, and on Mac OS, choose Distiller > Preferences.

4 Select the Ask for PDF File Destination option, and click OK.

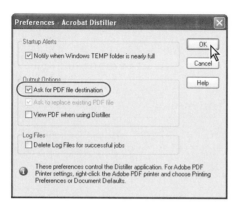 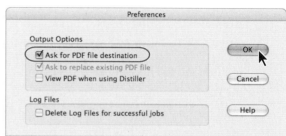

5 In the Acrobat Distiller window, choose Smallest File Size from the Default Settings pop-up menu.

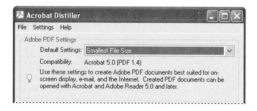

6 Choose Settings > Edit Adobe PDF Settings, and click Images.

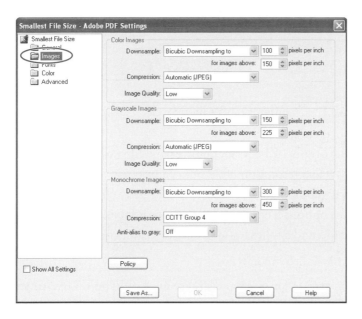

The default compression values associated with the Smallest File Size settings are displayed. You'll now adjust several options to produce your own custom setting (using the Smallest File Size settings as your base) for optimizing onscreen PDF display.

7 In the Color Images area, choose Average Downsampling To from the Downsample (Windows) or Sampling (Mac OS) pop-up menu.

Average downsampling averages the pixels in a sample area and replaces the entire area with the average pixel color at the specified resolution. A slower but more precise approach is to use bicubic downsampling, which uses a weighted average to determine pixel color. Bicubic downsampling yields the smoothest tonal gradations. Subsampling, which chooses a pixel in the center of the sample area and replaces the entire area with that pixel at the specified resolution, significantly reduces the conversion time but results in images that are less smooth and less continuous.

8 Enter **72** ppi for the Downsample (Windows) or Sampling (Mac OS) value and for the
For Images Above option. (These are much lower values than you would normally use.)

This will downsample the original PostScript color image file (assuming the image
resolution is above 72 ppi) to a resolution of 72 ppi. Values that you enter in the Color
Images section of the dialog box affect only color images. Any changes you make to the
grayscale or monochrome options have no effect on color images. Distiller recognizes the
type of PostScript image file, and applies the appropriate color, grayscale, or monochrome
compression settings.

In general, the resolution setting for color and grayscale should be 1.5 to 2 times the line
screen ruling at which the file will be printed. (As long as you don't go below this recommended resolution setting, images that contain no straight lines or geometric or repeating
patterns won't be affected by a lower resolution.) The resolution for monochrome images
should be the same as the output device, but be aware that saving a monochrome image
at a resolution higher than 1500 dpi increases the file size without noticeably improving
image quality.

Resampling resolution and printer resolution

*The following table shows common types of printers and their resolution measured in dpi, their default
screen ruling measured in lines per inch (lpi), and a resampling resolution for images measured in pixels per
inch (ppi). For example, if you were printing to a 600-dpi laser printer, you would enter 170 for the resolution at which to resample images.*

Printer resolution	Default line screen	Image resolution
300 dpi (laser printer)	*60 lpi*	*120 ppi*
600 dpi (laser printer)	*85 lpi*	*170 ppi*
1200 dpi (image setter)	*120 lpi*	*240 ppi*
2400 dpi (image setter)	*150 lpi*	*300 ppi*

—From the Complete Acrobat 7.0 Help.

Note: The minimum resolution of images that will be downsampled is determined by the sampling value you choose.

9 Leave the Compression set to Automatic (JPEG) to allow Acrobat to determine the best compression method for color and grayscale images, and leave the Image Quality set to Low.

10 Since the Color.ps file you'll be converting contains no grayscale or monochrome images, you'll leave the default values in these sections.

Now you'll save the custom setting that you have specified so that you can use it again in the future.

11 Click Save As. Save the custom setting using the default name **SmallestFileSize(1)**. Click Save to complete the Save process. (You cannot overwrite or delete the default Adobe PDF Settings.)

Your custom setting will now be available from the Adobe PDF Settings menu, along with the default settings.

12 On Windows, click OK.

13 Leave the Distiller window open.

Methods of compression

Distiller applies ZIP compression to text and line art, ZIP or JPEG compression to color and grayscale images, and ZIP, CCITT Group 3 or 4, or Run Length compression to monochrome images.

You can choose from the following compression methods:

*• **ZIP** works well on images with large areas of single colors or repeating patterns, such as screen shots and simple images created with paint programs, and for black-and-white images that contain repeating patterns. Acrobat provides 4-bit and 8-bit ZIP compression options. If you use 4-bit ZIP compression with 4-bit images, or 8-bit ZIP with 4-bit or 8-bit images, the ZIP method is lossless, which means it does not remove data to reduce file size and so does not affect an image's quality. However, using 4-bit ZIP compression with 8-bit data can affect the quality, since data is lost.*

***Note:** The Adobe implementation of the ZIP filter is derived from the zlib package of Jean-loup Gailly and Mark Adler, whose generous assistance we gratefully acknowledge.*

*• **JPEG** (Joint Photographic Experts Group) is suitable for grayscale or color images, such as continuous-tone photographs that contain more detail than can be reproduced onscreen or in print. JPEG is lossy, which means that it removes image data and may reduce image quality, but it attempts to reduce file size with the minimum loss of information. Because JPEG eliminates data, it can achieve much smaller file sizes than ZIP compression.*

Acrobat provides six JPEG options, ranging from Maximum quality (the least compression and the smallest loss of data) to Minimum quality (the most compression and the greatest loss of data). The loss of detail that results from the Maximum and High quality settings are so slight that most people cannot tell an image has been compressed. At Minimum and Low, however, the image may become blocky and acquire a mosaic look. The Medium quality setting usually strikes the best balance in creating a compact file while still maintaining enough information to produce high-quality images.

*• **CCITT** (International Coordinating Committee for Telephony and Telegraphy) is appropriate for black-and-white images made by paint programs and any images scanned with an image depth of 1 bit. CCITT is a lossless method. Acrobat provides the CCITT Group 3 and Group 4 compression options. CCITT Group 4 is a general-purpose method that produces good compression for most types of monochrome images. CCITT Group 3, used by most fax machines, compresses monochrome images one row at a time.*

*• **Run Length** is a lossless compression option that produces the best results for images that contain large areas of solid white or black.*

—From the Complete Acrobat 7.0 Help.

Processing the color file with custom settings

Now you're ready to try out your customized Adobe PDF Settings.

1 In Distiller, make sure that Smallest File Size (1) is selected in the Default Settings menu.

2 Choose File > Open. Select Color.ps in the Lesson06 folder, and click Open.

3 In the Specify PDF File Name dialog box (Windows) or the Choose Destination for PDF dialog box (Mac OS), navigate to the PDF folder in the Lesson06 folder, and click Save or Open to save the **Color.pdf** file that will be created.

The conversion of the PostScript file is shown in the Distiller window.

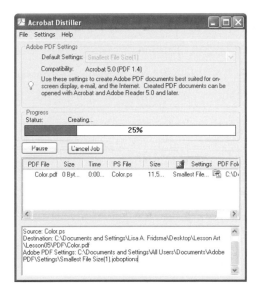

4 In Acrobat, choose File > Open. Select Color.pdf and Color3.pdf (the other PDF file created with the smallest file size setting) in the PDF folder in the Lesson06 folder, and click Open.

5 Choose Window > Tile > Vertically to display the files side-by-side, and use the Zoom In tool to view both files at 200% magnification. If needed, use the scroll bars to display the same area in each of the files.

Color3.pdf is smoother than Color.pdf. Because Color3.pdf has a higher resolution (100 ppi rather than 72 ppi), it contains more pixel detail and finer image quality.

Color3.pdf 33KB *Color.pdf 23KB*

6 Select the Hand tool.

7 Choose Window > Close All to close the files without saving them.

8 Minimize the Acrobat window, and exit or quit Distiller.

9 Compare the file size of the two images. On Windows use Windows Explorer; on Mac OS, use the list view in the Finder or choose Get Info from the File menu. Color3.pdf is significantly larger than Color.pdf.

Managing color

You can manage color when you create an Adobe PDF file, and you can manage color when you view an Adobe PDF file.

Managing color in Distiller or PDFMaker

When you use Distiller or PDFMaker to convert a file to Adobe PDF, you can choose to use the color management information contained in the source file, or you can modify any embedded color management information using the color settings in the Adobe PDF Settings file.

Managing color in Acrobat

Colors must often be converted when they are displayed to a monitor or sent to a printer. Any image in a file created by an ICC-compliant application such as Photoshop or Illustrator may have an ICC profile—a description of a device's color space—attached. Acrobat can interpret embedded ICC profiles to automatically manage color, and it can also assign ICC profiles to unmanaged color spaces. The Color Management preferences in Acrobat provide profiles for converting unmanaged color spaces.

Any color management embedded in a PDF file always takes precedence over the CSF setting.

For information on color management, see Lesson15, "Using Adobe Acrobat for Professional Publishing."

Reducing file size

As you saw in this lesson, the size of your PDF file can vary tremendously depending on the Adobe PDF Settings that you use when you create the file. Larger files, such as the Color2.pdf file offer great resolution for print purposes, but they are not necessarily a good size for emailing or posting on the web. If you have a large file of this type, you can often reduce the file size without having to regenerate the PDF file.

In this next section, you'll use the Reduce File Size command to dramatically reduce the size of the Color2.pdf file.

1 In Acrobat, open the Color2.pdf file in the PDF folder in the Lesson06 folder.

2 Choose File > Reduce File Size.

3 Choose the version of Acrobat that you want your file to be compatible with. We choose Acrobat 5.0 and later. Click OK.

When you choose the compatibility level, be aware that the newer the version of Acrobat that you choose, the smaller the file. If you choose compatibility with Acrobat 7.0, however, you should be sure that your intended audience does indeed have version 7.0 installed.

4 Save your modified file using a different name. We saved the file in the same directory using the name **SmallerColor2.pdf**. Click Save to complete the process.

It is a good idea to save the file using a different name so that you don't overwrite the unmodified file.

Acrobat automatically optimizes your PDF file, a process that may take a minute. Any anomalies are displayed in the Conversion Warnings window. If necessary, click OK to close the window.

5 Minimize the Acrobat window, and in Windows, use Windows Explorer to open the Lesson06 folder, and note the size of the Color2.pdf. In Mac OS, in the Finder, open the Lesson06 folder, and use the List View to view the size of the Color2.pdf file.

The file size is approximately 959KB. File size may vary slightly with your platform.

6 Now check the size of the SmallerColor2.pdf file.

7 The file size is approximately 120KB. Again, file size may vary slightly with your platform.

Choose File > Close and close your file and exit or quit Acrobat.

Review questions

1 Which of the default Adobe PDF Settings best balances file size with image quality?

2 What is sampling? What is downsampling?

3 Where can you change the Adobe PDF Settings?

Review answers

1 The Standard Adobe PDF Settings give the best balance of image quality with file size.

2 Sampling refers to reducing the number of pixels in an image to minimize the file size. Multiple pixels in the original image are combined to make a single, larger pixel that represents approximately the same image area. Downsampling is the same as sampling.

3 You can change the Adobe PDF Settings in a variety of places, including in Distiller, from the Start menu on Windows, from the Adobe PDF menu in Microsoft Office applications, and in the Properties dialog box accessed from the Print or Print Setup box of a number of authoring applications.

7 | Modifying PDF Files

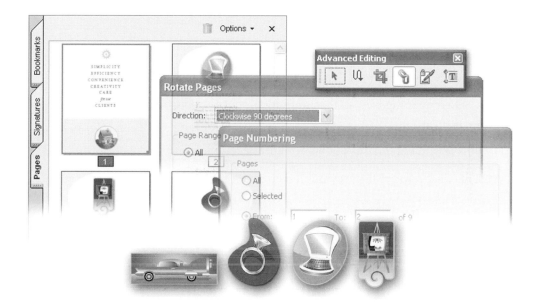

Once you have converted your document to Adobe PDF, you can use Acrobat to make final edits and modifications. You can add and edit actions, links, and bookmarks, you can insert, reorder, and extract pages, and you can set an opening view.

In this lesson, you'll learn how to do the following:

• Use page thumbnails to rearrange pages in a document and navigate through a document.

• Rotate and crop pages.

• Insert and extract pages from a document.

• Renumber pages.

• Create links and bookmarks.

• Add a page action so that a sound file plays when a page is opened.

• Set an opening view so that your document always opens at the same page and the same magnification.

This lesson will take about 60 minutes to complete.

If needed, remove the previous lesson folder from your hard drive, and copy the Lesson07 folder onto it.

Note: Windows 2000 users may need to unlock the lesson files before using them. For information, see "Copying the Classroom in a Book files" on page 4.

Opening and examining the work file

You'll work with a brochure that offers in-home services to busy families and professionals. The brochure has been designed both for print and for online viewing as an Adobe PDF file. Because this online brochure is in the developmental phase, it contains a number of mistakes. In this lesson you'll use Acrobat to correct the problems in this PDF document and optimize the brochure for online viewing.

1 Start Acrobat.

2 Choose File > Open. Select CustCare.pdf, located in the Lesson07 folder, and click Open. Then choose File > Save As, rename the file **CustCare1.pdf**, and save it in the Lesson07 folder.

Notice that the document opens with the Bookmarks tab open and that bookmarks for the pages in the brochure have already been created. Bookmarks are links that are generated automatically from the table-of-contents entries of documents created by most desktop publishing programs or from formatted headings in applications such as Microsoft Word. While these automatically generated bookmarks are usually adequate to navigate through a document, you can also set bookmarks to direct readers to specific sections in your document. You can also set the appearance of bookmarks and add actions to them.

Bookmarks for brochure

3 Use the Next Page button (▶) on the status bar to page through the brochure.

Notice that the bookmark that corresponds to the page that you are viewing is highlighted as you move through the pages.

4 With the Hand tool (🖐) selected, click the Contents bookmark to return to the first page of the brochure, which acts as the list of contents of the brochure.

5 Move the pointer into the document pane and over the text of the brochure. Notice that the titles in the list have already been linked, as shown by the hand changing to a pointing finger.

Move pointer over text.

When the file was converted to Adobe PDF, the entries in the formatted table of contents were linked automatically.

Certain page-layout and book-publishing programs, such as Adobe InDesign, Adobe PageMaker, and Adobe FrameMaker, work in conjunction with Acrobat to automate the creation of links and bookmarks during the conversion to Adobe PDF. On Windows, you can also preserve links created in Microsoft Office applications.

6 Click the Simplicity entry in the document pane to follow its link. (Be sure to click the entry in the table of contents, not the bookmark in the Bookmarks tab. Not all of the bookmarks work. You'll be fixing those later in the lesson.)

Notice that the page number on the page displayed in the document pane is 1, whereas the page number in the status bar shows the page as being page 5 of 7. Clearly the page is out of order.

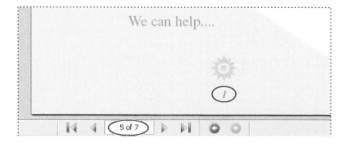

7 Click the Previous View button (⊙) to return to the contents.

Now you'll use page thumbnails to get a clearer picture of what's wrong with the organization of the brochure and correct it.

Moving pages with page thumbnails

Page thumbnails offer convenient previews of your pages. You can use them for navigation—they are especially useful if you are looking for a page that has a distinctive appearance. You can also drag them in the Pages tab to change the pagination in the document pane, which is what you'll do now.

1 Click the Pages tab in the navigation pane to see thumbnails of each page.

First you'll increase the size of the thumbnails so that you can more clearly see the content of the pages.

2 Click the Options button at the top of the tab, and choose Enlarge Page Thumbnails from the menu.

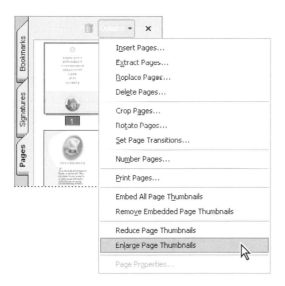

Now you'll widen the Pages tab so that you can see all the thumbnails without having to scroll.

3 Move your pointer over the margin between the navigation pane and the document pane. When the pointer changes shape (◀▌▶), drag to the right to widen the navigation pane. Adjust the width of the navigation pane so that you have two columns of page thumbnails.

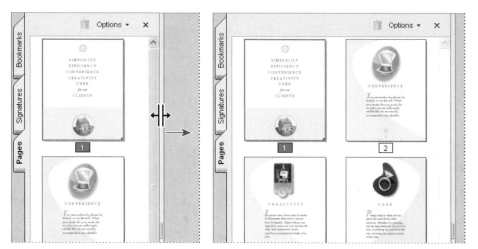

Drag the margin of the navigation pane to display page thumbnails in two columns.

Now you'll move two pages of the brochure that were incorrectly placed. As you noticed earlier, the page that is titled Simplicity is out of place. It should be the first page after the contents page. Also because the Efficiency page should follow the Simplicity page (based on the table of contents), you'll move the two pages together.

4 Click the page 5 thumbnail to select it.

5 Hold down Ctrl (Windows) or Command (Mac OS) and click the page 6 thumbnail to add it to the selection. Release the Ctrl or Command key.

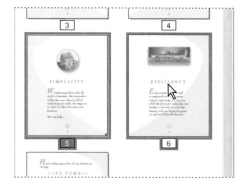

6 Drag the page 5 thumbnail image up until the insertion bar appears to the right of the page 1 thumbnail. The page 1 thumbnail represents the contents page. Because the page 6 thumbnail image is part of the selection, you're also moving that thumbnail image.

7 Release the mouse button to insert the page thumbnails into their new position.

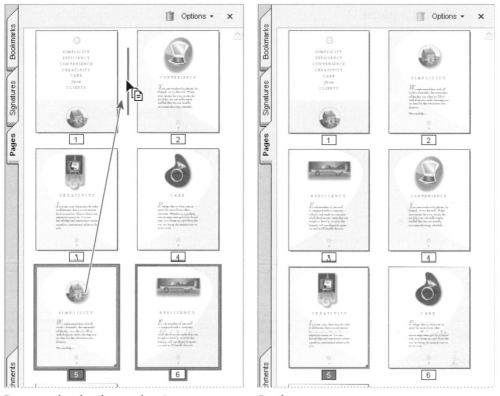

Drag page thumbnail to new location.   *Result*

The Simplicity page now follows the contents page, and the Efficiency page follows the Simplicity page.

8 To check the sequence of pages, click the First Page button (◀) on the status bar to go to the first page of the brochure, and then use the Next Page button (▶) to page through the brochure. Notice that as you page through the document, the corresponding page thumbnail is highlighted.

9 When you're satisfied that the pages are in the correct order, choose File > Save to save your work.

Editing Adobe PDF pages

If necessary, go back to the first page of the brochure (page 1 of 7). You'll notice that the first page, the contents page, is rather plain. To make the brochure more attractive, we've created a new cover page for you.

Rotating a page

You'll open a title page for the brochure, and then crop the new page to match the rest of the book.

1 Choose File > Open, navigate to the Lesson07 folder, and select the file Cover.pdf. Click Open. If necessary, click OK to close the Picture Tasks dialog box.

Now you'll rotate the new title page to the correct orientation.

2 Click the Pages tab.

3 Click the Options button at the top of the Pages tab, and choose Rotate Pages.

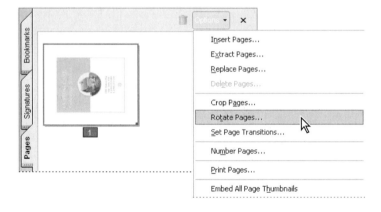

4 For Direction, choose Clockwise 90 degrees. Because you are only rotating one page, you can use the default settings. Click OK.

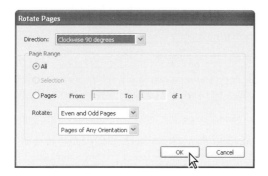

The page is rotated by 90° in the specified direction.

If you want to rotate all the pages in a file for viewing purposes only, click the Rotate Clockwise button (⬚) or Rotate Counterclockwise button (⬚) on the toolbar. If the Rotate View toolbar is hidden, choose View > Toolbars > Rotate View to display the toolbar. You can also choose View > Rotate View > Clockwise or Counterclockwise. When you close the file, however, the pages revert to their original rotation.

Rotating multiple pages

You can rotate one page or multiple pages within an Adobe PDF document using the Options menu of the Pages tab.

To rotate selected pages in an Adobe PDF document:

1. Click the Pages tab to show the page thumbnails for the document.

2. Select the page thumbnails corresponding to the pages you want to rotate. Click a page thumbnail to select it; Control-click (Windows) or Command-click (Mac OS) to add more page thumbnails to the selection.

3. Click the Options button at the top of the Pages pane to open the Options menu, and choose Rotate Pages.

4. For Direction, select Clockwise 90 degrees, Counterclockwise 90 degrees, or 180 degrees to specify the degree and direction of rotation.

If you select page thumbnails corresponding to the pages you want to rotate, the Selection button is highlighted. If you do not select page thumbnails in the Pages tab, you can choose to rotate all pages or a range of pages.

You can choose to rotate only odd or even pages, or you can choose to rotate both.

You can choose to rotate only landscape pages or portrait pages, or you can choose to rotate both.

5. When you have chosen which pages to rotate and the direction and degree of rotation, click OK to complete the task.

Inserting a page from another file

Now you'll use page thumbnails to insert the title page at the beginning of the brochure.

Because you'll be tiling windows vertically (stacking windows side-by-side) in this part of the lesson, you may prefer to adjust the width of the Pages tab to display the page thumbnails in one column. If you need help adjusting the width of the Pages tab, see ""Moving pages with page thumbnails" earlier in this lesson.

1 Choose Window > Tile > Vertically to arrange the two document windows side-by-side.

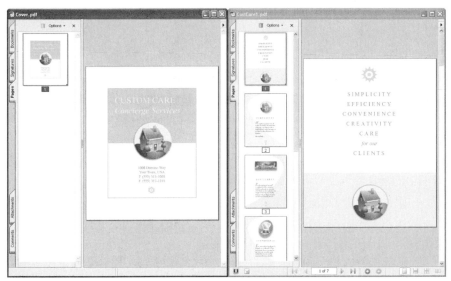

Tile the windows vertically to display two document windows side-by-side.

You can insert pages by dragging page thumbnails between Page tabs.

2 Select the page thumbnail for the title page in the Page tab of the Cover.pdf window, and drag the selected page thumbnail into the Pages tab for the CustCare1.pdf window. When the insertion bar appears before the page 1 thumbnail, release the mouse button. (If you have a single row of thumbnails, the insertion bar appears above the page 1 thumbnail.)

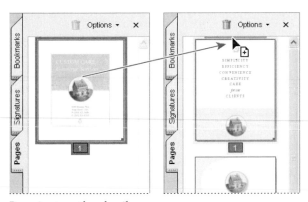

Dragging page thumbnails

The title page is inserted into the brochure in the correct location.

3 In the Cover.pdf document window, choose File > Close, and close the Cover.pdf file without saving any changes. Resize the CustCare1.pdf window to fill your document window.

4 Choose File > Save to save your work.

View the page thumbnails in the pages tab. Although the new cover page appears to be the same size as the other pages in the book, the image area is smaller. The cover image has a significant white margin around it. Now you'll crop the page to match the other pages in the book.

Cropping a page

You'll use the Crop Pages dialog box to enter dimensions for the imported page so that it matches the other pages in the document. You'll temporarily change the page units from inches to points, which will give you more control over the crop operation.

1 With the Page 1 thumbnail still selected in the Pages tab, click the Options button at the top of the Pages tab and choose Crop Pages.

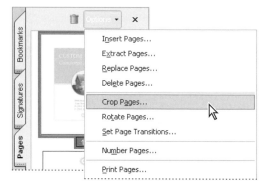

The Crop Pages dialog box appears, which lets you specify the units and margins for cropping the page.

2 Make sure that the Crop option is selected.

3 Select Points from the Units menu.

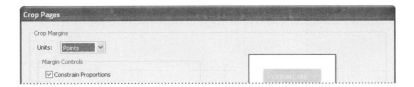

If you change the value for Units here, the change is temporary; if you change the value for Units in the Units & Guides preferences, the change remains in effect until changed again.

4 For Margin Controls, use the up and down arrows to enter the following values. You can Tab from one entry to the next. (If you type in the new values as opposed to using the up and down keys, be careful not to press Enter or Return after the last entry or you will execute the crop action automatically.)

- Top: **72**

- Bottom: **74**

- Left: **72**

- Right: **73**

Set location of left crop mark.   *Result*

Click in the preview area. A line representing the crop location appears both in the preview in the dialog box and in the document. You may need to drag the Crop Pages dialog box out of the way to view the crop line in the document. You can drag the dialog box by its title bar.

5 If needed, use the up and down arrows next to the margin values again to fine-tune the location of the crop line so that the crop lines align with the edges of the title border.

6 For Page Range, make sure that you are cropping only the selected page, page 1 of the document, and click OK.

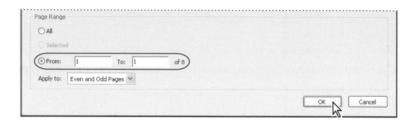

7 Choose File > Save to save the CustCare1.pdf file.

 *You can also use the Crop tool (*  *) to crop the page. Choose Tools > Advanced Editing > Crop Tool. Drag in the document pane to define the crop area, and then double-click in the crop area to open the Crop Pages dialog box and follow the relevant steps above to complete the crop operation. Because Acrobat automatically enters your top and bottom, right and left crop margins when you use this method, all you have to do is fine-tune the settings.*

Now you'll check the links on the Contents page of your brochure to make sure that online viewers navigate to the correct pages.

8 Click or drag in the page number area of the status bar to select the page number, type **2**, and press Enter or Return to return to the contents page.

Enter a page number and press Enter or Return to move to that page.

9 On the contents page, click each link in turn. (You must have the Hand tool selected.) Use the Previous View button () to return to the Contents page each time. Notice that the Creativity link takes you to the wrong page and that neither the Care link nor the Clients link is working.

Now you'll correct these broken links.

Editing links

1 Click in the page number area of the status bar to select the page number, type **2**, and press Enter or Return to return to the contents page if necessary.

2 On the contents page, click the Care link. Nothing happens. As you discovered just a few minutes ago, the Care link is not working.

3 Scroll down the page thumbnails in the Pages tab and notice that the Care page is page 7 in the brochure. You'll use this information to set the link correctly.

4 Choose Tools > Advanced Editing > Show Advanced Editing Toolbar to display the Advanced Editing toolbar.

5 Select the Link tool (). Notice that all the links on the page are outlined in black when the Link tool is active.

6 Move the pointer over the broken Care link. The link is selected when red handles appear on the link box. Right-click (Windows) or Control-click (Mac OS) in the link box, and choose Properties from the context menu.

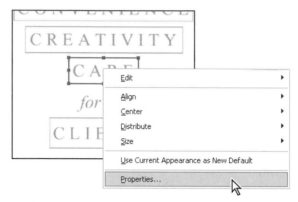

Red handles indicate that the link is selected.

7 Click the Actions tab in the Link Properties dialog box to set the correct destination for the link.

8 Choose Go To a Page View from the Select Action menu, and click Add.

9 Use the scroll bar on the right of the document pane to move to page 7. When the page number box reads 7 of 8, click Set Link.

10 In the Link Properties dialog box, click Close to apply your changes to the link.

11 Select the Hand tool () and test your link. When you are finished, click the Previous View button () to return to the contents page.

Earlier in this lesson, you noticed that the Creativity link incorrectly took you to the Care page. Now you'll correct the Creativity link.

12 Select the Link tool, and move the pointer over the Creativity link. When the red handles appear on the link box, double-click in the link box to open the Link Properties dialog box.

13 Click the Actions tab to correct the destination for the broken link.

The Actions window in the Link Properties dialog box shows that the link is to page 7, which is the Care page. You'll edit the link so that it goes to the Creativity page, page 6 in the brochure.

14 Make sure that Go To a Page View is selected in the Actions window, and click Edit.

15 Make sure that the Use Page Number option is selected, and change the entry in the Page text box from 7 to **6**. Click OK.

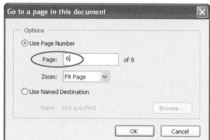

16 Click Close to apply your changes to the link.

17 Select the Hand tool and test your link. When you are finished, click the Previous View button to return to the contents page.

18 Choose File > Save to save your work.

19 Click the Close button on the Advanced Editing toolbar to close the toolbar.

Inserting PDF files

In Acrobat, you can insert a page, a specified range of pages, or all pages from one PDF document into another. Earlier in this lesson, you used page thumbnails to insert a page from one PDF document into another. Now you'll add client testimonials to the CustCare1.pdf file by inserting all the pages of another file (Clients.pdf).

1 Click the Bookmarks tab in the navigation pane to display the bookmarks. If needed, resize the navigation pane to view the entire bookmark text.

Although the Client Testimonials bookmark appears in the list, the brochure contains only a placeholder for the client testimonials. You'll insert the testimonials from another document.

2 Drag in the scroll bar in the document pane to go to the last page 8 (8 of 8) in the document, or click the Client Testimonials bookmark in the Bookmarks tab.

3 Choose Document > Insert Pages.

4 In the Select Files to Insert dialog box, select Clients.pdf in the Lesson07 folder, and click Select.

The Insert Pages dialog box appears.

5 For Location, choose Before.

6 Make sure that Page is selected and that the Page text box contains **8**. Then click OK.

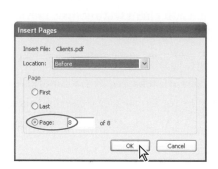 

The client testimonials are inserted where they belong.

7 Page through the document to verify that the testimonials have been inserted in the correct location.

8 Choose File > Save to save your work.

You'll need to delete the placeholder page, but first you'll add a bookmark for the cover that you added and then update the link for the Client Testimonials bookmark.

Replacing a page

Sometimes you may want to replace an entire page in a PDF file with another PDF page. For example, if you want to change the design or layout of a PDF page, you can revise the source page in your original design application, convert the modified page to PDF, and use it to replace the old PDF page. When you replace a page, only the text and graphics on the original page are replaced. The replacement does not affect any interactive elements associated with the original page, such as bookmarks or links.

To replace a page:

1. In the PDF file, navigate to the page that you want to replace.

2. Choose Document > Replace Pages.

3. In the Select File with New Pages dialog box, locate the replacement PDF page, and click Select.

4. In the Replace Pages dialog box, make sure that you are replacing the correct page with the corrected page, click OK and then Yes.

Looking at bookmarks

A bookmark is simply a link represented by text in the Bookmarks panel. While bookmarks that are created automatically by authoring programs such as Adobe InDesign, Adobe FrameMaker, Adobe PageMaker, or Microsoft Word are generally linked to headings in the text or to figure captions, you can also add your own bookmarks in Acrobat to create a brief custom outline of a document or to open other documents.

Additionally, you can use electronic bookmarks as you would paper bookmarks—to mark a place in a document that you want to highlight or return to later. Later in this lesson, you'll create custom bookmarks that are linked to an area on a page in the document.

Adding a bookmark

In this section of the lesson, you'll add a bookmark for the front cover of the brochure. First you'll display the page you want to bookmark.

1 Click the First Page button (◀) on the status bar to display the front cover of the brochure, and make sure that the Fit Page button (↕) is selected. A bookmark always displays a page at the magnification set when the bookmark was created.

2 In the Bookmark tab, click the New Bookmark icon (▦). A new, untitled bookmark is added below whatever bookmark was selected.

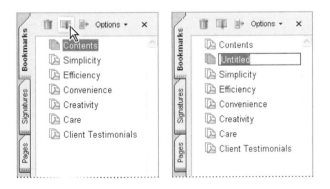

Anytime a bookmark is selected when you click the New Bookmark icon, the new bookmark is added below that bookmark.

3 In the text box of the new bookmark, type in the bookmark label that you want. We typed in **Front Cover**. Click anywhere in the Bookmarks tab to move the focus from the text box to the bookmark.

Now you'll move the bookmark into the correct location in the bookmark hierarchy.

4 Drag the bookmark icon directly up and above the Contents bookmark. Release the bookmark when you see an arrow and dotted line above the Contents bookmark.

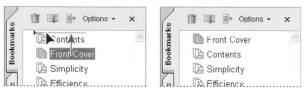

Drag the new bookmark to its correct location.

5 Choose File > Save to save your work.

Test your new bookmark by selecting another bookmark to change the document window view and then selecting the Front Cover bookmark again.

Changing a bookmark destination

1 In the Bookmarks tab, click the Client Testimonials bookmark. The document pane displays the place holder page.

2 In the Acrobat status bar, click the Previous Page button (◀) twice to go to page 8 (8 of 10) of the document, which is the page you want the bookmark to link to—the first page of the testimonials that you added.

3 Click the Options button at the top of the Bookmarks tab, and choose Set Bookmark Destination from the menu. Click Yes to the confirmation message to update the bookmark destination.

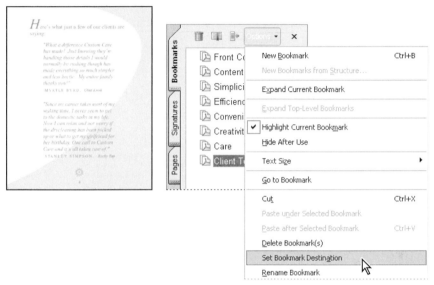

Go to page 8 in the document.   *With the bookmark selected, choose Set Bookmark Destination from the Options menu in the Bookmarks tab.*

If you wish, you can reset the destination for the Creativity bookmark using the same technique.

4 Choose File > Save to save the CustCare1.pdf file.

Linking a bookmark to an image or a block of text

In this section of the lesson, you'll create a bookmark whose destination is set automatically to the current document view that your screen displays. You'll create a bookmark for the company's address and link it to the contact information on the front page of the brochure.

1 In the Bookmarks tab, click the Client Testimonials bookmark to select it. Then click the New Bookmark icon at the top of the pane to add a new untitled bookmark at the end of the list of bookmarks.

2 Replace the text "Untitled," with **Contact Us**.

3 In the document pane, click the First Page button on the status bar to display the cover page. Then select the Zoom-In tool (🔍), and marquee-drag around the company's address and phone number at the bottom of the page. Our contact information filled the screen.

4 Choose Set Bookmark Destination from the Options menu in the Bookmarks tab. At the prompt, click Yes.

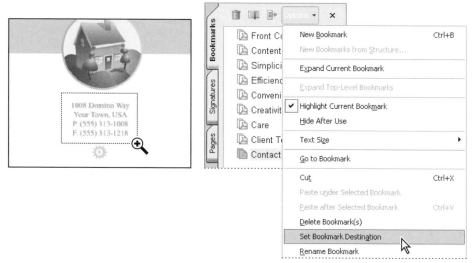

Use Zoom-In tool to magnify sidebar.   *Set bookmark destination.*

5 Select the Hand tool, and click any other bookmark. We clicked Convenience.

6 Then click the Contact Us bookmark and note how the magnification of the page changes.

7 Choose File > Save to save your work.

Other ways of creating bookmarks

You can add your own custom bookmarks and links to any PDF document using the tools in Acrobat. Here are some different methods to add new bookmarks.

Using keyboard shortcuts

You can create a bookmark using the keyboard shortcut for the New Bookmarks command. (Many Acrobat commands can be executed using keyboard shortcuts.)

1. To create a new bookmark using a keyboard shortcut, press Ctrl+B (Windows) or Command+B (Mac OS), and then name the bookmark. Click outside the bookmark to deselect it.

2. In the document window, navigate to the page that the bookmark should be linked to.

3. With the newly created bookmark selected in the Bookmarks tab, choose Set Bookmark Destination from the Options menu in the Bookmarks tab.

Automatically setting the correct link

You can create, name, and automatically link a bookmark by selecting text in the document pane.

1. Select the Select tool( ) in the toolbar.

2. Move the I-beam into the document page, and drag to highlight the text that you want to use as your bookmark.

Be sure to have the magnification of the page at the required level. Whatever magnification is used will be inherited by the bookmark.

Click the New Bookmark icon ( ) at the top of the Bookmarks panel. A new bookmark is created in the bookmarks list, and the highlighted text from the document pane is used as the bookmark name. By default, the new bookmark links to the current page view displayed in the document window.

Moving bookmarks

After creating a bookmark, you can easily move it to its proper place in the Bookmarks panel by dragging. You can move individual bookmarks or groups of bookmarks up and down in the Bookmarks list and you can nest bookmarks.

You'll nest the Simplicity, Efficiency, Convenience, Creativity, Care, and Client Testimonials bookmarks under the Contents bookmark.

1 Hold down Ctrl or Command and click the Simplicity, Efficiency, Convenience, Creativity, Care, and Client Testimonials bookmarks to select them all.

2 Position the pointer on one of the selected bookmarks, hold down the mouse button and drag the bookmarks up and under the Contents bookmark. When the arrow is below and to the right of the Contents bookmark icon, release the mouse.

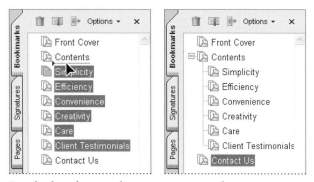

Drag bookmarks up and across. . .. . . to nest them.

3 Choose File > Save to save your work.

Deleting a page

Now you'll delete the customer testimonials placeholder page from the brochure.

1 Click the Last Page button (▶|) to go to the last page of the brochure, page 10 of 10, the customer testimonial placeholder.

2 Choose Document > Delete Pages.

3 Make sure that you are deleting page 10 to 10 of the brochure. Click OK. Click Yes to clear the confirmation box.

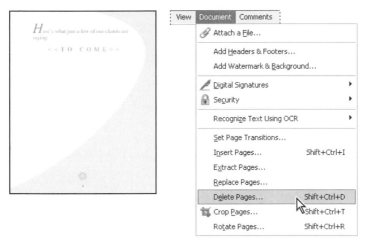

Go to page 10.   *Delete page 10.*

The page is deleted from the CustCare1.pdf file.

4 Choose File > Save, and save your work.

You can page through the brochure to check that the placeholder page has been deleted from the book.

Renumbering pages

You may have noticed that the page numbers on the document pages do not always match the page numbers that appear below the page thumbnails and in the status bar. Acrobat automatically numbers pages with arabic numerals, starting with page 1 for the first page in the document, and so on.

1 Click the Pages tab in the navigation pane to display the page thumbnails.

2 Click the page 2 thumbnail to go to the contents page.

The first two pages of the document contain front matter—the cover and the contents. You'll renumber these pages using lowercase roman numerals.

3 Click the Options button at the top of the Pages tab, and choose Number Pages.

4 For Pages, select From and enter pages from **1** to **2**. For Numbering, select Begin New Section, choose "i, ii, iii" from the Style menu, and enter **1** in the Start text box. Click OK.

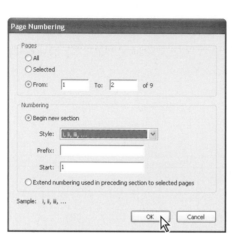

Renumber pages.

Result

5 Choose View > Go To > Page. Enter **1**, and click OK.

Notice that the number 1 in the status bar is now assigned to the first page of the brochure, the Simplicity page, matching the page number appearing at the center bottom of the page.

💡 *You can physically add page numbers to the pages of your Adobe PDF document using the Add Headers & Footers command. See "Adding header text and page numbers" in Lesson 4.*

Adding sound

Your brochure is almost finished. Just to add a distinguishing touch, you'll add a page action. You'll add a sound that plays when the first page of the PDF file opens.

1 In the Pages tab, select the page thumbnail for the cover page, the page i thumbnail.

2 With the page thumbnail selected, right-click (Windows) or Control-click (Mac OS) and choose Page Properties from the context menu.

3 In the Page Properties dialog box, click the Actions tab.

4 Choose Page Open from the Select Trigger menu.

5 Choose Play a Sound from the Select Actions menu, and click Add. (You may need to scroll down the Select Actions menu to see all the options available.)

6 In the Select Sound File dialog box, select the bell.wav file and click Select.

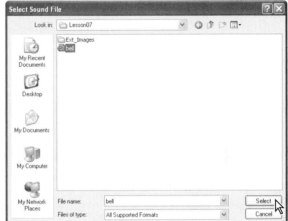

7 Click Close to apply the action to the page.

The bell will chime every time you return to the cover page in the PDF file.

8 Choose File > Save to save your work, and then choose File > Close to close the file.

You can check your sound effect by re-opening the file.

9 Choose File > Open, and open the CustCare1.pdf file. If your system is configured correctly, you should hear the door bell as the brochure opens. If your brochure didn't open to the cover page, click the First Page button on the status bar to move to the cover page and hear the sound.

For more information on sound system requirements and the types of sound file formats you can use with Acrobat, see "Using actions for special effects" in the Complete Acrobat 7.0 Help.

Setting an opening view

Lastly you'll set the initial view of the brochure to make sure that your brochure always opens at the cover page with the entire page displayed. If you were working with a longer document or a complex technical document, you might prefer to have the document open with the bookmarks displayed automatically to help the user navigate the document.

You should always set the opening view of a PDF document for your users, including the opening page number and magnification level, and whether bookmarks, page thumbnails, the toolbar, and the menu bar are displayed. You can change any of these settings to control how the document displays when it is opened.

1 If necessary, click the First Page button (⏮) to go to the first page of the brochure.

2 Choose File > Document Properties, and click the Initial View tab.

3 For Show, choose Page Only from the menu.

4 For Page Layout, choose Single Page from the menu.

5 For Magnification, choose Fit Page so that the user will see the entire front cover.

6 Make sure that the Open to Page option is set to "i".

7 Click OK to apply the changes.

The changes will be applied after you close the file.

8 Choose File > Close, and click Yes (Windows) or Save (Mac OS) in the alert box to save the changes before closing the file.

Changes do not take effect until you save and close the file.

9 Choose File > Open, and open the CustCare1.pdf file.

The file now opens with the first page displayed in the document window.

Setting up presentations

Generally when you make a presentation to a group of people, you want the document to take over the entire screen, hiding distractions such as the menu bar, toolbar, and other window controls.

You can set up any PDF file to display in full-screen view, and you can set a variety of transition effects and sound effects to play as you move between pages, and you can even set the speed at which pages "turn." You can also convert presentations that you've prepared in other programs, such as PowerPoint, to Adobe PDF, preserving many of the authoring program's special effects. For more information, see Lesson 12, "Creating Multimedia Presentations."

10 When you are finished, close the file, click the close box on the Advanced Editing toolbar, and exit or quit Acrobat.

Review questions

1 How can you change the order of pages in a PDF document?

2 How do you insert an entire PDF file into another PDF file?

3 Can you change the arrangement of bookmarks in the Bookmarks tab?

Review answers

1 You can change the page order by selecting the page thumbnails corresponding to the pages you want to move, and dragging them to their new locations.

2 To insert all the pages from a PDF file before or after any page in another PDF file, choose Document > Insert Pages, and select the file you wish to insert. If you want to combine two PDF files—that is, add one file to the beginning or end of another PDF file, you can use the Create PDF From Multiple Files command.

3 Yes. You can drag bookmarks up and down in the bookmarks tab. You can nest bookmarks. You can delete bookmarks (without deleting the referenced page). And you can add new, custom bookmarks. When you move bookmarks, you don't affect the link that the bookmark represents.

Lesson 8

8 More on Editing PDF Files

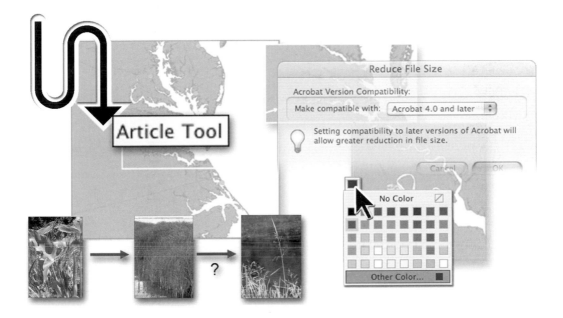

You can use Acrobat to make final edits and modifications to your PDF document. You can create article threads to lead readers through your document, and you can edit text. Powerful tools let you repurpose Adobe PDF content— you can save text in other file formats and save images in a variety of image formats. And before you share your Adobe PDF document, you can reduce the size of the file.

In this lesson, you'll learn how to do the following:

- Create, follow, and edit an article thread.

- Copy small amounts of text, and then copy all the text from a document in rich text format.

- Copy both individual images and all the art from a document.

- Create an image file from a PDF file.

- Reduce the file size of the finished Adobe PDF file.

This lesson will take about 45 minutes to complete.

If needed, remove the previous lesson folder from your hard drive, and copy the Lesson08 folder onto it.

Note: Windows 2000 users may need to unlock the lesson files before using them. For information, see "Copying the Classroom in a Book files" on page 4.

About this lesson

In this lesson, you'll work with a display poster created to summarize a current research project on wetland vegetation patterns. You'll add an article thread to make the poster easier to read on line, and then you'll copy text and images from the poster to use in a different project.

Viewing the work file

You'll start by opening a PDF version of the poster.

1 Start Acrobat.

2 Choose File > Open. Select FreshWater.pdf in the Lesson08 folder, and click Open. Then choose File > Save As, rename the file **FreshWater1.pdf**, and save it in the Lesson08 folder.

To make sure that readers see the entire poster, the Poster has been set to open in the Fit Page view and with the navigation pane closed.

Looking at articles

Although the poster has been converted to Adobe PDF for use online, it still uses the same layout as the printed poster, and the size restrictions of the screen can make the reading of presentations like this one quite difficult. Any documents created in a column format can be particularly difficult to follow using the traditional page-up or page-down tools of Acrobat.

Acrobat's article feature lets you guide users through material organized in columns or across a series of nonconsecutive pages, as in a magazine or journal article, for example. You use the Article tool to create a series of linked rectangles that connect the separate sections of the material and follow the flow of text. Some authoring programs generate article threads automatically when you convert the file to Adobe PDF.

In this part of the lesson, you'll learn how to create a customized article thread.

Opening the Articles tab

Before you create your article thread, you'll look at some different views available for reading the poster.

In the Fit Page view, the entire poster is visible, but the small type and three-column format make it difficult to read.

1 Click the Fit Width button ( ) and then the Actual Size button ( ). None of the three views offers particularly easy readability.

2 Select the Zoom In tool ( ), and click several times in the area of the ABSTRACT heading at the top of the first column. By the time the text is legible enough to read comfortably, you have to use the horizontal and vertical scroll bars to navigate through the poster.

3 Select the Hand tool, and click the Fit Page button to view the entire poster.

Now you'll discover how adding an article thread helps the reader navigate a complex document onscreen. First you'll open the Articles tab and dock it in the Navigation pane.

4 Choose View > Navigation Tabs > Articles.

5 Drag the Articles tab to the navigation pane to dock it, and click the close button on the Destination tab to hide the unwanted tab.

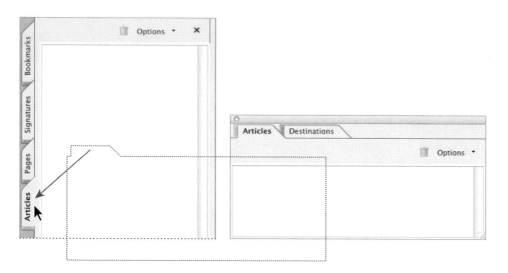

6 Click the Articles tab in the navigation pane.

The articles tab is empty. You'll create an article thread that will lead the onscreen reader through the poster at an optimal view for onscreen reading.

7 Choose Tools > Advanced Editing > Show Advanced Editing Toolbar. If necessary, drag the toolbar to the side so that you can see the title of the paper.

Defining an article

Now you'll create your own article thread to connect the heading and the three text columns.

1 Select the Article tool (⟲), and drag a marquee around the heading text. (When you first use the Article tool, it appears as a cross-hair pointer in the document window.) An article box appears around the enclosed text, and the pointer changes to the article pointer (▥).

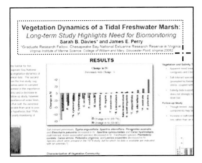

The 1-1 label at the top of the article box indicates that this is the first box of the first article in the file. Now you'll add another article box to continue the thread.

2 Go to the top of the left text column that starts with the Abstract, and drag a marquee around the column of text. An article box, labeled 1-2, appears around the enclosed text.

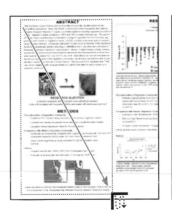

3 Go to the next column, and drag a marquee around the column of text in the center of the poster. Then drag a marquee around the column of text on the right.

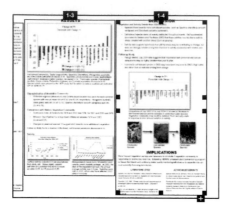

4 Press Enter or Return to end the article thread.

The Article Properties dialog box appears.

Note: You can also display the Article Properties dialog box by selecting an article in the Articles tab and choosing Properties from the Options menu.

5 Do the following:

• For Title, enter **Tidal Freshwater Marsh**, and press Tab. (The text that you enter here is the text that appears in the Articles tab.)

• For Subject, enter **Vegetation Dynamics**.

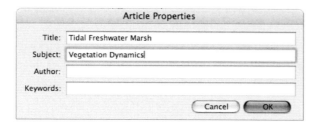

• Leave the Author and Keywords fields blank for this lesson, and click OK.

Subject, author, and keyword information is often used by search engines, and this information is included in the document metadata.

6 Choose File > Save to save your work.

Reading an article

In this section, you'll look at the various ways you can move through the article that you've just created.

1 Select the Hand tool ( ).

2 Double-click the Tidal Fresh Water Marsh article icon in the Articles tab. You may have to drag the Advanced Editing toolbar out of the way so that you can see the article icon in the Articles tab.

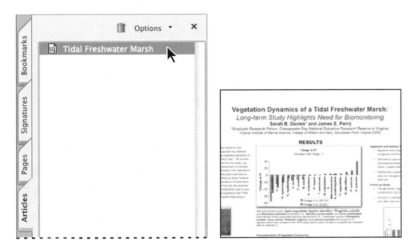

The contents of the first article box you created is centered on your screen.

You can control the magnification of article boxes by adjusting the Max "Fit Visible" Zoom Magnification preference, which you set in the Page Display Preferences dialog box.

3 Click in the document pane to move the focus from the navigation pane to the document pane.

4 Move through the article using any of these techniques:

• To advance through the article, press Enter or Return.

• To move backward through the article, hold down Shift and press Enter or Return.

• To move to the beginning of the article, hold down Ctrl (Windows) or Option (Mac OS) and click inside the article.

5 Click the Articles tab to close the navigation pane, and click the Fit Page button to view the entire poster again.

Adding the article thread makes it easy for the reader to step through the poster in a logical reading sequence without having to be concerned with scroll bars.

Now you'll make some editorial changes to your poster.

Editing text

You use the TouchUp Text tool to make last-minute corrections to text in a PDF document. You can edit text and change text attributes such as spacing, point size, and color. In order to add or replace text, you must have a licensed copy of the font installed on your system; however, you can change text attributes if the font is embedded in the PDF file.

You'll use the TouchUp Text tool to change the color of a heading.

1 Click the Fit Page button ( ) so that you can see the entire poster again.

2 Select the TouchUp Text tool ( ) on the Advanced Editing toolbar, and click in the document pane.

Acrobat may take a moment to load the system fonts. A bounding box then encloses the text that can be edited.

3 Drag through the first line of the poster title, "Vegetation Dynamics of a Tidal Freshwater Marsh."

4 Right-click (Windows) or Control-click (Mac OS), and choose Properties from the context menu.

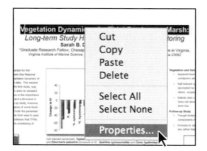

5 In the Text tab of the TouchUp Properties dialog box, click the Fill box, and choose a color for the line of text. (We used terra cotta.)

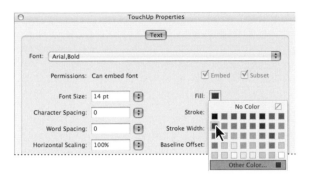

6 Click Close to close the dialog box, and click outside the text selection in the document pane to view the result.

You can experiment with changing other text attributes, such as the font size, and with adding color to other headings. To reopen the TouchUp Properties dialog box, with the TouchUp Text tool still selected, select the text that you want to edit, right-click (Windows) or Control-click (Mac OS), and choose Properties from the context menu.

7 When you are finished, select the Hand tool, and choose File > Save to save the file in the Lesson08 folder.

Copying tables

You can select and copy a table to the clipboard. You can also save it to a file that can then be loaded or imported to another application. If you have a CSV-compliant application on your system, such as Microsoft Excel, you can open the selected table directly in the application. If the document is tagged, you can click a table in a PDF document to select the entire table.

To copy a table using the Select tool:

1. Select the Select tool ( ).

2. Hold the pointer over the table. If the pointer becomes the table icon ( ), click in the table to select the entire table, or drag a box around the rows and columns to be copied.

3. Do one of the following:

• To copy the table to an open document in another authoring application, Ctrl-click (Windows) or Command-click (Mac OS) the table, and choose Copy As Table. Then paste the table into the open document.

• To copy the table to a file, Ctrl-click (Windows) or Command-click (Mac OS) the table, and choose Save As Table. Name the table, select a location and the format, and click Save.

• To copy the table directly to a spreadsheet, Ctrl-click (Windows) or Command-click (Mac OS) the table, and choose Open Table in Spreadsheet. Your CSV-compliant application, such as Excel, opens to a new spreadsheet displaying the imported table.

• To preserve formatting while copying a table to Excel, Ctrl-click (Windows) or Command -click (Mac OS) the table, and choose Copy As Table. In Excel, use the Paste Special command and select XML Spreadsheet.

• To copy a table in RTF, drag the selected table into an open document in the target application.

Note: Copying tables containing Asian languages is supported.

—From the Complete Acrobat 7.0 Help.

Copying text and images from a PDF file

Even if you no longer have access to the source file for your poster, you can reuse the text and images in other applications. For example, you might want to add some of the text or images to a web page. You can copy the text out of the PDF file in rich text format so you can import it into a different authoring application for reuse. You can save images in the file in JPEG or PNG format.

If you want to reuse only small amounts of text or one or two images, you can copy and paste text from a PDF file and copy images to the clipboard or to an image format file using the Select tool. (If the Copy, Cut, and Paste commands are grayed out, the creator of the PDF may have set restrictions on editing the content of the document.)

For complete information on copying text and images, see "Editing Adobe PDF documents" in the Complete Acrobat 7.0 Help.

Copying all the text and images

First you'll save all the text in rich text format.

1 Choose File > Save As, and for Save as Type (Windows) or Format (Mac OS), choose Rich Text Format (*.rtf).

2 Click the Settings button to open the Save As RTF Settings dialog box.

3 In the Save As RTF Settings dialog box, under Layout Settings, deselect the Retain Columns option.

4 Make sure that the Include Images option is checked if you want to save images in the RTF file. (If you wanted only the text in the file, you would uncheck this option.)

5 For Output Format, click JPG.

You'll let Acrobat determine the colorspace automatically.

6 Select the Change Resolution option, and choose 300 dpi from the menu. Images that are less than 300 dpi will not be downsampled. (If you do not select the Change Resolution option, images are created at the same resolution as in the PDF file.)

7 Make sure that the Generate Tags for Untagged Files option is selected, and click OK. (This option temporarily tags untagged files for the conversion process. Untagged files cannot be converted.)

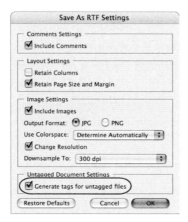

8 Click Save to complete the export of text and images.

The RTF file is saved as FreshWater1.rtf in the Lesson08 folder.

9 Minimize the Acrobat window, and open the text file (FreshWater1.rtf) using a text editing or authoring application, such as Microsoft Word. Notice that all the text is copied and that much of the spacing and formatting is retained to simplify re-use of the text. Images are included.

10 Close the RTF file and the authoring application when you are finished, and resize the Acrobat window.

You can export all the images in a PDF file in JPEG, PNG, TIFF, or JPEG2000 format using the Advanced > Export All Images command. Each image is saved in a separate file. (See "Converting PDF images to image files" in this lesson.)

Copying and pasting small amounts of text

As you saw in the prior section, copying all the text and images from a PDF file for use in another application is very easy. And it's equally easy to copy and paste a word, sentence, or paragraph into a document in another application using the Select tool.

1 In Acrobat, in the FreshWater1.pdf file, click the Select tool (I) and move the pointer over the text that you want to copy. Notice that the pointer changes when it is in the text-selection mode.

2 Drag through the text that you want to copy. We copied the body text of the abstract.

3 Choose Edit > Copy.

4 Minimize the Acrobat window, and open a new or existing document in an authoring application such as Microsoft Word, and choose Edit > Paste.

Your text is copied into the document in your authoring application. You can edit and format the text as you wish.

5 Close your document and authoring application (such as Word) when you are finished, and resize the Acrobat window.

Note: If a font copied from a PDF document is not available on the system displaying the copied text, the font cannot be preserved. A substitute font will be used.

Copying individual images

You can also copy individual images for use in another application using the Select tool or the Snapshot tool.

1 In the Acrobat document pane, click outside the text that you selected in the previous section of the lesson to deselect the text.

2 Using the Snapshot tool (⬛) on the toolbar, move the pointer over the map at the bottom of the first column in the document window.

The Snapshot tool allows you to copy both text and image. However, the resulting image is in bitmap format and the text is not editable.

3 Marquee-drag to enclose the map image at the bottom of the page.

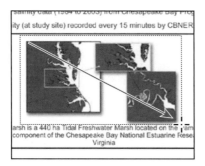

4 Click OK to clear the message box.

The image is copied to your clipboard.

If you click anywhere in the page (as opposed to marquee-dragging) with the Snapshot tool selected, the entire page is copied to the clipboard.

5 On Windows, choose Window > Clipboard Viewer to display the clipboard. On Mac OS, in the Finder, choose Edit > Show Clipboard.

The Select tool allows you to copy images as well as text. When you move the Select tool over an image, the pointer changes (-¦-). To copy an image with the Select tool, simply click in the image in your PDF document. The image is highlighted and a Copy Image to Clipboard message box displays. Click in this dialog box to copy the image to your clipboard. Also, once your image is selected, you can right-click the image, and choose the Save Image As command in the context menu to save the image in a bitmap (Windows), PICT (Mac OS), or JPEG format file.

6 When you're finished, close the clipboard viewer.

You can easily convert any clipboard image to Adobe PDF using the File > Create PDF > From Clipboard Image command.

Acrobat 7.0 Professional: Editing Images using the TouchUp Object tool

You use the TouchUp Object tool to make last-minute corrections to images and objects in an Adobe PDF document. For major revisions, use your original authoring application, and then regenerate the PDF document.

You can use the TouchUp Object tool context menu to perform some editing tasks on images without starting an external editing application. To open the context menu, right-click (Windows) or Control-click (Mac OS) the text using the TouchUp Object tool. Using the TouchUp Object tool can change how a document reflows and can affect accessibility. For example, changing the location of an object affects the order in which that object (or its alternate text) is read by a screen reader.

To edit an image or object with the TouchUp Object tool:

1 Choose Tools > Advanced Editing > TouchUp Object Tool, or select the TouchUp Object tool on the Advanced Editing toolbar.

2 Right-click (Windows) or Control-click (Mac OS) the image or object, and then choose a command.

• Delete Clip deletes objects that are clipping the selected object. For example, if you scale text and the resulting characters are clipped, selecting this option shows you the complete characters.

- *Create Artifact removes the object from the reading order so it isn't read by a screen reader or the Read Out Loud command.*

- *Edit Image, which appears when a bitmap image is selected, opens Adobe Photoshop, for example.*

- *Edit Object, which appears when a vector object is selected, opens Adobe Illustrator, for example.*

- *Properties allows you to edit properties for the content, tag, and text, such as adding alternate text to an image to make it accessible.*

Converting a PDF page to an image format file

Earlier in this lesson, you copied the text and images in the poster so that you can repurpose the content for your web page, but you may also want to have an image of the poster. You can easily create a TIFF version of the poster.

Converting PDF pages to image files

1 In Acrobat, select the Hand tool.

2 Choose File > Save As, and choose TIFF for Save as Type (Windows) or Format (Mac OS). Rename the file **FreshWater1.tif**.

3 Click Settings to review the monochrome, grayscale, and color settings, as well as the color management, colorspace, and resolution options. (For information on these Settings options, see "Copying images" in the Complete Acrobat 7.0 Help.) Click Cancel to use the default settings.

4 Click Save to convert the poster to TIFF format.

You can experiment with different Settings values and compare file size and image quality for the Settings you choose.

You can open and view the FreshWater1.tif file. When you are finished, close the TIFF files and the associated viewing application.

Converting PDF images to image files

If you want to use the art from the poster, it would be useful to have all the art in image file format. In this last section of the lesson, you'll extract all the art into separate PNG files. You can also extract art into TIFF, JPEG, and JPEG2000 file formats.

1 In Acrobat, choose Advanced > Export All Images.

2 Choose PNG for Save as Type (Windows) or Format (Mac OS).

3 Click Settings, and review the options. For information on these Settings options, see "Copying images" in the Complete Acrobat 7.0 Help.We used the default values.

4 Click Cancel to return to the Export All Images As dialog box without making any changes.

5 For Save In (Windows) or Where (Mac OS), select the Ext_Images folder in the Lesson08 folder.

6 Click Save to save the files to the Extracted folder.

Each piece of art is saved in a separate file. Open one or more of the files using Photoshop or an equivalent application, such as Preview (Mac OS) or Windows Picture and Fax Viewer (Windows).

7 When you are finished, close the PNG files and the associated viewing application, and resize the Acrobat window.

The JPEG file format allows you to save a lot of data in a small file space. Unfortunately, you lose image quality each time you re-save a JPEG file. TIFF is an excellent file format for preserving image quality, but TIFF files are very large. Consider editing your images in TIFF format and then saving the final images in JPEG format.

Reducing the file size

Before you share your PDF file, it's a good idea to make sure that the file is as small as possible. You'll use the Reduce File Size command to do this. First though, you'll check the file size.

1 In Acrobat, choose File > Document Properties. In the Description tab of this dialog box, check the file size.

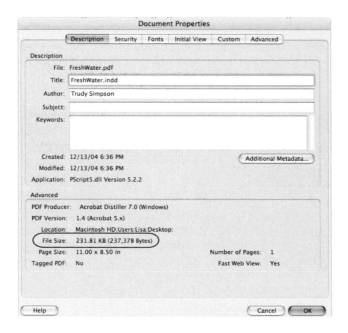

The file size is approximately 237 KB. File size may vary slightly with your platform.

2 Click Cancel to close the dialog box.

Now you'll see the result of using the Reduce File Size command.

3 Choose File > Reduce File Size.

4 Choose the version of Acrobat that you want your file to be compatible with. We choose Acrobat 4.0 and later. Click OK.

When you choose the compatibility level, be aware that the newer the version of Acrobat that you choose, the smaller the file. If you choose compatibility with Acrobat 7.0, you should be sure that your intended audience does indeed have version 7.0 installed.

5 In the Save As dialog box, save your modified file using a different name. We saved the file in the same directory using the name **SmallerFreshWater1.pdf**. Click Save to complete the process.

When you're using the Reduce File Size command, it is always a good idea to save the file using a different name so that you don't overwrite the unmodified file.

Acrobat automatically optimizes your PDF file, a process that may take a minute. Any anomalies are displayed in a Conversion Warnings window.

6 Using the same method as you used in Step 1, check the size of the SmallerFreshWater1.pdf file.

The file size is approximately 197 KB. Again, file size may vary slightly with your platform.

Choose File > Close and close your file. If necessary, close the Advanced Editing toolbar, and exit or quit Acrobat.

Exploring on your own: Using photo print sizes and layouts

The Picture Tasks plug-in is specifically designed to allow you to extract JPEG formatted pictures sent to you in an Adobe PDF file that was created with Adobe Photoshop Album, Adobe Photoshop Elements 2.0, or Adobe Acrobat using JPEG source files. With Picture Tasks, you can export and save the pictures to your local machine, and edit them using Photoshop or Photoshop Elements. You can also print them locally using standard photo print sizes and layouts.

In Acrobat for Windows, you can share pictures on the Internet or send them to an online service provider to have prints directly mailed to you.

1 Open Acrobat and in Acrobat, choose File > Open, and open the Domino_Dog.pdf file in the Lesson08 folder.

Because this PDF file was created from a JPEG file, the Picture Tasks message box opens automatically.

2 Click OK to clear the message box.

3 Click the Pictures Tasks button () on the Acrobat toolbar, and choose Print Pictures from the menu.

4 In the Print dialog box, click Next.

This is where you select your printer, your print size and layout, and your print options. We chose a print size of 5x7 inches using the same image twice.

5 When you're ready, simply click Print. (Click Cancel to exit the process without printing the file.)

6 When you're finished, close Acrobat and the Domino_dog.pdf file.

To get additional information on all the tasks you can accomplish using the Picture Tasks button, choose How To ... Picture Tasks from the Picture Tasks button menu. The Picture Tasks How To page links to wizards to help you perform each task, as well gives a link to the Picture Tasks Help.

Exploring on your own: Optimizing for page-at-a-time downloading

If you're distributing your documents on the web or via a company intranet, you should use the Fast Web View option to remove unused objects, consolidate duplicate page backgrounds, and reorder objects in the PDF file format for *page-at-a-time downloading*. With page-at-a-time downloading (also called byte-serving), the web server sends only the requested page of information to the user, not the entire PDF document. This is especially important with large documents, which can take a long time to download from the server.

In Acrobat 7.0, the default General preferences are set to always optimize for fast web view during a Save As operation. So first you'll check whether your file is already optimized for Fast Web View.

1 Open Acrobat.

2 Choose File > Open, and open the Illus_Opt.pdf file in the Lesson08 folder.

3 Choose File > Document Properties, and click the Description tab.

4 At the bottom right of the dialog box, you'll see that the document is not optimized for Fast Web View. Click Cancel to exit the dialog box.

To restructure the document for Fast Web View, you'll check your preferences to make sure that the Save As Optimizes for Fast Web View option is on and then re-save the file.

5 Choose Edit > Preferences (Windows) or Acrobat > Preferences (Mac OS), and select General in the left pane.

6 Under Miscellaneous, make sure that the Save As Optimizes for Fast Web View option is checked. (This option is checked by default.) Click OK.

7 Choose File > Save As and save the file using the same file name and location to overwrite the non-optimized file. If you recheck the Document Properties, you'll see that your file is now optimized for fast web view.

8 Choose File > Close to close the file.

9 Exit or quit Acrobat.

Now when users view your file on the Web, only the requested page of information will be downloaded, rather than the entire PDF file. This shortens perceived download times with large documents.

Review questions

1 When you're reading an article on-screen, where can you adjust the view magnification?

2 What kinds of text attributes can you change from within Acrobat?

3 How do you copy text from a PDF file?

4 How can you copy photographs or images from a PDF file?

Review answers

1 You can adjust the view magnification of articles in the Page Display preferences. Choose Edit > Preferences (Windows) or Acrobat > Preferences (Mac OS), and select Page Display in the left pane. Set the Max Fit Visible Zoom option to the desired value, and click OK to apply the change.

2 You can use the TouchUp Text tool to change text formatting—font, size, color, letter spacing, and alignment—or to change the text itself.

3 If you're copying a couple of words or sentences, you use the Select tool to copy and paste the text into another application. If you want to copy all the text from a PDF document, you use the File > Save As command and save the PDF file in a text format.

4 You can copy photographs or images from a PDF file in several ways:

• You can copy an image using the Select tool.

• You can copy an image using the Snapshot tool.

• You can save each image in a PDF file to an image format using the Advanced > Export All Images command.

9 Making Documents Accessible and Flexible

The accessibility and flexibility of your Adobe PDF files determine how easily vision- and motion-impaired users and users of hand-held devices and ebook readers can access, reflow, and if you allow it, reuse the content of your files. You control the accessibility and flexibility of your Adobe PDF files through the amount of structure you build into the source file and how you create the Adobe PDF file.

In this lesson, you'll do the following:

- Check the accessibility of a tagged PDF file.

- Reflow a document.

- Learn to scroll through a document automatically.

- Review keyboard shortcuts.

- Review the Acrobat features that make it easier for vision- and motor-impaired users to work with Adobe PDF files.

- Change your on-screen display to enhance readability.

 - *Improve the flexibility and accessibility of a PDF file.*

This lesson will take about 45 minutes to complete.

If needed, remove the previous lesson folder from your hard drive, and copy the Lesson09 folder onto it.

Note: *Windows 2000 users may need to unlock the lesson files before using them. For information, see "Copying the Classroom in a Book files" on page 4.*

About this lesson

In this lesson, you'll look at what constitute flexible and accessible documents. In the first part of the lesson, you'll examine a tagged PDF document and see how easy it is to reflow the document and extract content. Then, if you're working with Acrobat Professional, you'll examine an unstructured document and make it accessible. In the second part of the lesson, you'll look at the Acrobat 7.0 features that make it easier for motion- and vision-impaired users to access PDF files.

About flexibility

An Adobe PDF file is considered to be flexible when the content can be easily reused—that is, content can be reflowed for viewing on non-traditional monitors, such as hand-held devices, and when tables, text, and graphics can be exported for use in other applications if allowed by the creator of the Adobe PDF file. The degree of flexibility of a PDF file depends on the underlying logical structure of the document. (See "Reflowing a flexible PDF file" and "Saving as accessible text" in this lesson.)

About accessibility

By making your PDF documents more accessible to users, you can broaden your readership and better meet government standards for accessibility. Accessibility in Acrobat 7.0 falls into two categories:

• Accessibility features that help authors create accessible documents from new or existing PDF documents. These features include simple methods for checking accessibility and adding tags to PDF documents. (See "Looking at accessible documents" in this lesson.) In Acrobat Professional, you can also correct accessibility and reading-order problems in PDF files by editing the PDF file structure.

• Accessibility features that help readers with motion or vision limitations to navigate and view PDF documents more easily. Many of these features can be adjusted by using a wizard, the Accessibility Setup Assistant. (See "Using the Accessibility Setup Assistant" in this lesson.)

About structure

For Adobe PDF files to be flexible and accessible they must have structure, and Adobe PDF files support three levels of structure—tagged, structured, and unstructured. Tagged PDF files have the most structure. Structured PDF files have some structure, but are not as flexible or accessible as tagged PDF files. Unstructured PDF files have no structure. As you will see later in this lesson though, you can add limited structure to unstructured files. The more structure a file has, the more efficiently and reliably its content can be reused.

Structure is built-in to a document when the creator of the document defines headers, columns, adds navigation aids such as bookmarks, and adds alternative text descriptions for graphics, for example. In many cases, documents are automatically given logical structure and tags when they are converted to Adobe PDF. (PDF files created with earlier versions of Acrobat may not have structure.) The best way to create a structured, reusable PDF document is to create a well-structured document in your original authoring application.

When you create Adobe PDF from Microsoft Office files or from files created in later versions of Adobe FrameMaker, InDesign, or PageMaker, or when you create Adobe PDF using Web Capture, the resulting PDF files are tagged. The most built-in structure is obtained when you create a document that has defined structure and convert that document to give tagged PDF files.

In Acrobat Professional if your PDF documents don't reflow well, you can correct most problems using the Content tab in the navigation pane or the TouchUp Reading Order tool. However, this is not as easy as creating a well-structured document in the first place. For more information, see "Making files flexible and accessible" later in this lesson.

For an in depth guide to creating accessible PDF documents, visit the Adobe website at http://access.adobe.com.

Looking at accessible documents

In the first part of this lesson, you'll examine a tagged PDF file created by converting a Microsoft Word document using PDFMaker on Windows.

Working with a tagged Adobe PDF file

First you'll look at the accessibility and flexibility of a tagged PDF file that was created from a Word file.

1 Choose File > Open, and open the Tag_Wines.pdf file in the Lesson09 folder.

2 Choose File > Save As, and save the file as **Tag_Wines1.pdf** in the Lesson09 folder.

Checking for accessibility

It's always a good idea to check the accessibility of any Adobe PDF document before you distribute it to users, and the Acrobat Quick Check feature tells you right away if your document has the information necessary to make it accessible. At the same time, it checks for protection settings that would prohibit access.

1 Choose Advanced > Accessibility > Quick Check.

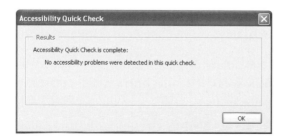

The message box indicates that the document Tag_Wines1.pdf has no accessibility issues.

2 Click OK to close the message box.

💡 *You can add security to your PDF files and still make them accessible. The 128-bit encryption offered by Acrobat 7.0 Standard prevents users from copying and pasting text from a PDF file while still supporting assistive technology. You can also use the Enable Text Access for Screen Reader Devices for the Visually Impaired option to modify security settings on older PDF documents to make them accessible without compromising security.*

Now you'll take a quick look at how flexible a tagged PDF file is. First you'll reflow the PDF file and then you'll save the contents of the PDF file as accessible text.

Reflowing a flexible PDF file

First you'll adjust the size of your document window to mimic the smaller screen of a hand-held device.

1 Click the Actual Size button (⬜) in the Acrobat toolbar to display the document at 100%.

2 Click the Windows minimize button to reduce the size of the document pane, or position the pointer over the bottom corner of the application window and drag until the document pane is the desired size. We made our Acrobat window small enough that the width of a full page (at 100%) could not be displayed on the screen.

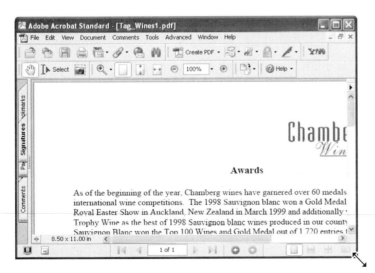

Reduce the size of the document window.

Your goal is to size the Acrobat window so that the ends of the sentences in the document pane are cut off.

3 Choose View > Reflow.

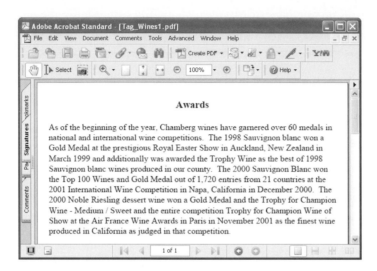

The content of the document is reflowed to accommodate the smaller document screen. You can now read an entire line of text without using the horizontal scroll bar.

When you reflow text, artifacts such as page numbers and page headers often drop out because they are no longer relevant to the page display. Text is reflowed one page at a time, and you cannot save the document in the reflowed state. Later in this lesson, you'll see some less successful results when you try to reflow a document created without structure or with less structure.

Now you'll examine the effect of changing the magnification.

4 Click the arrow next to the magnification box on the toolbar, and choose 400% from the menu.

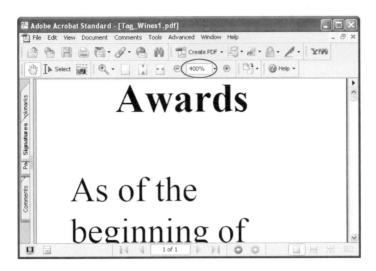

5 Scroll down the page to see how the text reflows. Again, because the text is reflowed, you don't have to use the horizontal scroll bar to move back and forth across the page to read the enlarged text. The text is automatically contained within the document pane.

6 When you've finished viewing the reflowed text, maximize the Acrobat document window and click the Fit Page button ([↕]) on the toolbar to view the entire page of the PDF file.

Now you'll see how efficiently Acrobat saves the contents of a tagged document for reuse in another application.

Saving as accessible text

1 Choose File > Save As, and in the Save As dialog box, choose Text (Accessible) for Save as Type (Windows) or Format (Mac OS), and click Save.

By default, your file is saved with the same file name and in the same folder, but with a .txt extension.

2 Minimize the Acrobat window using the Windows or Mac OS controls, and then navigate to the Lesson09 folder.

3 Double-click on the Tag_Wines1.txt file to open the file in any simple text editor that you have on your system.

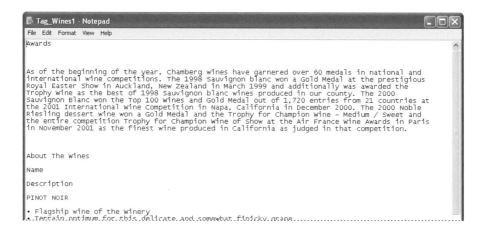

If necessary, scroll down the document and notice how the format of the table is translated into a format that is easily interpreted by a screen reader.

4 When you have finished examining the accessible text, exit or quit your text editor and close the Tag_Wines1.txt file, and then maximize the Acrobat window.

5 In Acrobat, choose File > Close to close the Tag_Wines1.pdf file.

With Acrobat you can make documents more readily accessible to all types of users. But Acrobat also offers tools to make it easier for motion- and vision-impaired users to access PDF files. For information on using these tools, see "Using the Acrobat accessibility features" later in this lesson.

Looking at the reading order

A well-designed, accessible online document will have a logical reading order. As you saw earlier in this lesson, you can quickly and easily check the accessibility of any PDF document. Now, you'll look at the accessibility of a couple of pages of a printed guide that has been converted to a PDF file. This guide was designed to be printed, so no attempt was made to make it accessible.

1 Choose File > Open, and open the file AI_pp.pdf in the Lesson 09 folder.

2 Choose Advanced > Accessibility > Quick Check. The message box indicates that the document has no structure. As a result, it might be necessary to change the reading order.

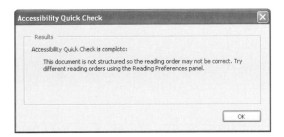

3 Click OK to close the message box.

You'll check the effect of changing the reading order preferences, but first you'll listen to a page read out loud.

4 Choose View > Read Out Loud > Read This Page Only. To stop the reading, press Shift+Ctrl+E (Windows) or Shift+Command+E (Mac OS).

As you listen to the reading, notice that the captions of the first two figures are read, followed by the left column of text. Then the caption of the third figure is read, followed by the right column of text. You'll fix this error by changing the reading order preferences.

5 Choose Edit > Preferences (Windows) or Acrobat > Preferences (Mac OS), and select Reading in the left pane.

6 From the Reading Order menu, choose Use Reading Order in Raw Print Stream to use the word order in the PDF document's print instructions. Click OK to apply the change.

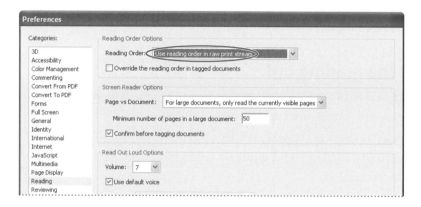

7 Choose View > Read Out Loud > Read This Page Only. To stop the reading, press Shift+Ctrl+E (Windows) or Shift+Command+E (Mac OS).

This time as you listen to the reading, notice that the left column is read first, followed by the right column, followed by the captions of the illustrations. This is a more logical reading order.

If you are going to be using the text-to-speech function in your future work, you should restore the recommended reading order preference (Infer Reading Order From Document option).

You can add tags to a PDF document in both Acrobat Standard and Acrobat Professional. using the Advanced > Accessibility > Add Tags to Document command. However, you can only correct tagging and order errors in Acrobat Professional. In the next section, you'll view the results of adding tags. If you have Acrobat Professional, you'll also correct order errors.

Making files flexible and accessible

Some tagged Adobe PDF documents may not contain all the information necessary to make the document contents fully flexible or accessible. For example, if you want to reuse the document in another format or make all items fully available to a screen reader, the PDF document should contain alternate text for figures, language properties for portions of the text that use a different language than the default language for the document, and expansion text for abbreviations. (Designating the appropriate language for different text elements ensures that the correct characters are used when you reuse the document for another purpose, that the word can be pronounced correctly when read out loud, and that it will be spell-checked with the correct dictionary.)

You can add alternate text and multiple languages to a tag using the Tags tab. (If only one language is required, it is easier to choose the language in the Document Properties dialog box.) You can also add alternate text using the Touchup Reading Order tool.

As you saw earlier in this lesson, if the document you are reading is accessible, you can zoom in to magnify the view and then reflow text so that you don't have to scroll back and forth across the page when you magnify the view. Now you'll look at how this page reflows.

1 Click the Actual Size button ( ) in the Acrobat toolbar to display the document at 100%.

2 Click the Windows minimize button to reduce the size of the document pane, or position the pointer over the bottom corner of the application window and drag until the document pane is the desired size. We made our Acrobat window small enough that the width of a full page could not be displayed on the screen (at 100%).

3 Choose View > Reflow.

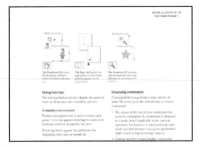
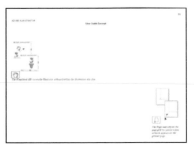

The text reflows well, but the figures are out of sequence.

The reflow operation for this page is less than perfect; it mirrors the reading order before you changed the Reading preferences.

4 Click the Fit Page button to restore the view. Resize the Acrobat window as required.

In this section of the lesson, you'll improve the flexibility and accessibility of the page. First you'll add tags to as many elements as possible using Acrobat.

5 Choose Advanced > Accessibility > Add Tags to Document.

Note: In Acrobat Professional, an Add Tags Report is displayed to the right of the document pane. Leave this pane open if you are using Acrobat Professional.

6 Click the First Page button (🔼) to return to page 1, and then test the effectiveness of this auto-tagging operation by reflowing the document again using View > Reflow

For this page, adding tags did not improve the reflow of the document.

7 If you are using Acrobat Professional, leave the file open. If you are using Acrobat Standard, choose File > Close to close your work. You needn't save your work.

When you add tags to a document, Acrobat adds a logical tree structure to the document that determines the order in which page content is reflowed and read by screen readers and the Read Out Loud feature. On relatively simple pages, the Add Tags to Document command can work well. On more complex pages—pages that contain irregularly shaped columns, bulleted lists, text that spans columns, etc.—the Add Tags to Document command may not be sufficient, as with this page.

To correctly tag these more complex pages you need to use the Content tab in the Navigation pane or the TouchUp Reading Order tool, which are available only in Acrobat Professional. If you are using Acrobat Standard, skip to the section "Using the Acrobat accessibility features" later in this lesson.

Acrobat 7.0 Professional: Viewing the results of adding tags

While Acrobat can track the structure of most page elements and tag them appropriately, as you saw in the prior section of the lesson, pages with complex layouts or unusual elements may not always result in successfully tagged PDF documents and may require editing. When you tag a PDF file using Acrobat Professional, Acrobat returns a confidence log report in the How To window that lists pages where problems were encountered and suggestions for fixing them.

It's a good idea to check these items in the PDF document to determine what corrections if any, need to be made. Use the report to navigate to the problem areas of your PDF document by clicking the links for each error. Then use the TouchUp Reading Order tool to correct the problem.

The confidence log report is a temporary file and can't be saved. The Full Check feature generates an accessibility report that can be saved.

Editing the reading order

As you saw in the prior section of the lesson, when the Add Tags to Document command finishes in Acrobat Professional, an Add Tags Report is displayed to the right of the document pane. As you look at this report, you see that the figures are missing alternate text. You'll add this text, but first you'll correct the reading order.

1 Choose File > Save As, and save the file as Access_AI_pp.pdf in the Lesson09 folder.

2 Choose View > Reflow to exit the reflow mode. (There will be a check mark next to Reflow if you are in the Reflow mode.)

3 *Choose Tools > Advanced Editing > TouchUp Reading Order Tool.*

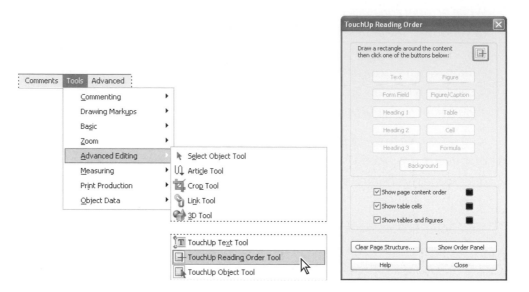

Whenever you select the TouchUp Reading Order tool, the TouchUp Reading Order dialog box opens. You'll use this dialog box to edit the reading order. Each element on the PDF page in the document pane is numbered and shaded.

First you'll review the extent of the reflow problems.

4 *Choose View > Reflow. If necessary, drag the TouchUp Reading Order dialog box out of the document pane.*

As before, the two images (leftmost and center) are followed by the left column of text. Then follows the rightmost image and the right column of text.

5 *Click the Fit Page button to restore the view.*

Notice also that the rightmost and leftmost images and captions are formatted differently from the center image. You'll group the images and captions for the first and third figures.

6 *To group the image and caption for the first figure, marquee drag (with the TouchUp Reading Order tool still selected) to enclose the figure and caption. When your selection is complete, click the Figure/Caption button in the TouchUp Reading Order dialog box.*

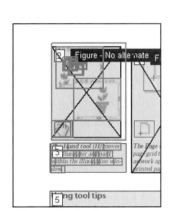 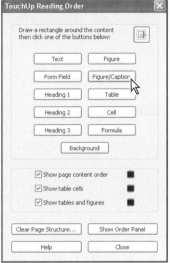 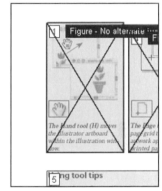

7 *Repeat step 6 for the third figure/caption set.*

To hide the alternate text labels, click the Show Tables and Figures option in the TouchUp Reading Order dialog box.

Now you'll look at the numbering of the elements on the page and adjust the reading order.

8 *Click the Show Order Panel button in the TouchUp Reading Order dialog box to open the Order tab.*

First you'll delete the header text because you don't want it to be read by a screen reader.

9 *In the Order tab of the Navigation pane, select the ADOBE ILLUSTRATOR element and then click the garbage can icon.*

10 *Arrange the elements on the page in the correct order by dragging them up and down in the tab. We used the order shown in the illustration below. If necessary, increase the size of the Order panel so that you can see all the elements on the page.*

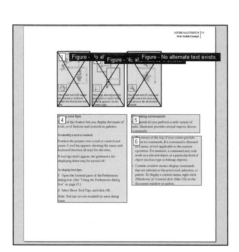 

11 *When you're finished, choose File > Save.*

12 *Close the Order navigation pane.*

13 *Choose View > Reflow to check the results of your work. When you are finished, click the Fit Page button to restore the view.*

Adding Alt Text (alternative text)

Non-text elements in your document, such as figures and multimedia elements, won't be recognized by a screen reader or Read Out Loud feature unless they are accompanied by alternate text. When you reviewed the Add Tags Report, you noticed that all the figures are missing Alt Text. You'll add alternate text now for three of the figures. First though, you'll close the Add Tags Report.

1 *Click the Hide button or Close button to close the Add Tags Report.*

2 With the TouchUp Reading Order tool still selected, right-click (Windows) or Control-click (Mac OS) on the leftmost figure, and choose Edit Alternate Text from the menu. In the Alternate Text dialog box, enter the text you want the Screen Reader to use. We entered: **Figure shows Hand tool being used to drag the artboard across the Illustrator window**. Then click OK.

You can use the same procedure to create alternate text for the other two figures if you wish.

 If the Show Tables and Figures option is selected in the TouchUp Reading Order dialog box, the alt text will be displayed in a label in the document pane.

3 To check your alternate text, choose View > Read Out Loud > Read This Page Only. You'll hear your alternate text. To stop the reading, press Shift+Ctrl+E (Windows) or Shift+Command+E (Mac OS).

Notice that only the alternate text is read. If you want both the alternate text and the caption of the figure to be read, don't combine the figure and caption elements.

4 Choose File > Close to close your work without saving your changes, and click the close button to close the TouchUp Reading Order dialog box. Select the Hand tool.

For an in depth guide to creating accessible PDF documents, visit the Adobe website at http://access.adobe.com.

Acrobat 7.0 Professional: Checking reading order

Acrobat 7.0 Professional allows you to check the reflow and reading-order of PDF files and improve the accessibility of non-text elements in a document using the Touchup Reading Order tool and the Tags tab.

If your document is a fillable PDF form or contains images, you must add alternate text for these items to make them fully accessible. For example, you can add alternate text in the form field's Properties dialog box. A screen reader will then read this alternate text rather than simply read the name of the type of form field when a user tabs through the form fields.

To add instructional information to a form field:

1. With the appropriate form field tool selected, do one of the following to open the form field's Properties dialog box:

- *Double-click the form field.*

- *Click the More button on the Properties toolbar.*

2. In the General tab, type instructional text into the Tooltip box.

Using the Acrobat accessibility features

Many people with vision and motor impairments use computers, and Acrobat has a number of features that make it easier for these users to work with Adobe PDF documents. These features include:

- Automatic scrolling.

- Keyboard shortcuts.

- Support for several screen-reader applications, including the text-to-speech engines built-in to Windows and Mac OS platforms.

- Enhanced on-screen viewing.

You'll learn more about these features in the following sections.

Using the Accessibility Setup Assistant

Both Acrobat 7.0 and Adobe Reader have an Accessibility Setup Assistant that launches automatically the first time the software detects a screen reader, screen magnifier, or other assistive technology on your system. (You can also launch the Assistant manually at any time by choosing Advanced > Accessibility > Setup Assistant.) This Assistant walks you through the options that mostly control how PDF documents appear on screen but also include the option that sends print output to a Braille printer.

A full explanation of the options that can be set in the Accessibility Setup Assistant is available in the Complete Acrobat 7.0 Help. The options available depend on the type of assistive technology you have on your system, and the first panel of the Accessibility Setup Assistant requires you to identify the type of assistive technology you are using:

• Select Set Options for Screen Readers if you use a device that reads text and sends output to a Braille printer.

• Select Set Options for Screen Magnifiers if you use a device that makes text appear larger on the screen.

• Select Set All Accessibility Options if you use a combination of assistive devices.

• Select Use Recommended Settings and Skip Setup to use the Adobe-recommended settings for users with limited accessibility. (Note that the preferred settings for users with assistive technology installed are _not_ the same as the default Acrobat settings for users who are not using assistive technology.)

In addition to the options you can set using the Accessibility Setup Assistant, you can set a number of options in the Acrobat or Reader preferences that control automatic scrolling, reading out loud settings, and reading order. You may want to use some of these options even if you don't have assistive technology on your system. For example, you can set your Multimedia preferences to hear available descriptions for video and audio attachments.

If you opened the Accessibility Setup Assistant, click Cancel to exit the dialog box without making any changes.

About automatic scrolling

When you're reading a long document, the Acrobat automatic scrolling feature saves a lot of keystroke and mouse actions. You can control the speed of the scrolling, you can scroll backwards and forward, and you can exit automatic scrolling with a single keystroke.

Now you'll test the automatic scroll feature.

1 If necessary, resize your Acrobat window to fill your desktop and select the Hand tool, and then choose File > Open, and open the AI_Access.pdf file.

2 Choose View > Automatically Scroll.

3 You can set the rate of scrolling using the number keys on your keyboard. The higher the number, the faster the rate of scrolling. Try pressing 9 and then 1, for example, to compare rates of scrolling. To exit automatic scrolling, press the Esc key.

About keyboard shortcuts

Many keyboard shortcuts are listed to the right of the menu command in Acrobat. Also, many tools can be selected with a single keystroke. But before these keyboard shortcuts are available, you may have to change your General preferences.

1 Move your pointer over the Select tool on the toolbar and notice that the tooltip displays Select Tool. Do not select the Select tool at this time, but keep the Hand tool selected.

2 If you don't see a keyboard shortcut in the tooltip, choose Edit > Preferences (Windows) or Acrobat > Preferences (Mac OS), and select General in the left pane.

3 Click the check box for the Use Single-Key Accelerators to Access Tools option. The option is on when the check box contains a check mark.

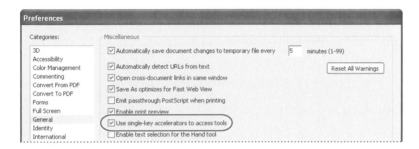

4 Click OK to apply your change.

5 Move your pointer over the Select tool again, and notice that the tooltip now contains the name of the tool plus the keyboard shortcut, V. Pressing the V key will select the Select tool. Again, don't select the Select tool but move the pointer into the document pane, and press the V key on your keyboard. The pointer changes from the Hand tool ( ) to the Select tool ( ).

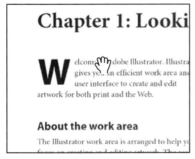
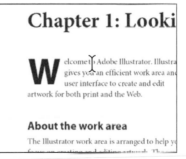

Pointer changes from Hand tool to Select tool. Note the icon for the tool changes as you move the cursor over text.

Now you'll use another keyboard shortcut to reselect the Hand tool.

6 Press H on your keyboard to select the Hand tool again.

For most common commands and tools, the keyboard shortcut is displayed next to the command or tool name if you have the preferences set to use single-key accelerators. A list of the keyboard shortcuts that are not displayed next to the associated command or tooltip is available in the Complete Acrobat 7.0 Help.

You can use the keyboard to control Acrobat within Microsoft Internet Explorer in Windows. If the focus is on the web browser, any keyboard shortcuts you use act according to the web browser settings for navigation and selection. Pressing the Tab key shifts the focus from the browser to the Acrobat document and application, so navigation and command keystrokes function normally. Pressing Ctrl + Tab shifts the focus from the document back to the web browser.

Changing background color

Now you'll experiment with changing the color of the background. Note that these changes affect only the on-screen display on your own system; they do not affect the printed document, nor are they saved with the document for display on systems other than your own.

1 Choose Edit > Preferences (Windows) or Acrobat > Preferences (Mac OS), and select Accessibility in the left pane.

2 Click the check box to select the Replace Document Colors option.

3 On Windows, select Custom Color.

4 Click the Page Background color square to open the color tab.

5 You can select a color from the color picker or you can select a custom color. We choose pale gray.

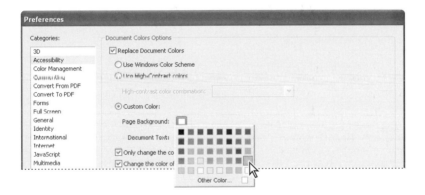

6 Click OK to apply your changes.

7 When you are finished, you can leave your background color as is, or return it to white.

⚲ *You can change the background color of form fields and the color of form fields when your pointer moves over them in the Forms preferences. You can change the background color, which is black by default, for full-screen presentations in the Full Screen preferences. You can change the color of the underline used by the spell check feature to identify misspelled words in the Spelling preferences.*

Smoothing text

Acrobat allows you to smooth text, line art, and images to improve on-screen readability, especially with larger text sizes. If you use a laptop or if you have an LCD screen, you can also choose to use CoolType to optimize your display quality. These options are set in the Page Display preferences.

Magnifying bookmark text

You can increase the text size used in bookmark labels.

1 Click the Bookmarks tab to display the Bookmarks.

2 Choose Text Size > Large from the Options menu of the bookmarks tab.

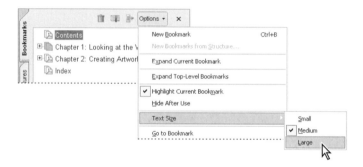

3 When you're finished, restore your bookmark text size to medium.

You should experiment with screen display options and other accessibility controls to find a combination that best suits your needs.

Setting screen reader and reading out loud preferences

After you have installed your screen reader or similar application and set it up to work with Acrobat, you can set the screen reader preferences in Acrobat. You set these preferences in the same panel in which you set the Read Out Loud feature preferences that control the volume, pitch, and speed of the speech; the nature of the voice; and the reading order preferences.

Note: *Newer systems (both Windows and Mac OS platforms) have built-in text-to-speech engines. Although the Read Out Loud feature can read the text of a PDF file out loud, it is not a screen reader. Not all systems support the Read Out Loud feature.*

In this section, you'll look at the preferences that affect the reading out loud of Adobe PDF documents. Unless you have text-to-speech software on your system, you do not need to set these preferences.

1 If your system has text-to-speech software, choose View > Read Out Loud > Read This Page Only. You will hear the currently displayed page read aloud. To stop the reading, press Shift+Ctrl+E (Windows) or Shift+Command+E (Mac OS).

You can experiment with the following reading options.

2 Choose Edit > Preferences (Windows) or Acrobat > Preferences (Mac OS), and select Reading in the left pane.

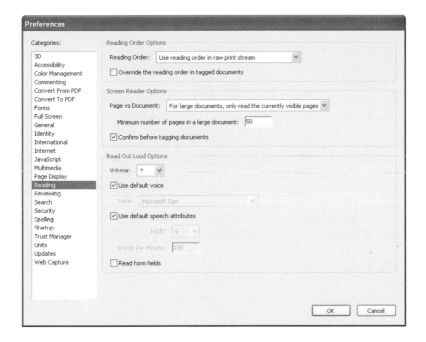

You can control the volume, pitch, speed, and voice used. If you use the default voice, you cannot change the pitch and speed of delivery.

If your system has limited memory, you may wish to reduce the number of pages before data is delivered by page. The default value is 50 pages.

3 You need to click OK in the Preferences dialog box to apply any changes that you make. Or you can click Cancel to exit the Preferences dialog box without making any changes.

4 To test your settings, choose View > Read Out Loud > Read This Page Only.

5 To stop the reading, press Shift+Ctrl+E (Windows) or Shift+Command+E (Mac OS). You set the reading order options here also.

When you are finished, choose File > Close. You need not save your work. Then exit or quit Acrobat.

Review questions

1 How do you check whether or not a file is accessible?

2 Can you make an unstructured document accessible?

3 What is the difference between changing the magnification when viewing a standard PDF file and changing the magnification when viewing a reflowed PDF file?

4 Where do you turn keyboard shortcuts on or off?

Review answers

1 Choose Advanced > Accessibility > Quick Check.

2 You can often improve the accessibility of an unstructured document by choosing the Advanced > Accessibility > Add Tags to Document command. If you can't improve the accessibility sufficiently, try saving the PDF file in accessible text format.

3 When you change the magnification when viewing a standard PDF file, you may need to use the horizontal scroll bars to read the full width of a line of text. When you change the magnification when viewing a reflowed PDF file, the text is reflowed to fit in the visible area; you never have to scroll horizontally to view text.

4 You turn keyboard shortcuts on or off in the General preferences, using the Use Single-Key Accelerators to Access Tools option.

Lesson 10:

10 | Using Acrobat in a Document Review Cycle

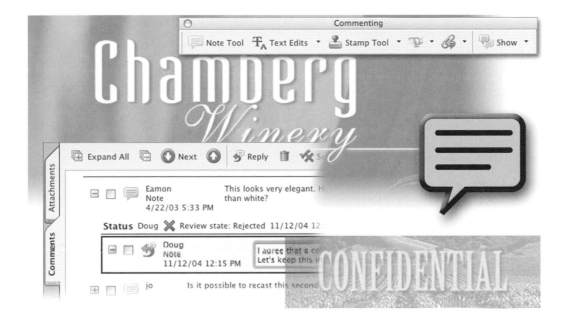

Acrobat can play an effective role in streamlining your document review cycle. You can distribute a PDF document to an audience of reviewers, and you can receive comments back in the form of notes, text, sound files, stamps, attached files, drawing markups, and text markups added to the file. You can track the review process and then collate the comments and compile them in a single file for easier viewing.

In this lesson, you'll learn how to do the following:

- Manage, create, and respond to comments.

- Change the appearance of comments.

- Export and import comments.

- Summarize and print comments.

- Create custom stamps to apply to your PDF documents.

This lesson will take about 60 minutes to complete.

If needed, remove the previous lesson folder from your hard drive, and copy the Lesson10 folder onto it.

Note: *Windows 2000 users may need to unlock the lesson files before using them. For information, see "Copying the Classroom in a Book files" on page 4.*

About the review process

There are several ways to use Acrobat in a review process depending on the formality of the review, the number of people involved, the interactivity of the review process, and the access of reviewers to a common server.

The simplest and least formal way to send a PDF document for review is to open the document that you want to have reviewed and click the Email button (📧) on the Acrobat toolbar. Acrobat automatically launches a new message window in your default email application and attaches the PDF document that you have open. All you have to do is provide the email addresses of the recipients and type a message for your reviewers. Reviewers receive the entire PDF file and can return comments to you as an FDF file (see "Exporting and importing comments" in this lesson) or they can return the complete, annotated PDF file. Because you may not have a review partner available as you work on this lesson, you'll work with this informal review process, though this isn't the recommended Acrobat review process. Although this informal review process is very easy, you have to manage the review process and the review comments manually—you don't have access to the full power built into Acrobat's tracked email-based review process, which is the recommended review process.

If you want more control over the review process—for example, if you want to track several documents that are being reviewed, send reminder messages to reviewers, or invite additional reviewers to join the process—you should use the File > Send for Review command to set up a tracked email-based review. Even though an email-based review is easy to set up, the management tools it offers are powerful. With this process, the PDF file is packaged in a way that automatically opens the Commenting and Drawing Markups toolbars for the recipients, opens the How To page on commenting topics, and provides instructions for returning comments. You'll see this process in action if you have the time and resources to work through the "Exploring on your own" section at the end of this lesson. This tracked email-based review process is particularly helpful if you are working with reviewers who are new to the commenting process.

If all your reviewers have access to a shared server, you can also set up a browser-based review in which reviewers can review and respond to each other's comments interactively. For more information, see "Setting up a browser-based review" in the Complete Acrobat 7.0 Help.

 On Windows, you set your default email application in the Programs tab of the Internet Options panel or the Internet Properties panel of the Windows Control Panel. On Mac OS, you set your default email application in the Default Email Reader menu in the Preferences for Mail (the email application included with Mac OS).

Opening the work file

First you'll work with a poster for the Chamberg winery. This poster, which is ready for a final review, was sent as a simple email attachment to just a few colleagues. You'll examine comments that reviewers have added to the poster and add several of your own comments before sending the annotated poster off to the designer.

1 Start Acrobat.

2 Choose File > Open. Select Poster.pdf in the Lesson10 folder, and click Open. Then choose File > Save As, rename the file **Poster1.pdf**, and save it in the Lesson10 folder.

 You should save your work regularly. However, Acrobat 7.0 does have an Autosave feature that protects against loss of all your work if you have a system failure or power outage, for example. The autosave options are set in the General preferences.

Working with comments

Acrobat's comment feature lets you attach comments to an existing document. These comments can be in the form of notes, text, sound files, stamps, application files, drawing markups, and text markups. Multiple reviewers can comment on and incorporate their comments into the same document being reviewed.

Important: Comments that you add to a tagged document are not tagged for accessibility unless you enable comment tagging before you add any comments. To enable tagging, choose View > Navigation Tabs > Tags, and then choose Tag Annotations from the Options menu in the Tags panel. This option is only available if you are adding comments to a tagged document. (The file you have open is not tagged.)

Opening the commenting toolbars

You add comments to a PDF document using tools on the Commenting toolbar and the Drawing Markups toolbar. The Commenting toolbar contains the Note tool, the text editing tools, the Stamp tool, the highlighter tools, and the file attachment tools. The Drawing Markups toolbar contains the Callout tool, the Cloud tool, the Dimensioning tool, the Text Box tool, and the drawing tools.

1 Click the Comment & Markup button on the Acrobat toolbar to open the Commenting toolbar. Be sure to click the Comment & Markup button and not the arrow next to the button.

2 Now click the arrow next to the Comment & Markup button, and choose Show Drawing Markups Toolbar from the menu to open the Drawing Markups toolbar.

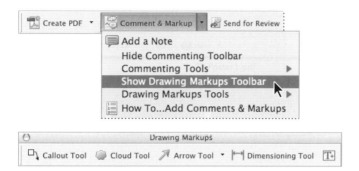

You can leave the two toolbars floating or you can dock them in the toolbar area. For help with moving the toolbars, see Lesson 2, "Getting to Know the Work Area."

Looking at other reviewer's comments

1 Click the Comments tab in the Navigation Pane to display the Comments List across the bottom of the Acrobat window. The Comments tab is at the bottom left of the Acrobat window.

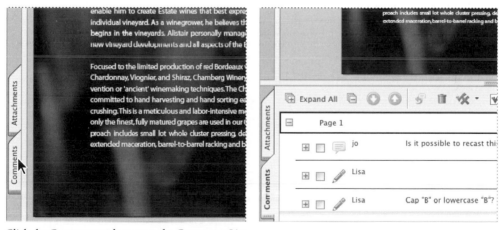

Click the Comments tab to open the Comments List.

A list of comments associated with the open document appears. By default, the list is sorted by page. You can sort the list by a variety of criteria, including type, author, and date. You'll resort the list by author.

2 Click the Sort By button (⏷) on the Comments List toolbar, and choose Author. Click OK to close the message box.

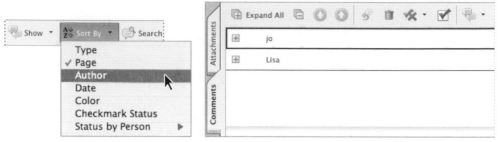

Sort annotations by author.   *Result*

3 Click the plus sign next to the author jo to expand the comments for that reviewer. Scroll down the Comments List and then click the plus sign next to the author Lisa to expand the comments for that reviewer. Continue to scroll down the Comments List.

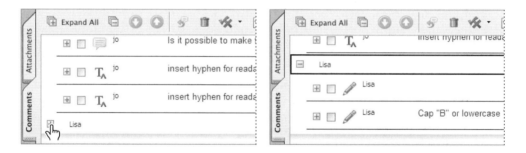

4 Use the scroll bar at the right of the Comments List to scroll back up through the Comments List, and click the first yellow note listed under jo to highlight that comment on the page. You can read the comment in the Comments List. You can also display the contents of a comment automatically when your mouse rolls over the comment icon in the document pane.

5 Roll your mouse over any of the notes in the document pane to display the note's content.

💡 *You can use the Show button (▤) in this toolbar to show and hide comments by type or by author.*

Now you'll look at the preferences that control how comments behave.

6 Choose Edit > Preferences (Windows) or Acrobat > Preferences (Mac OS), and select Commenting in the left pane. You can also open the Preferences dialog box by clicking the Show button (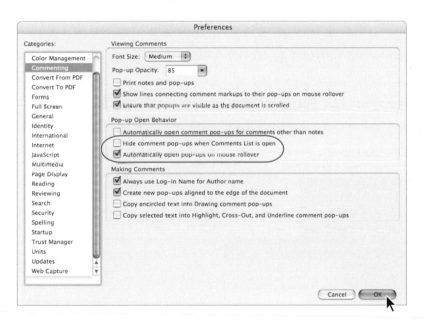) on the Commenting toolbar, and choosing Commenting Preferences.

These Commenting preferences control how comments appear, whether pop-ups open automatically, and authoring options. Notice that you can set the preferences to copy any text that you enclose with a drawing tool or highlight, cross out, or underline into the associated pop-up window.

7 Click the Hide Comment Pop-ups When Comments List Is Open to deselect this option (the box is empty when the option is deselected). This new setting will allow pop-ups in the document pane to remain open when the Comments List is open.

8 Select the Automatically Open Pop-ups on Mouse Rollover option, and click OK to close the Preferences dialog box and reset the preferences.

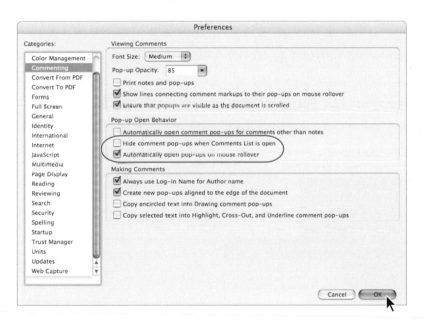

9 Move your pointer into the document pane and position it over one of the note comments. The pop-up windows should be visible when you roll the mouse over the comments and text markups.

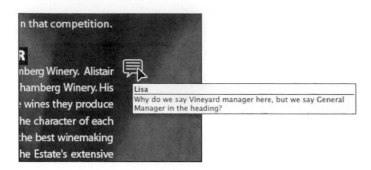

💡 *If you edit the text associated with a comment in the Comments List, the text in the comment in the document pane is updated automatically.*

Now you'll examine the different types of comments that appear on the page and the different colored notes.

10 If any note windows are open, click their close box to close them.

11 Double-click the blue note on the page to open the note and keep it open regardless of where the mouse is.

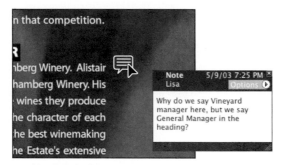

Double-click the blue note to open it and keep it open.

Reviewers can easily customize the appearance of their comments. You'll learn how to do this later in this lesson (see "Setting the appearance of comments" later in this lesson).

12 Click the close box at the top of the note window when you have finished reading the note.

Comments in the form of stamps, drawing markups, and text markups can also have pop-up windows associated with them.

Except for text markups (highlighting, underlining, and crossing out), comments can be easily moved around on a page. You can drag any comment and release it when it is in the desired location.

Now you'll look at some text mark-ups.

13 Use the right scroll bar in the Comments List to scroll down until you see the last two comments from jo. Both are text insertions. Click the plus sign for the first text insertion to open the associated pop-up window. (You can also click in the text of the comment in the Comments List to open the associated pop-up window in the document pane.) The comment is difficult to see in the Fit Page view that the document opened in.

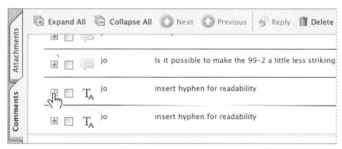

Click the plus sign in the Comments List to open the pop-up window in the document pane.

14 Select the Zoom-In tool (🔍) and drag around the last paragraph of text in the document pane to enlarge it. Now you can clearly see the text insertions.

💡 *The poster is a single-page document, but if your PDF document had multiple pages, clicking on a comment in the Comments List would automatically move the view in the document pane to the page on which the comment is displayed.*

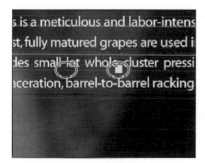

If you're concerned that the designer will miss the insertion of the hyphens, you can add a callout. Callout markups are useful when you want to draw attention to an area of the document but not obscure the document.

15 Select the Callout tool (⌐\) in the Drawing Markups toolbar, and click in the text between the two insertion carats.

A text box with an arrow pointing to the insertion point is added. You'll add text in the text box and then change the location and properties of the text box so that it doesn't obscure the text.

16 Click in the text box to create an insertion point, and type in a message. We typed, **Please don't forget these hyphens**.

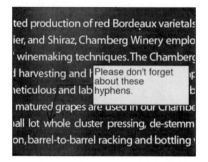

17 Click the Callout tool again and move the cursor (⌶) into the text box area. Right-click (Windows) or Control-click (Mac OS) and choose Properties from the menu.

Now you'll change the appearance of the text box.

18 We increased the thickness of the pointer line from 1 pt to 3 pt so that it would be more obvious; we changed the text box Fill color to pink; we changed the border color to blue (this is also the color of the arrow); and we typed in an Opacity value of 50%. Click Close to apply the selections you have made.

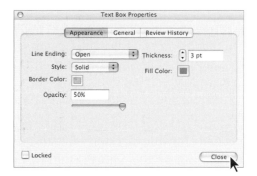

19 Select the Hand tool ( ) and click outside the text box to deselect it. Then drag the pink text box over to the margin so that it doesn't obscure the text. As you move the cursor over any corner of the text box, the cursor turns into a double-headed arrow. Drag to enlarge or reduce the text box. (You may need to adjust the magnification of the document to have the margin visible in the document pane.)

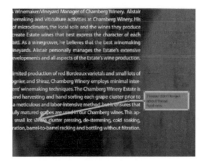

20 Click the Fit Page button to view the entire poster.

You can search for text in a comment using the Search command on the toolbar of the Comments List. Clicking the Search button ( ), opens the Search PDF window where you can enter your search string. Any comments containing the search string are highlighted in the Results window. The first search result is opened in the document window and in the Comments List.

Soon you'll add a variety of your own comments to this document and respond to the existing comments, but first you'll customize your note style.

Setting the appearance of comments

As you just saw, you set the appearance of comments in the Appearance tab of the Properties dialog box. You can also set the appearance of comments in the Properties toolbar. The Properties toolbar is unusual in that its contents change depending on the tool selected. The name of the toolbar also changes to reflect the name of the tool selected. In this section, you'll use the Properties toolbar to change the appearance of your notes.

1 Choose View > Toolbars > Properties Bar.

If you didn't dock or move the Commenting and Drawing Markups toolbars, you may need to reposition the Properties toolbar so that it doesn't hide either of the other toolbars.

2 Drag the Properties toolbar by its title bar so that it doesn't hide either of the commenting toolbars.

3 Click the Note tool ( ) on the Commenting toolbar. The Properties bar becomes the Note Tool Properties toolbar and shows the properties that you can change for notes.

When the Note tool is selected, the Properties toolbar shows the properties that can be set for notes.

Now you'll change the color of your notes.

4 On the Note Tool Properties toolbar, click the arrow next to the color square and choose a color from the color palette. We chose teal.

💡 *Reviewers often use the same color for all their annotations and drawing and mark-up tools.*

Now you'll change the icon associated with the Note tool.

5 Click the Icon button (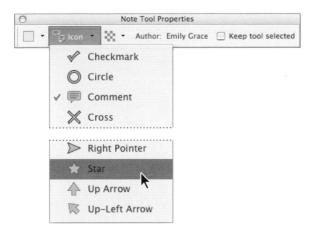)on the Note Tool Properties toolbar, and select an image to associate with the Note tool. We chose the Star.

6 Click the Opacity button (▒) on the Note Tool Properties toolbar, and set the opacity of the note icons. We chose 60%.

If you want to keep the current tool selected after you have added a comment, click the check box next to the Keep Tool Selected option. (The option is on when the check box contains a check mark.) Because we're adding different types of comments, we chose not to select this option.

💡 *You can change the color associated with any text edit tools, any markup tools, or any drawing tools using the Properties toolbar. Select the tool whose color you want to change and then use the Properties toolbar to change the color. You must change the color associated with the tool before using the tool. To apply the color change to all subsequent uses of the tool, use the tool in the document pane and then right-click (Windows) or Control-click (Mac OS) on the mark-up and choose Make Current Properties Default from the context menu.*

Changing the author name for comments

You cannot change the author name from the Properties toolbar. You can only change the author name in the General tab of the Properties dialog box, but first you must change the Commenting preferences to turn off the option to use the log-in name as the author name.

1 Click the Show button (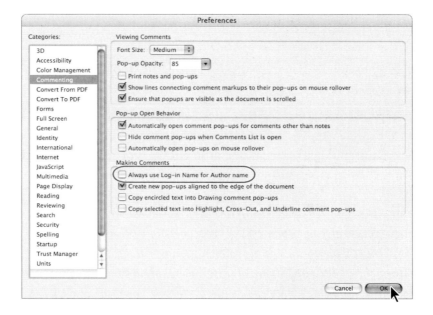) on the Commenting toolbar, and choose Commenting Preferences.

2 In the Making Comments section of the Commenting Preferences dialog box, click the check box to turn off the Always Use Log-In Name for Author Name option in the commenting preferences. (The option is off when the box is empty.) Then click OK to close the Preferences dialog box and apply your change.

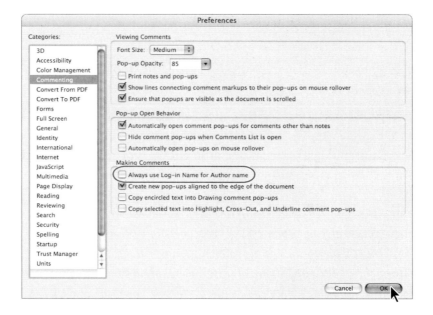

Now you'll change the author name.

3 With the Note tool ( ) selected, click anywhere on the poster to add a note.

4 Right-click (Windows) or Control-click (Mac OS) on the title bar of the note, and choose Properties from the context menu.

5 Click the General tab, and enter your author name. We entered **Doug** as the author. Be aware that this author name will be used for all comments, not just notes, until you change it again.

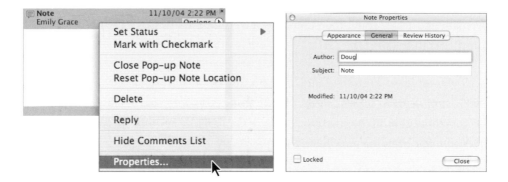

6 Click Close.

Now that you've set the color, opacity, icon, and author name for your notes, you'll make these the default properties. If you don't make these the default properties, your new setting will apply only to the current note and not to any subsequent notes that you add.

7 Close the open note window, and right-click (Windows) or Control-click (Mac OS) on the note icon. Then choose Make Current Properties Default from the context menu.

8 Choose File > Save to save your work.

When you are finished with this lesson, you should be sure to reset the appearance and author information for your notes to better suit your needs.

To change the properties of any object, right-click (Windows) or Control-click (Mac OS) the object, and choose Properties from the context menu.

Exporting and importing comments

As you have seen, the poster has been reviewed by several different reviewers. One reviewer, however, has placed comments on a separate copy of the poster. You'll export this reviewer's comments from their copy of the poster and place them in a Forms Data Format (FDF) file. You'll then combine the comments in this FDF file with the existing comments in the poster.

If you review a document outside a tracked email-based review and need to email the review comments to someone, it is usually easier to export your review comments to an FDF file and simply email the FDF file. Because the FDF file contains just the comments, it is much smaller than the annotated PDF file.

1 Choose File > Open. Select Review.pdf, located inside the Lesson10 folder, and click Open.

This file contains an orange note adjacent to the poster title. You'll read the note after you've imported it into your poster.

2 Choose Comments > Export Comments.

In Acrobat Professional for Windows, you can export comments to a file, to AutoCAD, or to Word. If you are using Acrobat Professional for Word for this lesson, choose Comments > Export Comments > To File.

3 Name the file **Comments.fdf**, and save it in the Lesson10 folder.

4 Choose File > Close to close the Review.pdf file without saving any changes.

Now you'll import the comment from the Comments.fdf file into the Poster1.pdf file, so that you have all the comments in a single document. First take a moment to compare the size of the Comments.fdf file and the Review.pdf file in the Lesson10 folder. (If you need help comparing the size of files, see "Using the Default Adobe PDF Settings" in Lesson 6.) The Comments.fdf file is only several KB, whereas the Review.pdf file is approximately 90 KB. (File size may vary depending on the platform you are working on.)

5 With the Poster1.pdf document active, choose Comments > Import Comments.

6 Select Comments.fdf, located in the Lesson10 folder, and click Select. Click Yes to close the message box.

7 If necessary, click the Comments tab to reopen the Comments List.

8 Scroll to the top of the Comments List.

The Comments List now lists comments from Eamon, as well as those from other reviewers.

With Acrobat 7.0 you can even import comments into a PDF document after the document has been revised. For more information, see "Migrating unresolved comments to a revised PDF document" in the complete Acrobat 7.0 Help.

9 Click the plus sign next to the name Eamon to expand the comment list, and then click the plus sign next to the note icon to open the pop-up in the document pane.

Click on a note in the Comments List to open the note in the document pane.

The imported comment opens in the correct location on the page.

10 Choose File > Save to save the Poster1.pdf file.

Importing Adobe PDF comments directly from one file into another

You can import comments directly from one PDF document to another. In the PDF document that you want to consolidate comments in, choose Comments > Import Comments. Choose Adobe PDF Files for Files of Type (Windows) or Show (Mac OS), and select the file from which you want to import comments. Click Select to import the comments directly without creating an FDF file.

Importing Adobe PDF comments into a Word document (Windows)

In some instances, reviewers make comments in an Adobe PDF document that was created from a Microsoft Word document in Windows. If you need to make changes to the Word document based on these comments, it may be easier for you to import the comments directly into the Word document, rather than switching back and forth between the Word document and Acrobat. You can use Acrobat or Word to export comments from the PDF document into Word and you can import comments in Word 2002 and later. The PDF document must be created from Word and include tags.

Importing Adobe PDF comments into an AutoDesk AutoCAD drawing (Acrobat Professional only)

If you have Acrobat Professional, you can import Adobe PDF comments directly into your AutoDesk AutoCAD drawings.

—See "Exporting comments to a Word document (Windows)," "Exporting markups to an AutoCAD drawing," and "Exporting and Importing Comments" in the Complete Acrobat 7.0 Help.

Setting the review status and replying to comments

Before you add comments of your own, you'll use the Reply command to respond to the existing comments. First you'll reply to Eamon's note that you just imported.

1 If necessary, double-click on the orange note in the document pane to open it and keep it open.

Eamon would like to have color applied to the text to soften it, but the poster is running over budget as is, so you'll decline to implement Eamon's suggestion.

2 Click the Set Status button (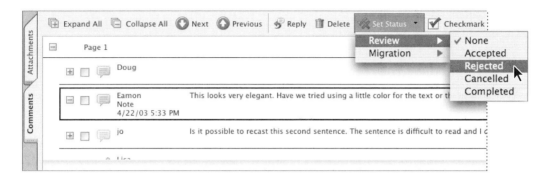) on the Comments List toolbar, and choose Review > Rejected from the menu.

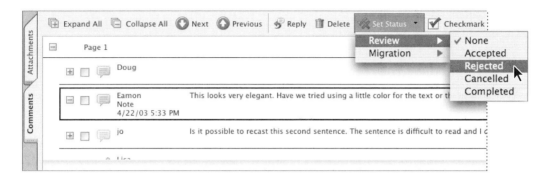

The status of the comment is recorded in the Comments List.

Now you'll explain your decision to Eamon.

3 Select Eamon's comment in the document pane or in the Comments List, and then click the Reply button (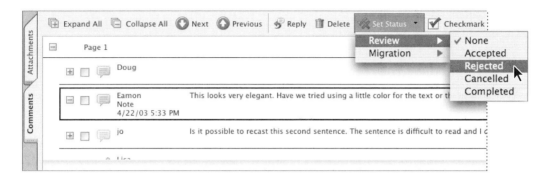) in the Comments List toolbar.

You'll enter your reply in the pop-up window that opens automatically below Eamon's note in the Comments List. You could also enter your reply directly in the reply pop-up window that opens in the document pane. (You can also open a reply window directly in a pop-up window by choosing Reply from the comment's Options menu.)

4 Type in your reply. We typed in, "**I agree that a color would be great, but unfortunately adding a color to the text would take us over budget. Let's keep this in mind for the next run.**"

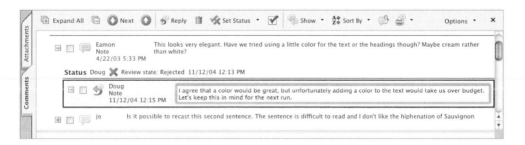

Your reply to Eamon's comment is also displayed automatically at the bottom of Eamon's comment. Notice also, that the same comment is displayed in the pop-up window.

💡 *You can set the status of a comment without creating a reply.*

5 When you're finished, close the note.

Now you'll deal with the comment about the capitalization of the names of wines.

6 In the Comments List, scroll down to view the three Pencil comments applied by Lisa, and click the second pencil icon to select the second comment.

7 Click the Reply button on the Comments List toolbar.

8 Click in the text box in the Comments List to create an insertion point, and enter your response. We entered, "**We need to use initial capitals for all wine names. Please be sure that the source text file for this poster is also corrected. I've attached a copy of the source file for you.**" (You'll learn how to attach the source file later in this lesson.)

If you are participating in an email or browser-based review, you should be aware that if you simply add your reply in the original text box (as opposed to using the Reply feature), your reply may be lost when comments are merged.

💡 *When you reply to a drawing or highlight markup, an icon is added to the markup in the document window to emphasize that a comment has been added.*

You can also add text formatting to your pop-up windows. In this case, you want to emphasize that the source text file needs to be updated. You can only add text formatting to a message in an associated pop-up window; you cannot add text formatting in the Comments List.

9 In the document pane, double-click the pencil comment that you replied to. Your reply is attached to the pencil comment. (You can also open the comment by double-clicking the pencil icon in the Comments List.)

10 Click in the text box pop-up window between the first and second sentences, and then drag to select the entire second sentence.

11 In the Pop-up Text Properties toolbar, choose the desired text formatting. We chose Italic (I) and Underline ($\underline{U}$). Click outside the text selection to see the effect of the fomatting. Note that changing the color from the Properties Bar changes the color of the note, not the color of the text in the note.

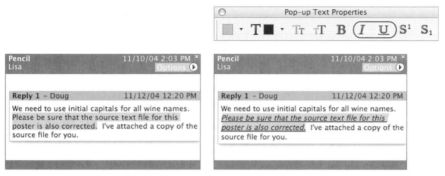

You use the Pop-up Text Properties toolbar to apply formatting to text in pop-up windows.

You can continue exploring the options available through the Comments List to expand and collapse comments, browse through comments, delete comments, sort comments, print comments, and search comments.

12 When you are finished, close all the pop-up windows at once by choosing Show > Close All Pop-ups in the Comments List toolbar, and click the Comments tab to close the Comments List.

13 Choose File > Save to save your work.

Before you go any further, you'll turn off the option to open pop-ups on a mouse rollover.

14 Choose Edit > Preferences (Windows) or Acrobat > Preferences (Mac OS), and choose Commenting. Deselect the Automatically Open Pop-ups on Mouse Rollover option, select the option Automatically Open Comment Popups for Comments Other Than Notes, and click OK to apply the change.

You can use check marks in the Comments List to keep track of which comments you have read and responded to. These check marks are for your personal use, however; they are not available to other users.

Marking up a document

As you saw in the earlier part of this lesson, you can easily add notes (the equivalent of sticky notes) to a document and respond to these notes. You can also mark up a document with the text markup tools and the drawing tools, and you can add text edit comments to indicate where text should be added, deleted, or replaced. You can add stamps, such as confidential notices, and you can even attach files and sound clips. You can also point to a specific location on a page and add a comment using the callout tool.

Marking up a document with text markup tools

You use the text markup tools in Acrobat—the Highlighter tool, the Cross-Out tool, and the Underline Text tool—to emphasize specific text in a document, such as a heading or an entire paragraph. You can also add a message associated with a text markup. Text markups are saved as comments and appear in the Comments List.

Note: *In Acrobat Professional, you can edit actual text in a PDF file using the TouchUp Text tool.*

You'll highlight text in the poster, and then add a message associated with the highlighted text.

1 Click the Fit Width button (⟷) on the Acrobat toolbar, and scroll down in the document pane until you can see the first paragraph of the poster.

2 Select the Highlighter or Highlight Text tool (⫶) in the Commenting toolbar, and drag the I-beam to highlight the last sentence in the first paragraph. The sentence begins with, "The 2000 Noble Riesling … ."

💡 *Don't forget that you can change the appearance properties of any of the tools, including the color of the highlight, in the Properties toolbar or in the Appearance tab of the Properties dialog box, as you did for the Note tool in "Setting the appearance of comments" in this lesson.*

3 In the associated pop-up window, and type in your message. We typed, "**This sentence needs editorial help. At a minimum, replace the first "and" with a comma.**"

4 Click the pop-up window's Close button to close the pop-up window.

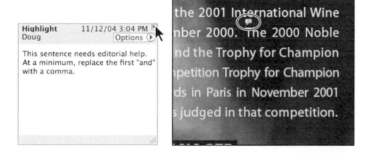

Notice the icon associated with the highlighting. This icon indicates to a reader that a pop-up note contains additional information about the text markup.

5 Choose File > Save to save your work.

Editing text

In this section, you'll use the text editing tools to indicate the required correction to a subheading on the poster, as suggested by one of the reviewers.

1 Click the Text Edits button (𝐓ₐ) in the Commenting toolbar, and read the Indicating Text Edits dialog box that opens automatically the first time you use this tool. When you have read the tips on text editing, click OK to close the dialog box. (Click the Don't Show Again option if you don't want the dialog box to be displayed again.) Then, in the poster, click just before the word GENERAL to create an insertion point in the second heading "WineMaker and General Manager." Drag to select the word "GENERAL." You may need to scroll down the page to see the heading.

2 Click the arrow next to the Text Edits button on the Commenting toolbar, and choose the Replace Selected Text tool.

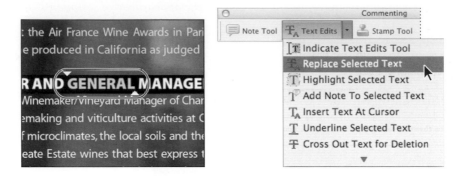

The word is automatically struck out and a text box opens in which you type the replacement text.

3 In the Replacement Text pop-up, we typed **VINEYARD**.

4 Click the pop-up window's Close button to close the pop-up window.

Now that you've made the correction to the heading, Lisa's note is no longer relevant so you'll delete it.

Deleting a comment

You can easily delete unwanted comments from a document.

1 Using the Hand tool, move the pointer over the blue note. The contents of the note are displayed, so you're sure to select the correct note to delete.

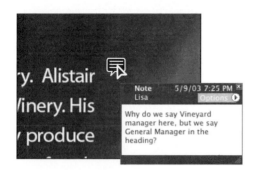

2 Right-click (Windows) or Control-click (Mac OS) on the note icon, and choose Delete from the context menu.

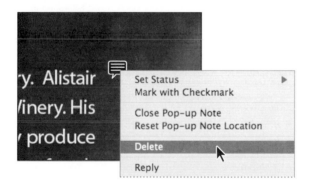

Note: If you try to delete a comment in this way and the Delete command is missing from the menu, the comment may be locked. You must unlock a comment before you can delete it. To determine if a comment is locked, right-click (Windows) or Control-click (Mac OS) on the comment, and choose Properties from the context menu. Then click the General tab.

3 Choose File > Save to save the Poster1.pdf file.

If you have a number of comments close together or even overlapping, deleting a specific comment can be difficult using the method describe above. In this case, you can more safely delete comments from the Comments List.

You've responded to several of the comments, and you can continue experimenting with this part of the lesson if you wish. You can create a thread of replies for any comment.

Now though, you'll move on to add a few more of your own comments to the poster before you send it off to the designer.

Adding a file attachment

You use the Attach a File as a Comment tool in Acrobat to embed a file at a specified location in a document so that the reader can open it for viewing. You can attach any type of file, including an audio file, as a file attachment. To open an attached file, however, the reader must have an application that can recognize the attachment.

Several reviewers observed that the sentence construction and capitalization of the text of the poster needed attention. Unfortunately the text for this poster was taken verbatim from another document. To ensure that the same corrections are made in the source document, Expansion.doc, you'll attach that document to the poster.

1 Click the Fit Page button to view the entire poster.

2 Select the Attach a File as a Comment tool (📎) in the Commenting toolbar.

💡 *Only files added using the Commenting toolbar are tracked with other comments in an email-based or browser-based document review. Files attached using the Attach a File tool (📎) on the main Acrobat toolbar are not tracked automatically in the document review process.*

3 Click in the blank space to the left of the poster heading.

4 In the dialog box, select Expansion.doc, located in the Lesson10 folder, and click Select. Be sure the Files of Type (Windows) or Show (Mac OS) option is set to All Files.

5 On the Appearance tab of the File Attachment Properties dialog box, select the Attachment icon to represent this type of file attachment. We used the Paperclip icon.

6 Click the Color button to select a color for the icon. We chose teal.

7 Click the General tab, and for Description, enter **Source file to be corrected**. Then click Close.

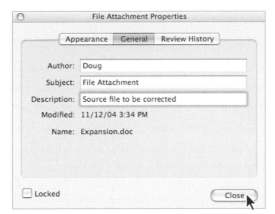

A paperclip appears on the page.

8 Click the Attachments tab in the navigation pane.

Details of the attached file, including the description you entered are displayed You can open the attachment by double-clicking the icon in the Attachments tab or by double-clicking the icon in the document pane.

If you have the appropriate application installed on your system, you can open the file that you have just attached.

9 Double-click the paperclip to open the file. Click OK or Open to confirm that you want to open the file. When you have finished viewing the file, close it, and exit or quit the associated application.

10 Choose File > Save to save your work.

11 Click click the Comments tab to return to the Comments List.

Notice that after you add the file as a comment a paperclip is displayed at the far left of the status bar at the bottom of the Acrobat document pane. Move the mouse over this paperclip to get more information. Anytime a PDF file has special properties, an explanatory icon is displayed in this area.

Marking up a document with drawing tools

Acrobat's drawing tools let you emphasize a specific area of a document, such as a graphic or table. The Pencil tool creates a free-form line; the Pencil Eraser tool lets you erase any part of a drawing you have created. The Rectangle tool creates a rectangular boundary, the Oval tool creates an elliptical boundary, the Arrow tool creates a line with an arrow head at one end, and the Line tool creates a straight line between two specified points. The Polygon tool creates a closed shape with multiple segments, and the Polygon Line tool creates an open shape with multiple segments. The Cloud tool is similar to the Polygon tool, but gives a rounded cloud effect. The Dimensioning tool allows you to measure distances in a PDF document. You can add a message associated with any drawing markup to comment on the area of the page being emphasized. Drawing markups are saved as comments and appear in the Comments List.

You'll add a rectangle to the poster indicating where you would like to see the copyright notice attached, and then add a message associated with the rectangle.

1 Click the arrow (down pointing triangle) next to the Arrow tool on the Drawing Markups toolbar, and select the Rectangle tool (▢) from the menu.

2 Drag to create a rectangle at the bottom of the poster, directly under the text column and the same width as the text column. This is where you want the designer to place the copyright notice.

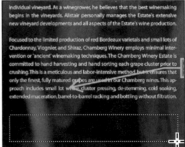

Drag to select Rectangle tool.

Drag to create a rectangle to contain the copyright notice.

3 In the pop-up window, type the message text as desired. (We typed **Please place a copyright notice here.**) Then close the pop-up window.

4 Choose File > Save to save your work.

Now you'll use the Dimensioning tool to accurately indicate the position of the copyright notice on the finished poster.

5 Click the Zoom In tool (⊕), and marquee-drag around the box you just added. Be sure to include the last couple of lines of the paragraph above in your selection.

6 Select the Dimensioning tool (⊢⊣) on the Drawing Markups toolbar.

7 In the document pane, position the crosshair on the base of the last line of text in the poster and then drag to the top line of the box that you just inserted to show the position of the copyright notice.

Acrobat adds a double-headed arrow that spans the distance between the last line of text and the top of the copyright box. Now you'll specify the required dimension for the designer.

8 Simply type in the required distance. We typed **One inch**. Select the Hand tool and click anywhere in the document pane to see the end result.

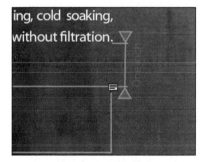

The added text is also displayed in the Comments List. You may need to expand the author comments (we used Doug as the author) to see the added comment.

9 Choose File > Save to save your work.

10 Close the Commenting, Drawing Markups, and Properties toolbars.

11 Click the Fit Page button.

Summarizing comments

At times you may want to review just the text associated with the comments so that you don't have to open each pop-up window individually. In this part of the lesson, you'll summarize the comments on the poster, compiling the text associated with all the comments in a new PDF document.

1 Click the Print Comments button on the Comments List toolbar, and select Create PDF of Comments Summary.

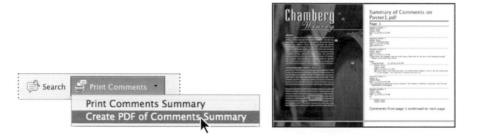

A summary of all the comments is displayed alongside the poster. Because the content of the comments exceeds one page, the poster page is repeated on multiple pages with the remaining comments. You can save this summary of comments and you can print it.

2 Chose File > Close or click the Close button to close the Summary of Comments on Poster1.pdf document and return to the Poster1.pdf document. You do not need to save the file.

If you want more control over how the summary of the comments is displayed, you can use the Summarize Options dialog box to determine whether to sort the summary of comments by page, author, date, or type, as well as to determine whether to include all comments or only the comments currently showing. You can preview the display options by clicking the buttons in the Choose a Layout panel.

3 In the Poster1.pdf document, choose Comments > Summarize Comments.

4 In the Summarize Options dialog box, click the Document and Comments with Connector Lines on Single Pages option.

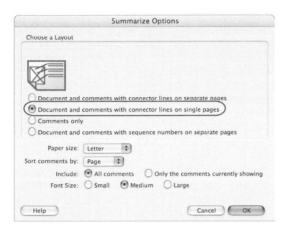

You'll use the default values for the other options.

5 Click OK.

A new PDF file named Summary of Comments on Poster1.pdf is created. This document displays the poster on the left side and the contents of the comments on the right, including the comment label, and the date and time the comment was added to the file. This time, however, you have lines that connect the comment to the associated text in the pop-up. Again, because the content of the comments exceeds one page, the poster page is displayed again on a second page with the remaining comments.

6 Choose File > Save As, rename the file **Summary.pdf**, and save it in the Lesson10 folder.

7 Choose File > Close and close the summary file.

If you are using Acrobat Standard, skip the next section and go to "Spell checking comments" later in this lesson.

Acrobat 7.0 Professional: Comparing two Adobe PDF documents

In Acrobat 7.0 Professional, you can compare two documents. You can compare an entire page or just the text on a page, including a font analysis. In this section of the lesson, you'll simply compare the Poster.pdf document with the Poster1.pdf document. You could, however, compare a PDF version of the revised poster with a PDF of the original poster to verify that all requested changes have been made.

1 *Choose Document > Compare Documents.*

2 *In the Compare (Older Document) section of the Compare Documents dialog box, click Choose to locate the file Poster.pdf in the Lesson10 folder. Then click Open.*

3 *Verify that Poster1.pdf is listed in the To (Newer Document) text box, and verify that Page by Page Visual Difference is selected.*

4 *From the drop down menu, select the type of comparison to be made. We chose Normal Analysis. (Since we haven't corrected any text at this point, a Textual Differences comparison would be meaningless.)*

5 *Choose whether to see a side-by-side comparison or a consolidated report. We chose Side by Side Report. Then click OK.*

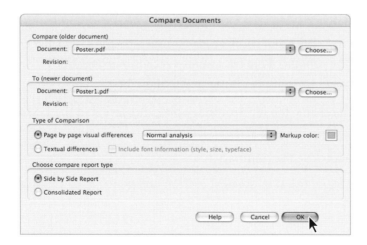

The two documents are displayed side-by-side with differences between the two highlighted.

6 *When you are finished reviewing the differences, click the Close button or choose File > Close. You do not need to save this comparison.*

Spell checking comments

When you looked at the summary of the comments, you may have noticed that one contains a typographical error—author jo typed "hiphenation" instead of "hyphenation."

You'll use the spell checking feature to quickly spell check all the comments added to the poster.

1 In the Poster1.pdf file, choose Edit > Check Spelling > In Comments and Form Fields.

2 In the Check Spelling dialog box, click Start.

Any unrecognized text string is displayed in the Word Not Found text box. "hyphenation" is the suggested correction for "hiphenation".

3 Click Change to accept the correction.

4 Click Done to close the spell checking operation without examining all the other options.

5 Choose File > Save, and save the corrected file in the Lesson10 folder.

Printing documents with comments

When you print a PDF file that contains comments, you can print the file so that the comment icons print or you can hide all the comment icons.

1 Do one of the following:

• To print the document with comment icons, choose File > Print. In the Print dialog box, choose Documents and Markups in the Comments and Forms text box. You'll see a preview of the print copy in the Print dialog box. Click Cancel to exit the Print dialog box without printing the file.

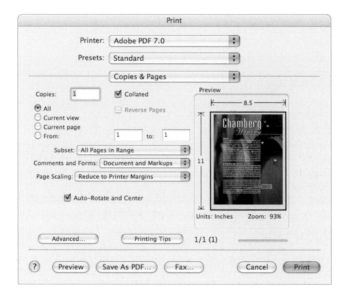

- To print a summary of the comments, choose File > Print With Comments Summary. In the Summarize Options dialog box, choose Comments Only and click Close or OK. In the Print dialog box, click Cancel to exit the Print dialog box without printing the comment summary.

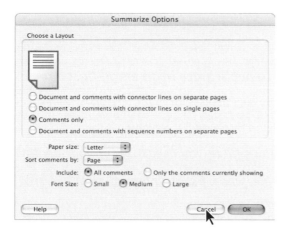

You can also summarize the comments and print both the document and the summary. The options for printing comments are the same as the layout options in the Comment Options dialog box—that is, printing comments on separate pages with connector lines, printing comments on the same page with connector lines, and printing only comments, or printing document and comments on separate pages but with sequence numbers. See "Summarizing comments" earlier in this lesson.

2 Choose File > Close to close the file when you have finished looking at the print options.

Acrobat 7.0 Professional: Inviting users of Adobe Reader to participate in reviews

If you are using Acrobat 7.0 Professional, you can include additional usage rights in a PDF document and invite Adobe Reader 7.0 users in addition to Acrobat users to participate in document reviews. (Adobe Reader 7.0 is a free download, available from the Adobe website.)

To invite users of Adobe Reader to participate in an email-based review:

1 *Choose File > Open, and reopen the file Poster1.pdf in the Lesson10 folder.*

2 *Choose File > Send For Review > Send By Email For Review.*

If this is the first time you have used this feature, you need to set up your identity.

1 *In the Identity Setup dialog box, enter your personal information. We entered a name and email address. Then click Complete.*

2 *In the Getting Started panel of the Send By Email For Review dialog box, browse to select the file you want reviewed and click Next.*

3 *In the Invite Reviewers panel, enter the email addresses of the reviewers. (Click the Address Book button if you want to copy email addresses from your address book.)*

4 *When you have entered email addresses for all your reviewers, click the Customize Review Options button.*

5 *In the Review Options dialog box, make sure the Also Allow Users of the Free Adobe Reader 7.0 to Participate in This Review option is selected. You can also elect to display the Drawing Markup Tools toolbar for these users. Click OK to return to the Invite Reviewers panel, and click Next to preview your invitation.*

6 *Click Send Invitation to initiate the review process.(Click Cancel to exit the process without initiating a review process.)*

You can also invite users of Adobe Reader to review a document using the Comments > Enable for Commenting in Adobe Reader command.

Additional usage rights, such as commenting rights, are document-specific. To include additional usage rights for browser-based reviews, you must use an additional Adobe server product, such as Adobe Document Server or Adobe Reader Extensions Server. (For more information, visit the Adobe website at www.adobe.com.)

When a PDF document with commenting rights opens in Adobe Reader, a Document Message Bar that provides instructions opens, along with the appropriate toolbar.

Note: *Participants must have email capabilities to review PDF documents that include additional usage rights.*

Exploring on your own: Custom stamps

The Commenting toolbar allows you to add stamps to your PDF document. Acrobat provides a number of traditional stamps, but you can also create custom stamps.

We've provided a PDF file with two images that you can use for practice, or you can use your own artwork or photos. You can create custom stamps from any supported image type files (JPEG, TIFF, BMP, PNG, etc.). The image files are converted to Adobe PDF automatically as you create the custom stamp. Be aware, though, that the image files must be sized correctly. You cannot resize the image once you have created a stamp. You can, however, fit the stamp within a rectangle that you drag with the stamp tool.

If you want to add an image to a document on a one-time basis, simply paste the image into the PDF document. The image that you paste in has all the attributes of a stamp—it can be resized, has editable properties, and can have an associated pop-up window.

Creating a custom stamp

1 Choose View > Toolbars > Commenting. (You don't need to have a document open.)

2 Click the arrow next to the Stamp tool (⊞), and choose Create Custom Stamp from the menu.

3 In the Select Image for Custom Stamp dialog box, click the Browse button to locate the image file that you're going to use to create the custom stamp. If you're creating a stamp directly from an image file (rather than a PDF file), be sure that you choose the appropriate file type from the Files of Type (Windows) or Show (Mac OS) menu. (You can also leave the type of file as All Supported Formats.) We selected the Stamps.pdf file in the Lesson10 folder.

4 Click Select, and preview the sample image. Because the target file contains more than one image, scroll through the pages to select the image that you want to use as the stamp. Our target file contains three images. We chose to use the image on page 1.

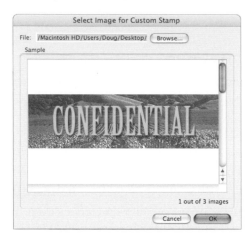

5 Click OK to return to the Create Custom Stamp dialog box.

Now you'll create a category for the stamp and give the stamp a name. The category name appears in the drop down menu associated with the Stamp tool on the Commenting toolbar. The stamp name appears in the category name's submenu.

6 Enter a name for the category of your stamp. We used **Chamberg**. A category may contain more than one stamp.

7 Enter a name for the stamp. We used **Confidential**.

8 Click OK.

That's all there is to creating custom stamps.

You can add, delete, or edit custom stamps using the Manage Custom Stamps dialog box. You access the Manage Custom Stamps dialog box from the Stamp tool pop-up menu.

Dynamic stamps use information from your system and from the Identity panel of the Preferences dialog box to add name, date, and time information to the stamp.

Now you'll add your custom stamp to a document.

Applying a custom stamp

1 Open the Review.pdf file in the Lesson10 folder.

2 Click the arrow next to the Stamp tool ( ), and choose Chamberg > Confidential from the menu.

3 Click on the document where you want the stamp to appear.

You can move the stamp by dragging it across the page of the document. You can resize the stamp by moving the pointer over a corner of the stamp until the pointer changes to a double-headed arrow, and then dragging the stamp out to the required size.

When you are finished, close Review.pdf without saving your work.

Exploring on your own: Email-based reviews

A tracked email-based review is easy to set up and yet gives you powerful tools for managing the review process. The Tracker monitors both the documents that you send for review and the reviewed documents that are returned to you. You can experiment with setting up an email-based review if you have an email address, a connection to the Internet, and a colleague to work with.

Setting up an email-based review

Note: *You cannot email a PDF document to yourself as part of an email-based review. Unless you have two separate email addresses, the process will not work. You need to collaborate with a colleague to complete this part of the lesson.*

1 In Acrobat, open the file that you want to send for review. We used the Stamps.pdf file.

2 Initiate the review process using the File > Send for Review > Send by Email for Review command.

The Send by Email for Review dialog box opens to guide you through the process.

If this is the first time you have used the Send by Email for Review process, you'll be asked to set up your identity. Subsequently, the Send by Email for Review dialog box opens automatically.

3 In the Getting Started panel, check that the correct file name is displayed.

4 In the Invite Reviewers panel, enter the email addresses of the people you want to send the file to. You can enter as many addresses as your email application supports.

5 Use the Customize Review options button if you want to specify a different email address for reviewers to return their comments to, if you want Acrobat to automatically display the drawing markup tools when a recipient opens the PDF file, and most importantly (if you are using Acrobat Professional), to allow users of Adobe Reader 7.0 to participate in the review process. Click OK when you have made your choices.

Specify whether to extend review rights to users of Adobe Reader and whether to display commenting tools.

6 Customize your email message in the Preview Invitation panel.

7 Send your invitation to complete the process.

Participating in an email-based review

Assuming you are the recipient of an email-based review request, you will receive a message with an .fdf attachment.

1 Double-click the email attachment to open it.

Acrobat opens and displays the document to be reviewed with the Commenting and Drawing Markups toolbars and Document Message Bar open if you have so specified.

 A document that is part of an email-based review will have a document status icon at the left of the status bar. Clicking this icon will open the informational Document Status dialog box.

2 When you have finished your review, return your comments using the Send Comments button on the Commenting toolbar.

Acrobat automatically opens your default email application and attaches the document to a pre-addressed and pre-written email message, returning the document to the sender.

Receiving review comments

When you receive a reviewed document as an email with a file attached, double-click the .fdf attachment to open it.

You should open the tracked PDF file to automatically merge comments and markups into your master (or tracked) file. The reviewer's comments are incorporated into the master copy of the document that you sent for review.

Each time you open an email reply to your request for review, comments are added to your master file.

Managing email-based reviews

All Adobe PDF documents that you have sent and received as part of an email-based or browser-based review are listed in the Tracker.

In Acrobat, you can open the Tracker by clicking the arrow next to the Send For Review button( ) on the Acrobat toolbar, and choosing Tracker. The Tracker pane offers powerful tools for managing your managed reviews.

All your email-based review documents are listed.

You can open the master file for an email based review by selecting the file in the Tracker file listing, and clicking the Open button. Similarly you can remove a file from the email-based review process, by selecting the file name and clicking the Remove button .

The Manage menu contains several commands that make contacting reviewers easy.

It is difficult to reproduce the rich experience of using the email review feature without a group of participants. We encourage you to experiment with this feature when you have a document to review with your colleagues.

Review questions

1 How can you send a PDF file out for review?

2 How can you consolidate comments made in several identical copies of a PDF file?

3 How can you change the author name on a note?

4 What are the advantages of using a structured email review process?

Review answers

1 There are several ways to send a PDF file for review. With the PDF file that you want to have reviewed open, do one of the following:

• Click the Email button on the Acrobat toolbar.

• To set up a more structured review, Choose File > Send for Review > Send by Email for Review.

• If all your reviewers have access to a common server, choose File > Send For Review > Upload for Browser-Based Review.

2 You can consolidate comments into one PDF file by exporting the comments from each copy of the PDF file to an FDF file and then importing all the FDF files into one PDF file. Or you can import the comments directly from the PDF files using the Comments > Import Comments command.

If you use the email-based or browser-based reviews, comments are consolidated automatically.

3 To change the author name on a note (or any pop-up window associated with a comment) you must first change the Acrobat Commenting preferences so that the system log-in name isn't used automatically for authoring comments. Then you can change the note's properties in the General tab of the Note Properties dialog box. Finally, you make the current note's properties the default values if you want to continue using the new author name.

4 When you start a review process using the Send by Email for Review command, the reviewer receives a copy of the PDF file along with instructions on how to complete the review and ready access to the How To page displaying related topics. A Send Comments button is added to the Commenting toolbar to facilitate return of the review comments. As the initiator of the review process, you can automatically consolidate all review comments as you open the documents returned by the reviewers. You also have access to a powerful set of review management tools.

11 | Adding Signatures and Security

You can digitally sign or certify Adobe PDF files to attest to the validity of the contents of the file. You can also protect your Adobe PDF files by applying security that limits how users can manipulate the contents of your files and even who can open your files.

In this lesson, you'll learn how to do the following:

- Create a digital ID.
- Digitally sign documents.
- Create a picture signature.
- Verify a digital signature.
- Certify a document.
- Apply password protection to a file to limit who can open it, and apply passwords to limit printing and changing of the file.

This lesson will take about 60 minutes to complete.

If needed, remove the previous lesson folder from your hard drive, and copy the Lesson11 folder onto it.

Note: Windows 2000 users may need to unlock the lesson files before using them. For information, see "Copying the Classroom in a Book files" on page 4.

Looking at your Security preferences

You can set the appearance of your digital signature, select your preferred digital signature signing method, and determine how digital signatures are verified in the Security preferences.

First you'll take a look at the default Security preferences.

1 Start Acrobat.

2 Choose Edit > Preferences (Windows) or Acrobat > Preferences (Mac OS), and select Security in the left pane.

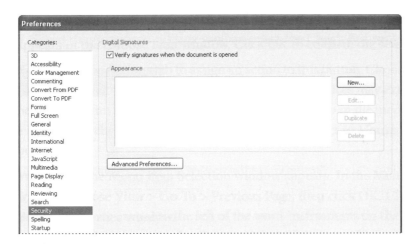

Unless you have already defined an appearance for your digital signature, the Appearance window is blank.

3 Click New to open the Configure Signature Appearance dialog box. This is where you will personalize your digital signature later in the lesson by adding a graphic to your signature. For the moment the Preview pane shows the default digital signature appearance. When you have reviewed the information contained in the default signature, click Cancel to return to the Preferences dialog box.

Now you'll specify a default signing method.

4 Click Advanced Preferences. The Digital Signatures Advanced Preferences dialog box opens with the Verification tab selected.

Notice that the option Require That Certificate Revocation Checking Be Done Whenever Possible When Verifying Signatures option is selected. This ensures that certificates are checked against a list of excluded certificates during validation.

5 In the Verification tab of the dialog box, make sure that signatures are verified using the document-specified method when a document is opened. You'll be prompted if you don't have the necessary software when you try to open a document.

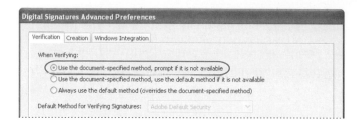

You can only change the default method for verifying signatures in this panel if you change this selection. You set the default method to be used when signing and encrypting documents in the Creation tab.

6 Click the Creation tab and check that Adobe Default Security is selected for the Default Method to Use When Signing and Encrypting Documents option.

On Windows, you have a Windows Integration tab where you can specify whether identities from Windows Certificates can be imported. and whether all root certificates in the Windows Certificates can be trusted. We recommend that you leave the defaults in this tab.

7 Choose Cancel and Cancel again to close the Preferences dialog boxes without making any changes, or choose OK if you changed any of the options.

For an in-depth discussion of security in Acrobat 7.0, see "About Security" and "Setting Digital Signature Preferences" in the Complete Acrobat 7.0 Help.

Opening the work file

In this lesson, you'll send an advertisement for Clarity skin lotion to the advertising agency for finalization. You've reviewed the document and made required changes, and now you'll sign the revised advertisement electronically.

Signing a document electronically offers several advantages, not least of which is that you can email the signed document rather than having to fax it. (You can even sign PDF documents in a web browser.) Although digitally signing a document doesn't necessarily prevent people from changing the document, it does allow you to track any changes made after the signature is added and revert to the signed version if necessary. (You can prevent users from changing your document by applying appropriate security to the document, as you'll see later in this lesson.)

Choose File > Open. Select Lotion.pdf in the Lesson11 folder, and click Open. Then choose File > Save As, rename the file **Lotion1.pdf**, and save it in the Lesson11 folder.

About digital signatures

A digital signature, like a conventional handwritten signature, identifies the person signing a document. Unlike traditional signatures on paper, however, each digital signature stores information about the person signing a document. Signatures help prevent unwanted changes to a PDF document. For example, an author may not want a PDF document with company letterhead to be changed after it's signed.

The first signature in a document is called the author signature. When you add the first signature to a document, you have the option of certifying the document. Certifying a document lets you attest to its contents and specify the types of changes allowed for the document to remain certified. Changes to the document are detected in the Signatures tab. Subsequent signatures to the document are called ordinary signatures.

To sign a document, you must select a digital ID, which contains the signature information that you can share with other users in a certificate. You can create a self-signed digital ID, or you can obtain a digital ID from a third-party provider. Using certificates, other users can validate your signatures, and you should validate the signatures of others.

Note: *For the latest information about digital signatures, choose Help > Online Support to open the Adobe Acrobat support page on the Adobe website, and then search for "digital signatures."*

—From the Complete Acrobat 7.0 Online Help.

Creating a digital ID

A digital ID lets you create a digital signature or decrypt a PDF document that has been encrypted. You can create a digital ID at the same time that you sign a document, but in this lesson you'll create your self-signed digital ID before you sign the document. (You can also get a digital ID from a third-party provider.)

You can create more than one digital ID to reflect different roles in your life. For this section of the lesson, you'll create a digital ID for T. Simpson, Director of Advertising. Later in the lesson, you'll experiment with creating a picture signature.

1 Choose Advanced > Security Settings.

2 In the Security Settings dialog box, click Digital IDs in the left pane. Then click the Add ID button (⊞).

In this lesson, you'll create a self-signed digital ID. With a self-signed ID, you share your signature information with other users using a public certificate. (A certificate is a confirmation of your digital ID and contains information used to protect data.) While this method is adequate for most unofficial exchanges, a more secure approach is to obtain a digital ID from a third-party provider.

3 In the Add Digital ID dialog box, select Create a Self-Signed Digital ID. Then click Next and click Next again to close the message box. (On Mac OS, you may not see the message box.)

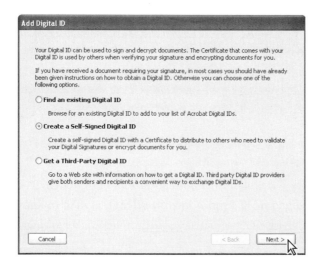

If you're working in Mac OS, you may need to skip step 4. If you're working in Windows, you'll choose where to store your digital ID. The PKCS#12 Digital ID File option stores the information in a file that you can share with others. A Windows Default Certificate Digital ID is stored in the Windows Certificate Store. Because you want to easily share your digital ID with colleagues, you use the PKCS#12 option.

4 Make sure that New PKCS#12 Digital File ID is selected, and click Next.

Now you'll enter your personal information.

5 Enter the name you want to appear in the Signatures tab and in any signature field that you complete, and enter a corporate or organization name (if necessary) and an email address. We entered **T. Simpson, Director** for the name, **Clarity** for the Organization Name, and **clarity@xyz.net** for the email address. Make sure that you select a Country/Region. We selected **US - United States**.

6 Choose a Key Algorithm to set the level of security. We chose **1024-bit RSA**. Although 2048-bit RSA offers more security protection, it is not as universally compatible as 1024-bit RSA.

Now you'll specify what the encryption applies to. You can use the digital ID to control digital signatures, data encryption (security), or both. When you encrypt a PDF document, you specify a list of recipients from your Trusted Identities, and you define the recipients' level of access to the file—for example, whether the recipients can edit, copy, or print the files. You can also encrypt documents using security policies.

For this lesson, you'll chose digital signatures.

7 From the Use Digital ID For menu, choose Digital Signatures and then click Next.

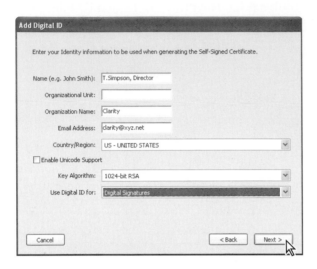

Now you'll save and safeguard your information.

8 If you want to change the location where your information is stored, click the Browse button and locate the required folder. For this lesson, you'll use the default. Now you must set a password. We used **Lotion123** as the password. Reenter your password to confirm it. Remember that the password is case-sensitive. Be sure to make a note of your password in a safe place. You cannot use or access your digital ID without this password.

*Note: Your password may not contain double quotation marks or the characters ! @ # $ % ^ & *, | \ ; < > _ .*

9 Click Finish to save the digital ID file in the Security folder.

Your new digital ID appears in the Security Settings dialog box. When you've finished checking your digital ID, click the Close button to close the dialog box.

Now you'll sign the advertisement and return it to the agency.

Signing the advertisement

1 Click the Sign button (🖊) on the toolbar, and choose Sign This Document from the menu.

Acrobat first reminds you that this document is not certified. (You'll certify a document later in this lesson.)

2 Click Continue Signing.

Now Acrobat reminds you that you need to create a signature field.

Note: *When you certify a document, you attest to its contents and specify the type of changes that a user can make to the document without invalidating the signature. When you sign a document, any subsequent changes to the document affect the validity of the signature.*

Because you want the advertising agency to know that the changes to this advertisement are approved and you want them to be sure that no additional changes have been made since the time you approved it, you'll create a visible signature field and sign the document. Later in this lesson you'll certify a document.

💡 *Any time you add a first signature to a document, you should consider certifying the document when prompted.*

3 Make sure that the Create a New Signature Field to Sign option is selected, and click Next.

4 Click OK to close the alert box, and drag to create a signature field. We dragged a signature field in the area below the headline.

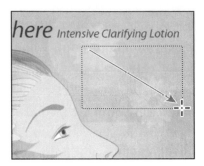

You may establish multiple identities, depending on your needs. If you have not established any identities except T. Simpson, skip step 5.

5 If you have any other identities defined, other than T. Simpson, you're asked to select your identity. Select the Digital ID that you just created, and click OK. We selected T. Simpson, Director.

6 In the dialog box, enter your password. We entered **Lotion123**.

7 Choose a reason for signing the document. We chose **I Am Approving This Document** from the drop down menu.

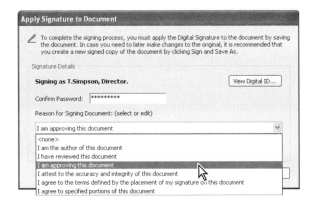

Before you complete the signature process, you'll change the appearance of your signature.

Adding an image to a digital signature

1 Click the Show Options button to display the signature appearance options.

2 Click the New button to open the Configure Signature Appearance dialog box where you can modify your signature appearance.

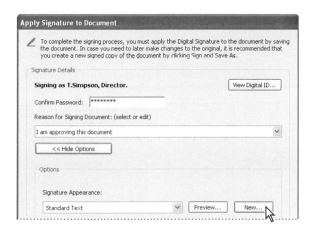

The Preview pane shows the default digital signature appearance.

First you'll name your signature and then add your corporate logo to the signature block.

3 In the Title text box, enter a name for your signature. We entered **Logo** because we're going to add our corporate logo to the signature line. You should use a name that is easy to associate with the contents of the signature.

4 In the Configure Graphic section of the dialog box, select the Imported Graphic option, and click the File button.

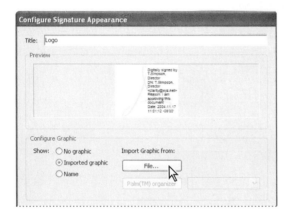

5 In the Select Picture dialog box, click the Browse button and locate the Clarity_Logo.pdf file in the Lesson11 folder. (Supported file types are listed in the Files of Type (Windows) or Format (Mac OS) menu.) Click Select, and then click OK to return to the Configure Signature Appearance dialog box.

💡 *You can also create a new signature appearance in the Security preferences.*

Now you'll specify the information to be included in the text block of your signature. You'll include your name, the reason for signing the document, and the date.

6 In the Configure Text area of the Configure Signature Appearance dialog box, leave Name, Date, and Reason selected. Deselect all the other options.

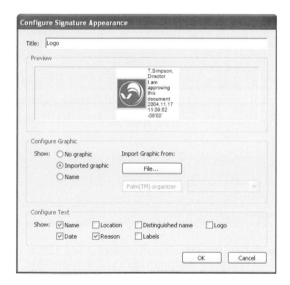

7 When you're happy with the preview of your signature block, click OK.

8 Click Sign and Save in the Apply Signature to Document dialog box to apply the signature. Click OK to close the alert box.

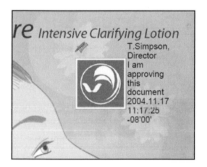

The recipient of the signed document needs your signer's certificate to validate the digital signature.

💡 *You can use the Signature tool to add a blank signature field to a document for someone else to sign.*

Modifying a signed document

Just for fun, you'll add a comment to the signed document to see how the digital signature information changes. But first you'll look at the signatures tab to see what a valid signature looks like.

1 Click the Signatures tab, and if necessary, drag the right margin of the Signatures panel so that you can see all the signature information. Expand the Signature is Valid and Time entries. Notice that the Signature tab contains more information than the digital signature.

Now you'll add a note to the advertisement and see how the addition changes the digital signature.

2 Choose Tools > Commenting, and click the Note tool (🗨).

3 Click anywhere on the document page to add a note. We added a note saying, "**Good work**."

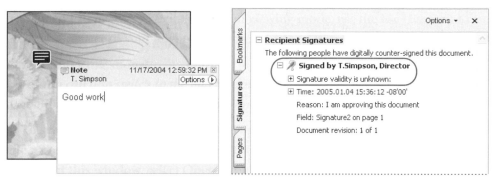

The signature is invalidated by the addition of a note.

As soon as you add the note, the status of the signature changes from valid to unknown.

4 Right-click (Windows) or Control-click (Mac OS) on the signature box in the document pane, and choose Validate Signature. The alert box explains that although the signature is valid, a change has been made. Click Close to close the warning box.

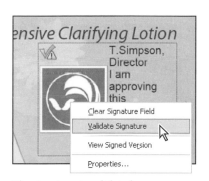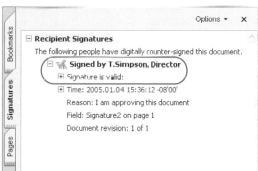

The signature is validated.

When you validate the signature, the information in the Signature tab changes again. Notice that the signature is represented as valid again but there is a cautionary icon ( ) that signifies that a change was made after the signature was applied.

Managing digital ID certificates

A digital ID certificate contains a public key that is used to validate digital signatures and to encrypt documents.

• Validating signatures. Before other users can validate your signature on documents they receive, they must have access to your certificate, which you can share with them. Likewise, other users can share their certificates with you so that you can build a list of trusted user certificates, called trusted identities, for validating signatures.

• Encrypting documents. If you're encrypting a document using certificates, you need access to the certificates of the people for whom you're encrypting the document. You can use a directory search to locate these trusted identities, or you can store users' certificates in your list of trusted identities. Acrobat keeps track of the trusted identities that you build.

You can also configure Windows Certificate Security to trust identities in the common Windows Certificate Store. Third-party providers may validate identities using other methods, or these validation methods may be integrated with Acrobat.

—From the Complete Acrobat 7.0 Online Help.

5 Expand the Signature Is Valid line in the Signature tab. You'll see that although the signature is validated, the document is reported as having been changed.

The signature is validated again but change information is included in the Signature tab.

6 Choose File > Save.

Even after you have saved the document, you can easily revert to the copy that was signed.

7 Right-click (Windows) or Control-click (Mac OS) on the signature box in the document pane, and choose View Signed Version.

The View Signed Version option allows you to recover your unchanged file.

8 Choose Window > Close All to close both files.

If a document has signatures on multiple versions of the document, you can view any previously signed version of the document by selecting the signature in the Signatures tab and then choosing View Signed Version from the Options menu. You can also compare two versions of a signed document.

Using the Signatures Tab

The Signatures tab lists all the signature fields in the current document. Each signature in the palette has an icon identifying its current verification status. The blue ribbon icon indicates that the certification is valid. The digital signature icon along with the name of the field in the Signature tab indicates the presence of the empty signature field. The checkmark icon indicates that the signature is valid. The question mark icon indicates that the signature could not be verified. The warning sign icon indicates that the document was modified after the signature was added.

You can collapse a signature to see only the name, date, and status, or you can expand it to see more information.

To display the Signatures tab:

Choose View > Navigation Tabs > Signatures, or click the Signatures tab on the left side of the document pane.

Tip: *You can right-click (Windows) or Control-click (Mac OS) a signature field in the Signatures tab to do most signature-related tasks, including adding, clearing, and validating signatures. In some cases, however, the signature field may become locked after you sign it.*

To expand or collapse a signature in the Signatures tab:

Click the plus sign (Windows) or triangle (Mac OS) to the left of the signature to expand it. Click the minus sign (Windows) or the rotated triangle (Mac OS) to the left of the signature to collapse it.

—From the Complete Acrobat 7.0 Online Help.

Certifying a PDF file

In the prior section of this lesson, you signed a PDF document to signify that you had approved the content and requested changes. You can also certify the contents of a PDF document. Certifying a document rather than signing it is useful if you want the user to be able to make approved changes to a document. As you saw in the previous section, if you sign a document, and anyone (even you as the signer) makes changes, the signature is invalidated. However, if you certify a document and a user makes approved changes, the certification is still valid. You can certify forms, for example, to guarantee that the content is valid when the user receives the form. You, as the creator of the form, can specify what tasks the user can perform. For example, you can specify that readers can fill in the form fields without invalidating the document. However, if a user tries to add or remove a form field or a page, the certification will be invalidated.

Now you'll certify a form to be sent to clients of a winery, asking them to estimate their purchases. By certifying the form, you are sure that the client fills out the form as you designed it, with no additions or deletions to the form fields.

1 Choose File > Open, and open the Final_Survey.pdf file in the Lesson11 folder.

2 Choose File > Document Properties, and click the Security tab.

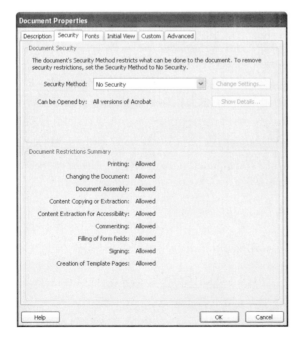

The information in the Document Properties dialog box shows that no security and no restrictions have been applied to the document.

3 Click Cancel to close the Document Properties dialog box without making any changes.

4 Choose File > Save As Certified Document.

5 Click OK to clear the message box. You'll use the digital ID that you created earlier in the lesson to certify the file.

6 From the Allowed Actions menu, choose Only Allow Commenting and Forms Fill-in Actions on This Document.

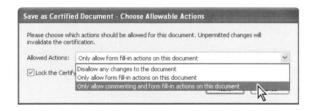

7 Leave the option checked that locks the certifying signature so that no one can modify or delete your certification. (The option is selected when a check mark is visible in the box.) Then click Next.

8 Click Next again to clear the warning box.

In the Select Visibility dialog box, if you choose the Show Certification on Document option, your signature will appear on the document alongside a blue ribbon certification. For this lesson, you'll choose not to show the certification on the form.

9 Sclect the Do Not Show Certification on Document option, and click Next.

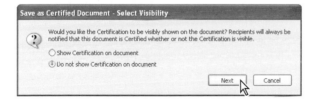

10 If you have created more than one digital ID, select the digital ID to use, and click OK. We selected T. Simpson, Director.

11 Enter your password. We entered **Lotion123**.

12 Choose a reason for signing the document. We choose to certify that we attested to the accuracy and integrity of the document.

13 Click the Sign and Save button and complete the certification process.

14 Click OK to clear the message box.

15 Click the Signatures tab to review what actions the certification allows.

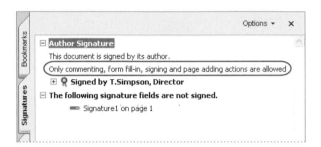

16 When you've finished reviewing the certification information, click the Signatures tab to close the Signatures panel.

Whenever you open a certified document, you'll see a Certification icon (♀) at the left of the status bar. You can click on this icon at any time to see certification information for the document.

Signing a certified document

Now you'll sign the document that you just certified to verify that filling in a signature field doesn't invalidate the certification.

1 Click the Sign button (✐) on the toolbar, and choose Sign This Document from the menu. Click OK to close the message box.

2 With the Hand tool selected, click in the signature box at the foot of the page.

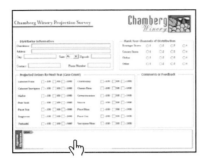

3 In the dialog box, if you have more than one digital ID defined, select your digital ID, and then click OK. We selected T. Simpson, Director.

4 Enter your password. We entered **Lotion123**.

5 Select a reason for signing the document if you wish. Then click Sign and Save to complete the process. Click OK to clear the alert box.

6 Click the Signatures tab, and expand the certification entry marked with the blue ribbon icon.

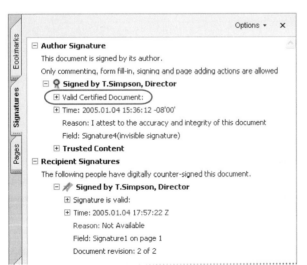

Notice that the certification is still valid even though a signature has been added. Remember that when you signed the document earlier in the lesson and then added a comment, your signature became invalid.

7 Choose File > Close.

Looking at security settings

As you have seen, you can digitally sign a document or certify a document to attest to the contents of the document at the time of signing or certification. There are times, however, when you simply want to restrict access to a document. You can do this by adding security to your Adobe PDF files.

When you open a document that has restricted access or some type of security applied to it, you'll see an icon in the bottom left of the status bar. Clicking this icon at any time opens a dialog box that tells more about the restrictions applied to the document.

1 Choose File > Open, and open the Secure_Survey.pdf file in the Lesson11 folder.

2 Click the Sign button ( ) on the Acrobat toolbar, and notice that the Sign This Document command is grayed out.

3 Choose Tools > Commenting > Show Commenting Toolbar, and again notice that all the commenting and text markup tools are grayed out. Then click the Close button to close the Commenting toolbar.

4 Click the Secure button ( ) on the Acrobat toolbar, and choose Show Security Settings for This Document.

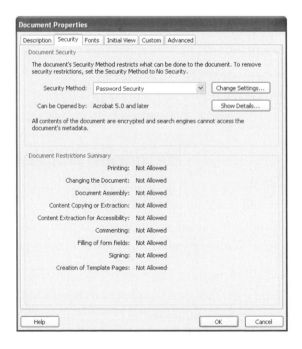

The dialog box lists the actions that are allowed and those that are not allowed. As you read down the list, you'll see that signing and commenting are not allowed, which is why the related tools are grayed out (steps 2 and 3).

5 When you have finished reviewing the information, click Cancel to close the Document Properties dialog box.

6 Choose File > Close to close the Secure_Survey.pdf file.

To view security settings of a PDF document opened in a browser, click the arrow icon above the vertical scroll bar on the right of the document, and choose Document Properties from the menu. Then click the Security tab.

Now you'll change the security settings for one of your own files.

Adding security to your PDF files

You can add security to your Adobe PDF files when you first create them or after the fact. You can even add security to files that you receive from someone else, unless the creator of the document has limited who can change security settings.

In Acrobat, you have several ways of adding security:

• You can apply password protection to your files to limit what a user can do with your files. For example, you can disallow printing, editing, or adding comments to your files.

• You can apply password protection to limit who can open your files.

• You can apply password protection to limit who can change the security settings on your files.

• You can encrypt your files to limit access to your files to a predefined set of users and to limit the types of actions they can perform on your files.

• You can certify your documents to attest to the contents and to allow users to make certain types of changes. Unlike a digital signature, a certification isn't invalidated if the user makes the approved types of changes.

• You can use eEnvelopes to protect your PDF documents in transit as outlined in the "Exploring on your own" section in this lesson.

In this part of the lesson, you'll add password protection to limit who can open your document and who can change the security settings.

💡 *You can save your security settings by creating a custom security policy. You can create three types of security policies: password security, public key certificate security, and Adobe Policy Server policies. Creating custom security policies allows you to apply the same security settings to any number of PDF documents without having to specify the settings each time. For information, see "Creating user security policies" in the Complete Acrobat 7.0 Help.*

Adding passwords

You can add two kinds of passwords to protect your Adobe PDF documents. You can add a Document Open password so that only users who have the password can open the document, and you can add a Permissions password so that only users who have the password can change the permissions for the document.

You'll add protection to your logo file so that no one can change the contents of the logo file and so that unauthorized users can't open and use the file.

1 Choose File > Open, and open the file SBR_Logo.pdf. Click OK to close the Adobe Picture Tasks dialog box.

2 Choose File > Save As, and name the file **SBR_Logo1.pdf** and save it in the Lesson11 folder.

3 Click the Secure button on the Acrobat toolbar, and choose Show Security Settings for This Document.

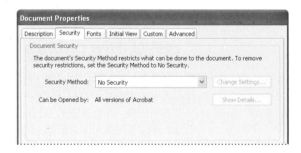

No security at all has been applied to this file. You'll first choose the type of security to add.

4 From the Security Method menu, choose Password Security. The Password Security Settings dialog box opens automatically.

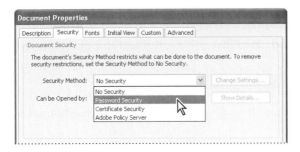

First you'll set the compatibility level.

The default compatibility level is compatibility with Acrobat 5 or later. If you're sure that all your users have Acrobat 5 or later, this compatibility level is the preferred setting. If you think that some of your users may still be running Acrobat 4, then you should select Acrobat 3 and later. Be aware, however, that this is a lower encryption level.

5 Select your compatibility level from the Compatibility menu. We used **Acrobat 5 and later**.

6 Check the box for the Require a Password to Open the Document option, and then type in your password. We typed in **SBRLogo**.

You'll share this password with anyone that you want to be able to open the document. Remember that passwords are case-sensitive.

Always record your passwords in a secure location. If you forget your password, you can't recover it from the document. You might also want to store an unprotected copy of the document in a secure location.

Now you'll add a second password that controls who is allowed to change printing, editing, and security settings for the file.

7 Under Permission, check the box for the Use a Password to Restrict Printing and Editing of the Document and its Security Settings, and type in a second password. We typed in **SBRPres**.

Note: *Your open password and permissions password can't be the same.*

8 From the Printing Allowed menu, choose whether to allow printing at all, printing at low resolution, or printing at high resolution. We chose Low Resolution (150 dpi).

9 From the Changes Allowed menu, choose the type of changes you will allow users to make. We chose **Commenting, Filling in Form Fields, and Signing Existing Signature Fields** to allow users to comment on the logo.

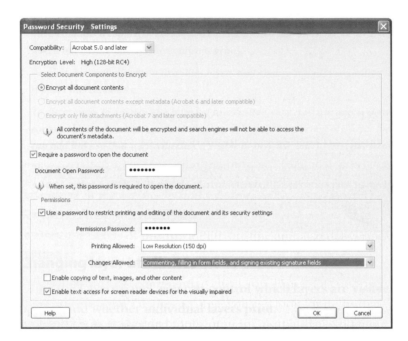

10 Click OK to apply your changes.

11 In the first dialog box, re-enter the Open Password. We entered **SBRLogo**. Then click OK, and click OK again to clear the alert box.

12 In the second dialog box, re-enter the Permissions Password. We entered **SBRPres**. Then click OK, and click OK again to clear the alert box.

Notice that the actions available to users don't appear to have changed. But if you click the Show Details button, you'll see the limitations applied.

13 Click OK and OK again to exit the Document Properties dialog box.

14 Click File > Save to save your work and apply the security changes.

15 Choose File > Close to close the SBRLogo1.pdf file.

Now you'll check the security that you've added to your file.

Opening a password-protected file

1 Choose File > Open and re-open the SBRLogo1.pdf file in the Lesson11 folder.

You're prompted to enter the required password to open the file.

2 We entered **SBRLogo**, and clicked OK. Then click OK to clear the Adobe Picture Tasks dialog box.

Now you'll test the Permissions Password.

3 Click the Secure button ( ) on the toolbar, and choose Show Security Settings for This Document from the menu.

4 In the Document Properties dialog box, try changing the Security Method from Password Security to No Security.

Acrobat prompts you to enter the Permissions password.

5 We entered **SBRPres** and clicked OK and then OK again.

All restrictions are now removed from the file.

6 Click OK to close the Document Properties dialog box.

7 Choose File > Close, and close the file without saving the changes.

Encrypting Adobe PDF files using certificates

When you encrypt a PDF file using a certificate, you specify a list of recipients and define the recipient's level of access to the file—for example, whether the recipients can edit, copy, or print the file. You can also encrypt a document using security policies.

Encrypting a document for a list of recipients begins by including your digital ID in the list, so that you later are able to open the document. You then select the digital ID certificates for those that you want to be able to open the document. You can obtain these certificates from your list of trusted identities, from files on disk, from an LDAP server, or from the Windows Certificate Store if you use Windows. After you build a list of recipients who have access to the file, you can apply restricted permissions on an individual basis.

Note: You can also create a security policy that stores certificate settings for easy reuse.

—From the Complete Acrobat 7.0 Help.

Exploring on your own: Using eEnvelopes

In Acrobat 7.0 you can attach files to a PDF document and encrypt only the file attachments. In this case, the PDF document in which the file attachments are embedded functions as an eEnvelope. Anyone can open the eEnvelope and view the cover page and even a list of contents, but the attachments can only be opened as defined by the security you apply. When the attachments are opened and saved, they are identical to the original. No encryption is applied.

Suppose that you want to send a copy of the Lotion advertisement to a satellite office. The advertisement is confidential at this point, so you want to be sure that no unauthorized person intercepts and opens it. To ensure this, you'll create an eEnvelope and attach the advertisement to it and apply security. In this part of the lesson, you'll use the wizard to walk you through the process; however, you can also create secure eEnvelopes manually.

1 In Acrobat, choose Document > Security > Secure PDF Delivery.

2 In the Choose the Files You Want to Include in Your eEnvelope panel of the Creating Secure eEnvelope dialog box, click the Add File to Send button. In the Choose the Files to Enclose dialog box, browse to select the file or files to add. We added the Lotion.pdf file in the Lesson11 folder. Note that you can add non-PDF files, and you can add more than one file. (Use Ctrl-click or Command-click to add multiple files from the same location, or add files one at a time if the files are located in different folders.) Click Open to add the files.

If you want to experiment with adding non-PDF files, try adding some of the lesson files from the Lesson03 folder.

The file or files you have added are displayed in the Currently Selected Files window. You can delete any file by selecting it and clicking the Remove Selected File(s) button.

3 Click Next to create your eEnvelope.

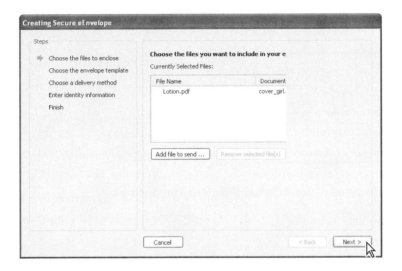

4 In the Choose the Envelope Template panel, select the template you want to use and then click Next. We choose the template2.pdf that has a date stamp.

5 For the delivery method, we elected to have the wizard email the completed envelope. Click Next and then click Yes to clear the message box.

6 In the Security Policy dialog box, first select the Show All Policies option. The policies available to you are listed. We chose Restrict Opening and Editing Using Password. When you have selected the necessary options, click Next.

7 Enter your personal information, and click Next.

8 Click Finish.

Now you'll choose your security settings.

9 We chose to use the default setting for the compatibility level and the document components to encrypt, and we chose to set a password requirement for opening the documents.

10 Click OK, and if you set a password requirement, you'll be asked to reenter the password.

After you complete this process, Acrobat will launch your default email program and create an email with the eEnvelope attached. Send the email to yourself to see what the finished product looks like.

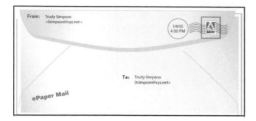

11 When you are finished, close Acrobat and close any open files.

Review questions

1 Where do you change the appearance of your digital signature?

2 How many digital signatures can you create?

3 Why would you want to apply password protection to a PDF file?

4 When would you apply permissions protection?

Review answers

1 You change the appearance of your digital signature in the Configure Signature Appearance dialog box. You can access this dialog box from the Security Preferences dialog box. You can also change the appearance of your digital signature in the Apply Signature to Document dialog box during the signing process.

2 You can have numerous digital signatures. You can create different digital signatures for the different identities that you use. You can have personal signatures, corporate signatures, family signatures, etc.

3 If you have a confidential document that you don't want others to read, you can apply password protection. Only users with whom you share your password will be able to open the document.

4 Permissions protection limits how a user can use or reuse the contents of your Adobe PDF file. For example, you can specify that users cannot print the contents of your file, or copy and paste the contents of your file. Permission protection allows you to share the content of your file without losing control over how it is used.

12 | Creating Multimedia Presentations

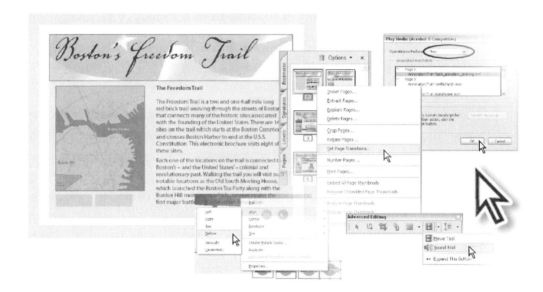

Adobe PDF is the perfect format for delivery of multimedia presentations. Whether you use PDF to deliver a presentation, or you distribute it across your entire organization, PDF is the complete solution for delivering interactive content, including movies and sounds.

In this lesson, you will learn how to do the following:

- Add and embed movies and animations into PDF files.

- Add and embed sounds into PDF documents.

- Control movies and sounds through buttons and page actions.

- Control transitions and timing of presentations using Full Screen mode.

If needed, remove the previous lesson folder from your hard drive, and copy the Lesson12 folder onto your hard drive.

Note: Windows 2000 users may need to unlock the lesson files before using them. For information, see "Copying the Classroom in a Book files" on page 4.

This lesson involves multimedia content that can be shared across multiple computer platforms, and uses several cross-platform formats for the sound and movie files. To view the animated .swf files included in this lesson, your computer needs to have the free Flash player installed; it is available at www.macromedia.com. To view the movie files used in this lesson, your computer needs to have the free QuickTime player installed. This Windows and Macintosh movie player is available at www.apple.com/quicktime.

You may see a Manage Trust for Multimedia Content window displayed at some point during this lesson. This allows you to verify whether you wish to allow multimedia content within a document to play. If this window is displayed, choose the Play multimedia content and add this document to my list of trusted documents option, and then click the Play button.

Getting started

In this lesson, you'll work on a multimedia tour of the Freedom Trail, a National Park that consists of a collection of historic locations in Boston, Massachusetts. The tour visits eight locations, and each location has its own separate page to which you will add a multimedia element, such as a sound or movie file. You will control the sounds, movies, and animations using buttons and page actions. You will also add navigational buttons for viewers to use to easily move through the document, as it will be presented in the full screen viewing mode, which hides the menus and palettes.

1 Start Adobe Acrobat 7.0 Professional.

2 To see what the finished file looks like, navigate to the Lesson12 folder and open the file Freedom_Trail_end.pdf. Your menu bars will be hidden when you open this file because it includes instructions to open in Full Screen mode. Use the navigational buttons in the document to move through each page. Notice the buttons, sounds, movies, and animations in the document.

3 When you have finished examining the completed PDF file, choose Ctrl+L (Windows) or Command+L (Mac OS) to return to a view that shows all your menus. You can keep this file open for reference while you work on the exercise, or you can close the file by choosing File > Close.

💡 *You can also use the Esc key to leave the full screen mode, but this option can be disabled in the Full Screen section of Acrobat's Preferences.*

4 Choose File > Open and choose the file Freedom_Trail_start.pdf in the Lesson12 folder.

Adding an interactive animation

If the Advanced Editing toolbar is not open, open it now via View > Toolbars > Advanced Editing. You will use this toolbar to add movies, animations, and sounds to your PDF presentation.

1 If necessary, navigate to page 1. Choose the Movie tool (▤) from the Advanced Editing toolbar.

The Movie tool and the Sound tool (◀») share the same position on the Advanced Editing toolbar. If the Sound tool is visible, click the arrow to the right of the Sound tool and choose the Movie tool (▦) from the menu that appears. To see both tools at the same time, choose Expand This Button, which adds both tools to the Advanced Editing toolbar, so they are both visible at the same time.

2 Using the Movie tool, click and drag a rectangle that completely encloses the tan box on the upper left side of the first page. This box has been placed for you to use as a guide. After you release the mouse, the Add Movie window appears.

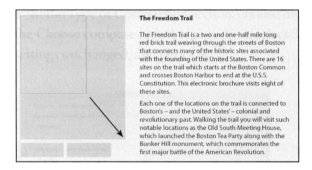

3 In the Add Movie window, select the Acrobat 6 and Later Compatible Media radio button. Click the Browse button (Windows) or Choose button (Mac OS) and choose the file named opening_animation.swf that is located in the movies folder in the Lesson12 folder. Click the Select button.

After selecting the file, choose the following options in the Add Movie Window:

- Deselect Snap to content proportions.
- Select Embed content in document.
- Select Retrieve poster from movie.

4 Now click OK. The animated movie file appears in the box you created with the Movie tool.

Note: When selecting movies or animations on a Windows computer, it may be necessary to select "Most Common Formats" from the Files of Type drop-down menu. When browsing for the files to input, this allows Acrobat to display most movie and sound formats.

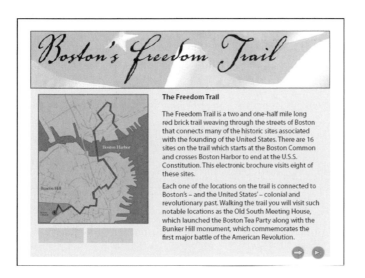

5 If necessary, change the position of the movie file by clicking and holding the mouse on the center of the movie file, and then dragging it to the desired location. To adjust the dimensions of the movie file proportionally, Shift-click the handles in the corner of the movie file and drag toward the center of the movie to reduce the size, or away from the center to enlarge the size.

Always use the Shift key when resizing a movie or animation file to ensure that it remains proportional. Clicking and dragging without the Shift key may cause the movie or animation to become distorted.

6 Choose the Hand tool ( ) from the Basic toolbar and move the cursor over the animated map. The cursor changes to a pointing finger ( ) to indicate that the content is interactive. Click on the center of the Flash animation. The animated map will play. This file also includes audio. If you cannot hear the audio, you may need to adjust the sound controls on your computer.

Note: When clicking on your movie file to play it, a window named Manage Trust for Multimedia Content may appear. If this window appears, select the second option Play the multimedia content and add this document to my list of trusted documents. This behavior is a feature of the Acrobat 7.0 Professional Trust Manager. See "Setting Trust Manager Preferences" in the Complete Acrobat 7.0 Help.

To stop an animated movie file, an action must be created that specifically tells Acrobat to stop the playback. Without an action stopping the playback, the file will continue to play, even after navigating to another page. It is advisable to always create an action that allows a user to stop a movie, animation, or sound file. This is described in Adding an action to stop the animation later in this lesson.

Adding a button

1 Choose the Button tool (■) from the Advanced Editing toolbar. Move your cursor to the upper left corner of the box that is positioned below and to the left of the animated map. Click and drag from the upper left corner of the box to the lower right corner. The Button Properties window opens after you release the mouse.

2 In the Button Properties window, choose the General tab and enter the button name **Start Introduction**. The button name is used by Acrobat to identify this button. The name is not visible to users and does not appear on the button itself.

3 Click on the Options tab in the Button Properties window and enter the Label name of **Start Introduction**. The label name appears on the face of the button and is the text that is visible to the viewer.

4 Click the Actions tab in the Button Properties window. For the Select Trigger option, keep the default selection of Mouse Up. This indicates that when the mouse is clicked and released, the action will occur. For the Select Action option, choose Play Media (Acrobat 6 and Later Compatible) and then click the Add button. The Play Media (Acrobat 6 and Later Compatible) window will open.

5 In the Play Media (Acrobat 6 and Later Compatible) window, leave the Operation to Perform option set to Play. In the Associated Annotation section of the window, choose Annotation from opening_animation.swf, which is listed under Page 1. Click OK in the Play Media (Acrobat 6 and Later Compatible) window and then click the Close button in the Button Properties window.

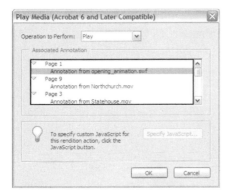

6 Choose the Hand tool ( ) and test your button by clicking the Start Introduction button.

Adding an action to stop the animation

1 Choose the Button tool ( ). Move your cursor to the upper left corner of the box that is positioned to the right of the Start Introduction button you created in the previous step. Click and drag from the upper left corner of the box to the lower right corner. The Button Properties window opens after you release the mouse. Choose the General tab and name the button **Stop Introduction**. For Tooltip, enter **Click to stop movie**. The tooltip appears when a user positions their cursor over the button.

2 Choose the Options tab in the Button Properties window. In the Label field type the words **Stop Introduction**.

3 Choose the Actions tab in the Button Properties window, and keep the Select Trigger option as Mouse Up. Choose Play Media (Acrobat 6 and Later Compatible) from the Select Action options and click Add. The Play Media (Acrobat 6 and Later Compatible) window opens.

Even though you are selecting Play Media as the action, this action is also used any time you want to start, stop, pause, resume, or restart a movie, sound, or animation.

4 In the Play Media (Acrobat 6 and Later Compatible) window, choose Stop from the Operation to Perform list and in the Associated Annotation portion of the window, choose Annotation from opening_animation.swf, which is listed under Page 1. Click OK and then click the Close button in the Button Properties Window.

5 Choose the Hand tool ( ) and click the Start Introduction button. After the animation starts to play, click the Stop Introduction button to stop the animation. In this exercise you have used the Stop and Start actions. Acrobat 7.0 Professional also includes actions for pausing and resuming the play of sounds and movies.

 If the Stop or Start Introduction buttons do not provide the desired results, you can edit their actions by choosing the Button tool ( ) and double-clicking either button and choosing the Actions tab, then selecting the action to be changed and clicking the Edit button. You may need to edit the action if the Stop Introduction button does not actually stop the media from playing. Because the default Play Media action is to play rather than stop a media element, you may accidentally set the Stop Introduction action to Play rather than Stop.

Adding a Show/hide field

Form fields, such as buttons, can be set to appear only when they are needed. For example, you can have a form field that only appears if a certain checkbox or button is selected, or when the mouse is in a certain location. In this exercise, you will use two overlapping images that have been placed in the PDF as buttons. One of the two images appears when you click a button, and disappears when you click a second button.

1 Navigate to page two. Select the Zoom In tool ( ). Click and drag a box around both the map, and the buttons below the map, so that both are visible in the document window.

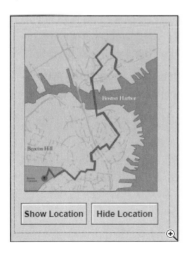

The red circle on the map with the number 1 in its center will be made to appear and disappear based upon which button is selected. You will start by making the circle hidden by default, and then require the viewer to click the Show Location button for the circle to appear.

2 Choose the Button tool (■) and move the cursor over the map, notice that it is labeled boston common location. Red handles around the corners appear when you move your cursor over this field, indicating that it will be selected if you click. Double-click on the boston common location button field to open the Button Properties window.

3 In the Button Properties window, choose the General tab and select Hidden from the Form Field drop-down menu. Click the Close button.

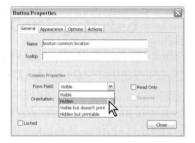

4 Select the Hand tool (✋). The red circle showing the location of the Boston Common along the trail is now hidden from view.

5 From the Advanced Editing toolbar, choose the Select Object tool (▶). Use this tool to edit all types of form fields, including buttons. Double-click the Show Location button. The Button Properties window appears.

6 In the Button Properties window, choose the Actions tab. For Select Action choose Show/Hide a field. Leave the Select Trigger set to Mouse Up and click the Add button.

7 In the Show/Hide Field window, choose the Show radio button on the right side of the window. From the list of fields, choose boston common location and click OK to close the Show/Hide Field window, then click Close to close the Button Properties window.

8 Choose the Hand tool and click on the Show Location button. The red circle appears on the trail map, showing the location of the Boston Common.

9 Choose the Select Object tool (▶) and double-click the Hide Location button, which is located immediately to the right of the Show Location button.

10 In the Button Properties window, choose the Actions tab. Leave the Select Trigger set to Mouse Up. For Select Action, click the menu and choose Show/Hide a field. Click the Add button. The Show/Hide Field window appears.

11 In the Show/Hide Field window, choose the Hide radio button on the right side of the window. Choose boston common location from the list of available form fields, and click OK. Click Close to close the Button Properties window.

12 Choose the Hand tool and alternate between selecting the Show Location and Hide Location button.

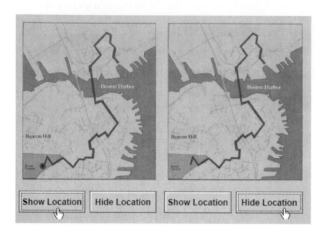

💡 *If the buttons do not work as expected, use the Select Object tool and right-click (Windows) or Ctrl-click (Mac OS) the Show Location or Hide Location button and choose Properties. Confirm that the actions applied to the buttons under the Actions tab are correct.*

Adding a movie clip and controlling it with buttons

1 Choose View > Fit Page or click the Fit Page button (⬍).

2 If necessary, open the Advanced Editing toolbar by choosing View > Toolbars > Advanced Editing.

3 Choose the Movie tool (▤) from the Advanced Editing toolbar. Both the Sound tool (◀») and the Movie tool are located in the same position in the toolbar. To change from the Sound tool to the Movie tool, click on the Sound tool and select the Movie tool from the menu that appears.

4 Using the Movie tool, click and drag to create a frame in the empty space on the page, immediately to the right of the Play Multimedia and Stop Multimedia buttons. After you have created the frame, the Add Movie window appears.

Note: You may see a dialog box informing you that Acrobat is initializing the authoring system.

5 In the Add Movie window, choose the Acrobat 6 and Later Compatible Media radio button and click the Browse button (Windows) or Choose button (Mac OS) to select the movie file. Navigate to the Lesson12 folder and choose Boston_Common.mov from the movies folder. Click the Select button, then click the OK button to close the Add Movie window. The movie is added to your page.

6 If necessary, move the file by clicking and dragging it so that it is positioned to the right of the Play and Stop buttons, and above the navigational buttons. The movie file should not be positioned on top of any other content.

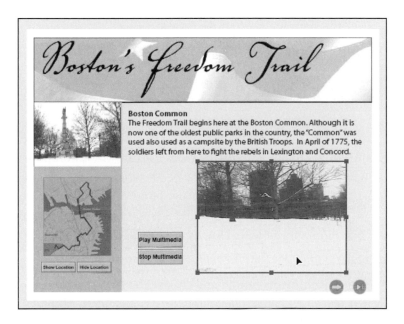

7 Choose the Hand tool (🖐) and move the cursor over the movie. The cursor changes to a pointing finger (👆) to indicate that the content is interactive. Click on the center of the movie file and the movie will play.

8 Choose the Select Object tool and double-click on the Play Multimedia button positioned to the left of the movie. Click the Actions tab and from the Select Action pull-down menu, choose Play Media (Acrobat 6 and Later Compatible). Leave the Select Trigger set at Mouse Up and click the Add button. The Play Media (Acrobat 6 and Later Compatible) window opens.

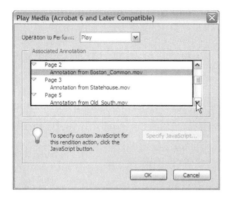

9 In the Play Media window, choose Annotation from Boston_Common.mov from the list of Associated Annotations and leave the Operation to Perform option set to Play. Click OK, then click Close to shut the Button Properties window.

You can test your first button if you wish. However, we will also be adding a stop action to the second button so users can have the option of stopping the movie.

10 Double-click the Stop Multimedia button and choose the Actions tab in the Button Properties window that appears. Keep the default Select Trigger set to Mouse Up. From the Select Action pull-down menu, choose Play Media (Acrobat 6 and Later Compatible) and then click the Add button. The Play Media (Acrobat 6 and Later Compatible) window opens.

11 In the Play Media (Acrobat 6 and Later Compatible) window, select Stop from the Operation to Perform options, choose Annotation from Boston_Common.mov from the list of Associated Annotations, and click OK. Click the Close button to close the Button Properties window.

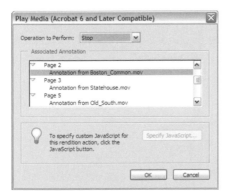

12 Choose the Hand tool () and click the Play Multimedia and Stop Multimedia buttons to start and stop the movie.

Adding, aligning, and duplicating navigational buttons

1 Click the Next Page button in the lower right corner of the document. Note that the button has an action that takes you to another page. Return to page 2.

2 Choose the Button tool (■) from the Advanced Editing toolbar. Click and drag a square that is approximately the same size as the other two buttons, to the left of the Next Page button.

When you finish drawing the frame for the button, the Button Properties window opens.

3 Click the General tab, and enter the name for the button as **Previous Page**.

4 In the Button Properties window, click the Appearance tab. Click the Fill color swatch and choose No Color from the available colors. This sets the fill color of the button to be transparent.

5 Click the Options tab, and in the Layout menu choose Icon Only. This causes Acrobat to display an imported picture as the face of the button.

6 For the Behavior option, choose Push. Three separate options appear in the State portion of the window after choosing Push for the Behavior options: Up, Down, and Rollover.

7 If it's not already selected, click the Up state and then click the Choose Icon button to select a graphic that will be positioned on the button as it is up. In the Choose Icon window that appears, click the Browse button and navigate to the buttons folder in the Lesson12 folder and choose previous_page.pdf to use as the button, then click Select. A preview of the button appears in the Choose Icon window. Click OK to confirm the selection of this graphic.

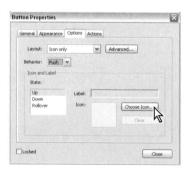

8 Choose the Rollover state and click the Choose Icon button to select a graphic that will appear on the button as the mouse rolls over. In the Choose Icon window that appears, click the Browse button and, if necessary, navigate to the buttons folder in the Lesson12 folder. Choose previous_page_rollover.pdf then click Select. A preview of the button appears in the Choose Icon window. Click OK to confirm the selection of this graphic.

9 Click on the Actions tab to assign an action to this button. Choose Execute a menu item from the Select Action menu. Note that the menu choices may extend both above and below the menu selection, so you may need to scroll up in the menu to locate the Execute a menu item choice. Leave the Select Trigger option set to Mouse Up and click the Add button.

Windows: The Menu Item Selection window appears. In the Menu Item Selection window, choose View > Go To > Previous Page, then click OK. Click Close to close the Button Properties window.

Mac OS: From the menu at the top of the window choose View > Go To > Previous Page, then click OK. Click Close to close the Button Properties window.

10 Select the Hand tool and click on the Previous Page button you created in the previous steps. After you have completed testing the button, return to page 2.

Adding a first page button

1 Choose the Button tool (■) from the Advanced Editing toolbar. Click and drag a square to the left of the Previous Page button that is approximately the same size as the other buttons. When you finish drawing the frame for the button, the Button Properties window opens. Click the General tab and enter the name for the button as **First Page**.

2 In the Button Properties window, click the Appearance tab. Click the Fill Color swatch and choose No Color from the available colors. This sets the background color of the button to be transparent.

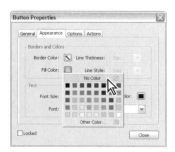

3 Click the Options tab, and in the Layout menu choose Icon Only.

4 For the Behavior option choose Push. Note that three separate options appear in the State portion of the window after choosing Push for the Behavior options: Up, Down, and Rollover.

5 Click the Up state and then click Choose Icon to select a graphic that will be positioned on the button by default. In the Choose Icon window that appears, click the Browse button, and navigate to the buttons folder in the Lesson12 folder, and choose first_page.pdf, then click Select. A preview of the button appears in the Choose Icon window. Click OK to confirm the selection of this graphic.

6 Choose the Rollover state and click Choose Icon to select a graphic that will be positioned on the button as the mouse rolls over it. In the Choose Icon window that appears, click the Browse button, and navigate to the buttons folder in the Lesson12 folder, and choose first_page_rollover.pdf to use as the button and click Select. A preview of the button appears in the Choose Icon window. Click OK to confirm the selection of this graphic.

7 Click on the Actions tab to assign an action to this button. Choose Execute a menu item from the Select Action menu. Note that the menu choices may extend both above and below the menu selection, so you may need to scroll up in the menu to locate this choice. Leave the Select Trigger option set to Mouse Up and click the Add button. The Menu Item Selection window appears.

8 In the Menu Item Selection window, choose View > Go To > First Page (Windows) or from the menu, select View > Go To > First Page (Mac OS), then click OK.

9 Click Close in the Buttons Property Window.

10 Choose the Hand tool ( ). Click on the buttons you have created to change from one page to another.

Aligning buttons

1 Choose the Select Object tool (⬀).

2 Shift-click to select each of the navigational buttons.

3 Right-click (Windows) or Ctrl-click (Mac OS) on any button and choose Align > Bottom from the context menu.

The buttons all align with the bottom edge of the button with the red outline.

Duplicating buttons

1 On page 2, confirm the four navigational buttons in the lower right corner are selected. If necessary, Shift-click each button to select them all with the Select Object tool.

2 Right-click (Windows) or Ctrl-click (Mac OS) on any of the four buttons, making certain that they remain selected.

3 Choose Duplicate from the contextual menu.

4 In the Duplicate Field window, enter in the From textbox **3** and in the To textbox **9**. Click OK.

5 Click on the Hand tool and begin navigating through the document, using the buttons you've created. The buttons now appear on pages two through nine. If content on the pages overlaps the buttons, use the Select Object tool to move or resize the buttons or objects as necessary.

Adding a sound file and adding two actions to one button

1 Navigate to page 3. If the Advanced Editing toolbar is not currently visible, choose View > Toolbars > Advanced Editing.

2 Select the Sound tool (◀)) and draw a small square at the bottom of the page on the white area near the edge. The size and exact location are not critically important, as the box will be hidden from view.

💡 *Remember that both the Sound tool (◀)) and the Movie tool (▦) are located in the same position in the toolbar. To change from the Movie tool to the Sound tool, you may need to click on the arrow to the right of the Movie tool and select the Sound tool from the menu that appears. To make both tools visible at the same time, click on the arrow next to either tool and choose Expand this Button from the menu that appears.*

3 In the Add Sound window, choose the Acrobat 6 (and Later) Compatible Media option. Click the Browse button to identify the location of the sound file that you are adding to the presentation. Navigate to the sound file Statehouse_audioclip.wav in the audio folder in the Lesson12 folder, and click Select to choose this file.

4 Click the Embed content in document checkbox, and then click OK to close the Add Sound window.

5 Double-click the frame that was created in the previous step. Note that the frame containing the sound includes a border.

6 In the Multimedia Properties window, click the Appearance tab and choose Invisible Rectangle from the Border Type drop-down menu. This removes the black border around the perimeter of the frame containing the sound, making the sound border invisible on the PDF page. Click the Close button to close the Multimedia Properties window.

Adding multiple actions to one button

Because the sound and movie files are added to this page separately, you will add two actions to a single button to cause both the sound and the movie to play at the same time.

1 Choose the Select Object tool (◣) and double-click the Play Multimedia button. The Button Properties window appears.

2 Click on the Actions tab. For Select Trigger, keep the default setting of Mouse Up and for Select Action, choose Play Media (Acrobat 6 and Later Compatible). Click the Add button.

3 In the Play Media (Acrobat 6 and Later Compatible) window, choose Play as the Operation to Perform. Choose Annotation from Statehouse_audioclip.wav from the list of Associated Annotations and click OK.

Do not close the Button Properties window, as you will add another action for this button. The second action will also be a Play Media (Acrobat 6 and Later Compatible) action, and will also occur when the mouse is clicked and released, so do not change these settings.

4 Click the Add button and choose Annotation from Statehouse.mov from the list of Associated Annotations in the Play Media (Acrobat 6 and Later Compatible) window. Click OK and then click the Close button in the Button Properties window.

5 Choose the Hand tool and click the Play Multimedia button to play both the sound clip and movie clip simultaneously.

Creating page actions to control multimedia clips

In the previous section, you controlled both sound and movie elements through a button action. You can also use other methods for starting or stopping a sound or movie file. Here you will create an action to cause a movie to play when a page is opened. When the page closes, you will have the movie stop playing.

When you play either sound or movie files in Acrobat, they continue to play until the file has reached its end or an action tells it to stop. For example, if you start playing the movie files on page 3, and then move to a different page before the movie is complete, it will continue playing even after you move to the other page.

1 Open the Pages panel by clicking the Pages tab on the left side of the screen, or choose View > Navigation Tabs > Pages.

2 In the Pages panel, right-click (Windows) or Ctrl-click (Mac OS) the page 3 thumbnail. From the context menu that appears, choose Page Properties.

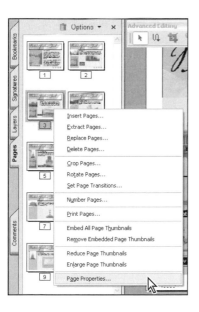

3 Click on the Actions tab in the Page Properties window. For Select Trigger, choose Page Close and for Select Action choose Play Media (Acrobat 6 and Later Compatible), then click the Add button. The Play Media (Acrobat 6 and Later Compatible) window appears.

4 In the Play Media window, choose Stop from the Operation to Perform menu and then choose Annotation from Statehouse.mov from the list of Associated Annotations. After making these selections, click OK. This action stops the movie from playing whenever the page is closed.

5 In the Page Properties window, for Select Trigger, choose Page Close and for Select Action, choose Play Media (Acrobat 6 and Later Compatible) and then click Add. Choose Stop for the Operation to Perform and choose Annotation from Statehouse_audioclip.wav as the sound file that will be affected by this action. Click OK, and then click Close to close the Page Properties window.

6 Choose the Hand tool (🖐) and click the Play Multimedia button. As the multimedia clips are playing, click on the next page button. Both the sound and movie files stop playing after you navigate to another page of the document.

Creating page actions to start multimedia clips

Just as you created a page action that stopped movie and sound files, you can also create a page action which plays a multimedia clip when a page is opened.

1 Navigate to page four. A movie file has already been placed on the page for you.

2 Open the Pages panel by clicking its tab on the left side of the screen or choosing View > Navigation Tabs > Pages and Right-click (Windows) or Ctrl-click (Mac OS) on the page thumbnail representing page four. Choose Page Properties from the context menu. The Page Properties window appears.

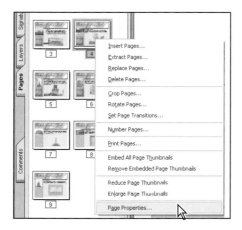

3 Click on the Actions tab and set the Select Trigger option to Page Open. Choose Play Media (Acrobat 6 and Later Compatible) and then click the Add button. The Play Media (Acrobat 6 and Later Compatible) window opens. Choose Play as the Operation to Perform. From the Associated Annotations list, choose Annotation from Granary.mov and click OK, then click Close to close the Page Properties window.

4 Choose the Hand tool (🖐). Using either the navigational buttons in this document or the previous page button, navigate to page 3, then return to page 4 to see the movie clip start playing automatically.

Opening a movie clip in a floating window

1 Navigate to page five. This page already includes a movie file along with a button to play the movie. This movie plays in the default location, in its current frame located on the document page. You will change the movie so that it plays in a separate window.

2 Choose the Select Object tool (↖) and double-click the movie frame. In the Multimedia Properties window that opens, choose the Settings tab. Select Rendition from Old _South.mov from the list of renditions, then click the Edit Rendition button.

Note: *You may need to scroll to locate this object.*

3 In the Rendition Settings window, choose the Playback Location tab. For Playback Location, choose Floating Window and keep this window open.

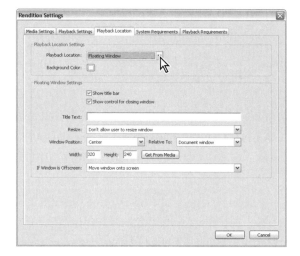

4 In the Floating Window Settings at the bottom of the window, click the Get From Media button to set the size of the window based upon the size of the movie file.

5 Choose the Playback Settings tab and select the Show Player Controls option. This allows viewers to pause, rewind, and adjust the sound volume of the movie file as it plays in the floating window. Click OK to close the Renditions Settings window.

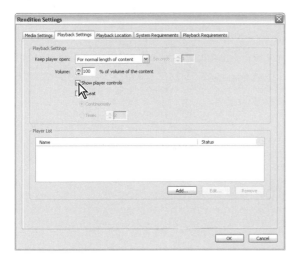

6 Click the Close button to close the Multimedia Properties window.

7 Choose the Hand tool ( ) and click the Play Multimedia button to see the movie play in a separate window.

Creating a full screen presentation with transitions

You will now view your PDF document without all the tools and menus by using the Full Screen viewing mode. You will also create transitions that vary how the screen changes from one page to the next.

1 Open the Pages panel. Shift-click to select both page 1 and page 2. Right-click (Windows) or Ctrl-click (Mac OS) on the thumbnail of either page. Choose Set Page Transitions from the context menu that appears.

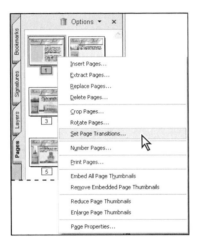

2 In the Set Transitions window, choose Fade from the Effect options. Check the Auto Flip checkbox, and choose 10 Seconds from the After drop-down menu. In the Page Range portion of this window, confirm that the option Pages selected in Pages panel is selected, and then click OK.

These choices will cause page 1 to fade into page 2 whenever the document is viewed using the Full Screen mode. Also, if the first page is not changed manually, it will automatically move to the next page after 10 seconds.

3 In the Pages panel, right-click on the page thumbnail for page 3. From the context menu, choose Set Page Transitions and from the Effect options, choose Random Transition. In the Page Range portion of the window, choose Pages Range and enter from **3** to **9**. Click OK after entering these settings.

4 Navigate to the first page of the document. To view the presentation using the Full Screen mode, choose Window > Full Screen View. Wait 10 seconds to test the automatic transition, or click the Next Page button to view the Fade effect as the page transitions from page 1 to page 2. To exit Full Screen viewing mode, use the Esc (Escape) Key on the upper left corner of your keyboard, or press Ctrl+L (Windows) or Command+L (Mac OS).

Note: You can also switch to the Full Screen mode by clicking the Full Screen Icon located in the bottom left corner of the document window.

5 To set the entire document to always open in the Full Screen viewing mode, choose File > Document Properties and select the Initial View tab. In the Window Options portion of this window, select Open in Full Screen mode and then click OK.

6 Choose File > Save. Close the document, and then reopen it. The file now opens directly in the Full Screen mode.

Exploring on your own: Creating multimedia presentations

1 On pages 6-9, add the following items. Additional multimedia files are located in the Lesson12 folder.

• Sound files for each page.

• Play buttons for the movie and sound clips on each page.

• Show/hide buttons for the map on each page.

2 Explore the full screen preferences by choosing Edit > Preferences (Windows) or Acrobat > Preferences (Mac OS) and selecting Full Screen.

• You can override the page transitions so that they use those set in the Preferences, and not those set in the file.

• If you do not want to use the Escape key to leave the Full Screen mode, deselect Escape key exits.

• Choose Loop after last page to have the file return to the first page after viewing the last page in a file.

3 Change the movie rendition settings to have the movie files play in their own window. Try having the movie files play both with and without a visible controller.

Review questions

1 Why would you convert an existing presentation to Adobe PDF? Why would you create a new multimedia presentation using the Sound and Movie tools of Adobe Acrobat 7.0 Professional?

2 Are you able to automatically start playing sound and movie files, and how would this be useful?

3 How can you make a form field, such as a button, invisible? If so, why would you do this?

Review answers

1 As a universally accepted file format, Adobe PDF files are not limited by the software on the recipient's computer or the fonts used when creating a file. Typical presentation software files require the recipients to have the presentation software on their computer, along with the same fonts used when the file was created. Presentations delivered as an Adobe PDF can be viewed by users on many computer systems—including Palm, Windows, Macintosh, and various forms of Unix.

2 Movie and sound files can start playing based upon a number of actions. These can include a page being opened or closed, or the mouse being moved to a certain location on the page. You can even have sounds or movies play because the viewer has moved his or her cursor to a certain form field. These automatic actions are helpful for delivering presentations with minimal effort on the part of the viewer.

3 Set a Button Field's properties to Hidden to keep it from displaying or printing. Buttons and form fields can be made visible or invisible for both on-screen and printing purposes. This can be useful if you want a button to be visible on screen, but not print. For multi-media purposes, you can have buttons that are not visible until a certain action occurs. Clicking on a portion of the document can cause a graphic or text to appear on the page.

13 | Using Acrobat's Engineering and Technical Features

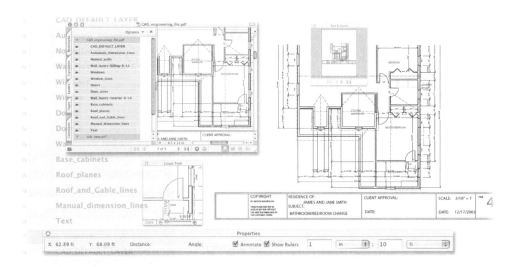

Adobe Acrobat Professional 7.0 lets you share technical drawings with clients and colleagues while maintaining control over your original files. You can clearly communicate project needs using special review and commenting tools designed for the needs of technical professionals.

In this lesson you will learn how to do the following:

- Merge separate PDF documents into one consolidated file.

- Use Layers created in an AutoCAD drawing.

- Work with Acrobat's measuring tools.

- Use navigational tools to easily move through PDF documents.

If needed, remove the previous lesson folder from your hard drive, and copy the Lesson13 folder onto your hard drive.

Note: Windows 2000 users may need to unlock the lesson files before using them. For information, see "Copying the Classroom in a Book files" on page 4.

Getting started

In this lesson, you'll work on the architectural plans for a home remodeling project that involves adding three new rooms to a home. You will combine three independent PDF files, work with the layers from the AutoCAD file, add measurements and comments, and use special navigational tools that make it easy to view these technical illustrations.

1 Start Adobe Acrobat Professional 7.0.

2 To see what the finished file looks like, navigate to the Lesson13 folder and open the file engineering_end.pdf. Notice the document contains several pages, including different views of this construction project.

3 You can keep this file open for reference while you work on this exercise, or you can close the file by choosing File > Close.

Merging documents

You will start by combining three separate Computer Aided Design (CAD) drawing files into one single PDF file. Sharing these files as PDF allows those who do not have specialized design software to view the drawings. Rather than having users open three separate files, all the files they need will be placed in one document.

1 Choose File > Open and navigate to the Lesson13 folder. Choose the file rear.pdf and click the Open button.

2 Click the Pages tab along the left side of the document window, or choose View > Navigation Tabs > Pages.

3 In the Pages panel, choose Options > Insert Pages. The Select File to Insert window appears.

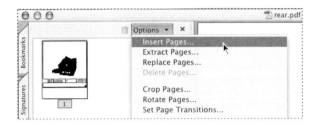

4 If necessary, navigate to the Lesson13 folder. Click once to select the file side.pdf. Ctrl-click (Windows) or Command-click (Mac OS) the floorplan.pdf file. Both the side.pdf and the floorplan.pdf file should be selected.

5 Click the Select button. The Insert Pages window opens.

6 In the Insert Pages window, confirm the pages are being inserted After Page 1, then click OK.

7 The PDF file now includes three pages showing different views of the building project.

Enhanced navigation tools: Pan & Zoom

Using the Pan & Zoom window, it is easy to focus on important portions of your documents.

1 Navigate to page 3, the floorplan view of the construction project.

2 Choose View > Fit Page.

3 Choose Tools > Zoom > Pan & Zoom Window. The Pan & Zoom window opens. If necessary, move the Pan & Zoom window to the side of the document window so that the architectural plans are also visible.

4 In the Pan & Zoom window, notice the red box surrounding the frame. Click the handle in the upper left corner of the red box. Drag the handle straight down, until the top line of the red frame is aligned with the top portion of the drawing.

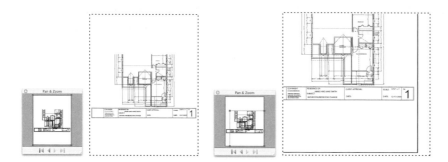

5 In the Pan & Zoom window, click and drag the lower left corner handle up and to the right. Stop when the bottom of the red frame is aligned with the bottom of the drawing.

6 Continuing to work in the Pan & Zoom window, click the handle in the upper right corner of the red box surrounding the window. Drag down and to the left. Stop when the focus of the document window is on the Master Bath.

Maintain a view that allows you to see this entire room. If necessary, click and drag the center of the red box in the Pan and Zoom window to reposition the visible portion of the page. You will be measuring several items in this area.

7 Click on the Close button in the upper corner of the Pan and Zoom window to close it.

Working with layers

This document was created using AutoCAD. Adobe Acrobat Professional 7.0 is able to preserve layers from AutoCAD and other programs such as Microsoft Visio. These layers can be enabled or disabled for viewing. This makes it easier to focus on the information in your file that is most relevant.

1 Click the Layers tab or choose View > Navigation Tabs > Layers to open the Layers panel.

2 If necessary, in the Layers panel, click the plus sign (+) (Windows) or triangle (▶) (Mac OS) located to the left of the floorplan section. This makes all the layers in the section available for modification.

If you can already see a number of layers visible under the floorplan heading, do not click the minus sign or triangle, as this will hide the layers for this portion of the PDF document.

3 In the Layers panel, click the Eye icon (👁) located to the left of the layer name for each of the following layers:

- Automatic_Dimension_Lines.

- Window_sizes.

- Door_sizes.

- Roof_planes.

All the text, lines, and other elements on these layers are now hidden from view.

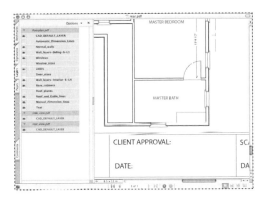

 💡 *The Eye icon in the Layers panel is used to represent layers that are visible. If the icon is not visible and a layer's objects are hidden, you can make a layer visible by clicking in the first column of the Layers panel, to the left of the layer name. By default, layers that are not visible do not print.*

About Adobe PDF layers

Acrobat supports the display, navigation, and printing of layered Adobe PDF content output by applications such as Adobe InDesign, AutoCAD, and Visio.

You can rename and merge layers, change the properties of layers, and add actions to layers. You can also lock layers to prevent them from being hidden.

You can control the display of layers using the default and initial state settings. For example, if your document contains a copyright notice, you can easily hide the layer whenever the document is displayed on-screen but ensure that the layer always prints.

Acrobat does not allow you to author layers that change visibility according to the zoom level, but it does support this capability.

To direct users to a particular layer set to a custom view, you can add bookmarks to a PDF document that contains layers. You can use this technique to highlight a portion of a layer that is especially important. You can add links so that users can click a visible or invisible link to navigate to or zoom in on a layer.

To create layers while exporting InDesign CS, or later documents, to PDF, make sure that Compatibility is set to Acrobat 6 (PDF 1.5) and that Create Acrobat Layers is selected in the Export PDF dialog box.

—From the Complete Acrobat 7.0 Help

Changing layer attributes

Using the Layers panel, you can control which layers are visible when a document is opened and whether individual layers print.

1 Right-click (Windows) or Ctrl-click (Mac OS) the Base_cabinets layer and choose Properties. The Layer Properties window opens.

2 In the Layer Properties window, for Default state, choose Off. For Print, choose Never Prints. Leave the other settings in this window unchanged, and click OK.

Using measuring tools

You will add some measurements to this file, helping to clarify the size of some of the windows in the drawing. Additionally, you will have Acrobat calculate both the area and perimeter of portions of the construction project.

Using rulers and the Distance tool

1 Choose View > Rulers to display rulers on the top and side of the document window.

2 Position your cursor over the horizontal ruler across the top of the document window. Click in the ruler and drag downward, stopping when the ruler guide is aligned with the top of the window on the right side in the Master Bath.

3 Click and drag a second ruler guide from the ruler at the top of the page, positioning the second guide along the bottom of the same window.

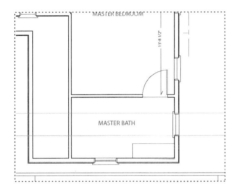

The guides extend to the ruler, allowing you to measure the distance or confirm alignment with other objects. Acrobat also provides measuring tools that can calculate the measurement for you.

4 Choose View > Toolbars > Measuring. The Measuring toolbar appears.

5 Click the Distance tool (⊶), and the Distance tool window is displayed.

6 In the Distance tool window, set the scale for the drawing by changing the 1 in = 1 in to 1 in = **10.75** ft.

7 Click once on the top of the window on the right side of the Master Bath, then click once on the bottom of the same window. Hold down the Shift key while clicking to keep the line straight.

The size of the opening is displayed in the Distance Tool window as approximately 2.5 ft.

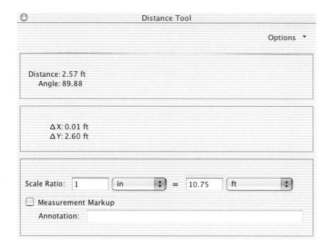

8 In the Distance Tool window, click the Measurement Markup checkbox. Repeat the process of measuring the window with the Distance tool (⤝). Acrobat creates an annotation showing the distance of the area you have measured. The distance is displayed when you roll your cursor over the annotation.

9 Repeat this process to measure the window along the bottom side of the drawing.

10 Click on the Close button in the upper corner of the Distance Tool window to close it.

Measuring perimeter and area

1 Using the Layers panel, click to turn off the following layers so they are not visible:

- Doors.
- Roof and gable lines.

2 If necessary, scroll up so the Master Bedroom is entirely visible.

3 Choose the Perimeter tool (⌐ₜ) and click in the upper left corner of the Master Bedroom. Proceed to click in all four corners of the room, moving counter-clockwise to the bottom left corner, the bottom right corner and the upper right corner. Hold down the Shift key to maintain a straight line as you click in each corner.

4 Move the cursor to the starting point—the upper left corner—and double-click. The perimeter of the room is displayed in the Perimeter tool window.

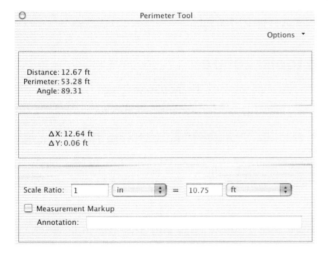

5 Close the Perimeter tool window, then choose the Area tool (◁), which displays the Area tool window. Click once in the upper left corner of the Master Bedroom, then in a counter-clockwise direction, click one time in each of the three remaining corners. Move the cursor over the original starting point, until the crosshair also displays a small open circle (+ₒ). Click to complete the measurement of the area of this room.

The area of the room is displayed in the Area tool window.

6 Click the Close button in the upper corner of the Area tool window and the measuring toolbar to close this window.

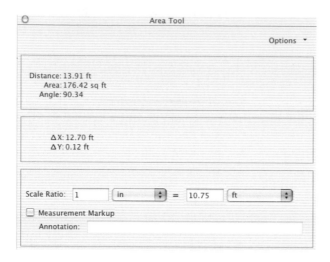

Enhanced navigation tools: Loupe

1 In the Pages panel, switch to the side view of the house on page two of the document.

2 Choose View > Fit Page.

3 Choose the Loupe tool (🔍) from the Zoom toolbar or choose Tools > Zoom > Loupe.

4 On the bottom row of the house's windows, locate the window in the center that is shorter than the other four. Click once in its center. The Loupe window opens, showing a magnified view of this window.

5 Along the bottom of the Loupe tool window, click and drag the slider to the right, increasing the magnification. Stop when the window fills the Loupe tool window.

Use the Loupe tool to view specific portions of your documents at a higher magnification, while maintaining a separate zoom level in the document window.

6 Close the Loupe tool window.

Using the Cloud Annotation tool

On technical drawings and illustrations with many straight lines, traditional notes and comments may not be clearly visible. Acrobat solves this problem with the Cloud Annotation tool.

Notice that the small window, which you magnified with the Loupe tool, contains four small panes in its top row, and four below. All the other windows in this construction project contain only three panes in each row. You can use Acrobat to add a comment for the designer, suggesting a change in the number of panes in this window.

1 Choose the Cloud Annotation tool ( ) by choosing Tools > Drawing Markups > Cloud tool, or click the tool in the Markups toolbar.

2 Click once in the upper left corner of this window, then travel in a counterclockwise direction and click in the lower left corner, and then the lower right corner of the window. Move to the upper right corner, and double-click. This completes the annotation.

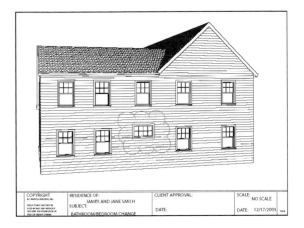

3 Choose the Hand tool ( ) and Right-click (Windows) or Ctrl-click (Mac OS) inside the cloud and choose Properties. The Polygon Properties window appears.

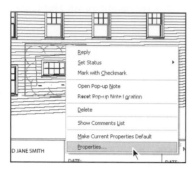

4 In the Appearance Tab, choose Cloudy 1 from the Style drop-down. Increase the thickness to 2 by clicking the upward facing arrow. Notice that the annotation changes appearance to reflect these modifications.

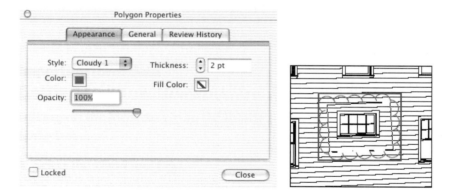

5 Click the Close button to close the Polygon Properties window. Click anywhere on the page outside the annotation to deselect the annotation.

Preparing engineering documents for distribution

Acrobat includes a variety of tools to make it easier for your audience to read and navigate through your documents, and for you to secure your projects from unauthorized viewing or editing.

Cropping pages

This document includes a large amount of empty space on both the top and bottom of the document. Before distributing the file, you will crop it so that the drawings are easier to view and navigate.

1 Choose View > Fit Page or click the Fit Page button (⬍).

2 Choose the Crop tool (⬚) from the Advanced Editing toolbar, or choose Tools > Advanced Editing > Crop tool. Your cursor changes to a plus sign (+).

3 Position your cursor below and to the left of the project information, along the left edge of the document itself. Click and drag up and to the right, creating a box that completely encloses the entire drawing on the page.

4 Press the Return or Enter key on your keyboard. The Crop Pages window opens. In the Page Range section of this window, select All, then click OK.

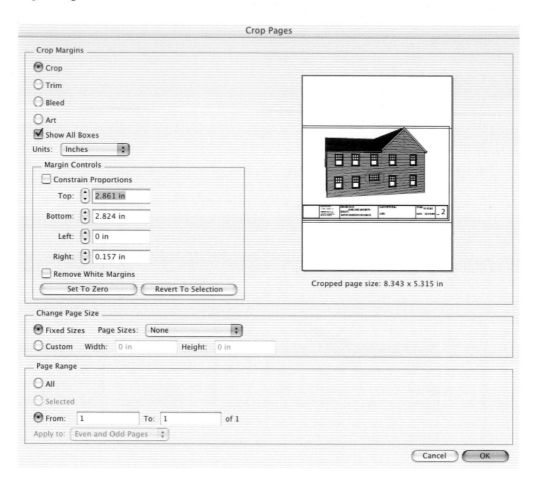

The white area surrounding the drawings is no longer displayed.

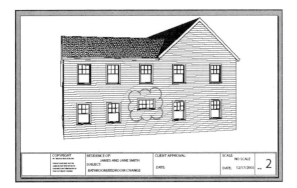

Set Initial View to show layers panel and page

Because this document contains layers that might need to be enabled or disabled, you will set the document to open with the Layers panel visible. This makes it easier for viewers to take advantage of the document layers.

1 Choose File > Document Properties.

2 Click the Initial View tab in the Document Properties window.

3 From the Show drop-down menu, at the top of the window, choose Layers Panel and Page. Keep this window open.

Set security to no changes

1 Click the Security tab along the left edge of the window.

2 From the Security Method drop-down menu, choose Password Security. The Password Security-Settings window opens.

3 From the Compatibility drop-down, choose Acrobat 7.0 and later.

The Acrobat 7.0 and later compatibility setting requires users to have either Adobe Reader 7.0 (or later) or Adobe Acrobat 7.0 (or later). It provides access to more advanced file features. If you need to have your documents accessed by users with older versions of Adobe Acrobat or Adobe Reader, you can always choose an earlier version under the Compatibility setting.

4 Choose the Encrypt all document contents option.

5 Click the Require a password to open the document checkbox, and for Document Open Password enter **engineering123**.

6 Click the checkbox for Use a password to restrict printing and editing of the document and its security settings. For Permissions Password enter **cad789**.

7 For Permissions, set the following:

• Printing Allowed: Choose Low Resolution (150dpi).

• Changes Allowed: Choose Commenting, filling in form fields, and signing existing signature fields.

8 Confirm that Enable copying of text, images, and other content is not checked.

9 Select the checkbox to select Enable text access for screen reader devices for the visually impaired.

Password Security – Settings

Compatibility: Acrobat 7.0 and later

Encryption Level: High (128–bit AES)

Select Document Components to Encrypt

⦿ Encrypt all document contents

◯ Encrypt all document contents except metadata (Acrobat 6 and later compatible)

◯ Encrypt only file attachments (Acrobat 7 and later compatible)

All contents of the document will be encrypted and search engines will not be able to access the document's metadata.

☑ Require a password to open the document

Document Open Password: ●●●●●●●●●●●●●

When set, this password is required to open the document.

Permissions

☑ Use a password to restrict printing and editing of the document and its security settings

Permissions Password: ●●●●●●

Printing Allowed: Low Resolution (150 dpi)

Changes Allowed: Commenting, filling in form fields, and signing existing signature fields

☐ Enable copying of text, images, and other content

☑ Enable text access for screen reader devices for the visually impaired

Help   Cancel   OK

10 Click OK to close the Password Security-Settings window. Confirm the passwords when requested.

Acrobat informs you that Password settings are fully supported by all Adobe products, such as the Adobe Reader, but recipients using some non-Adobe products may be able to bypass some of the Password Security settings. Click OK to close this window.

11 Close the Document Properties window then choose File > Save As. Navigate to your Lesson13 folder and enter the name **engineering_finished.pdf**. Click the Save button to save the file, then choose File > Close.

◯ *Adobe Acrobat Professional can also work with large-format documents, including ARCH, ISO, JIS, and ANSI.*

Comparing documents

Two separate cover letters have been written at different times to accompany this project. Only one of these letters is correct. You will use Acrobat to highlight the differences between the two letters, allowing you to determine which one should be used.

1 If necessary, close any open documents by choosing File > Close.

2 Choose Document > Compare Documents. The Compare Documents window opens.

3 In the Compare (older document) portion of the window, click the Choose button and navigate to the Lesson13 folder and select client_letter2.pdf. Click Open, and you are returned to the Compare Documents window.

4 In the To (newer document) portion of the window, click the Choose button and navigate to the Lesson13 folder and select client_letter1.pdf. Click Open, and you are returned to the Compare Documents window.

5 In the Type of Comparison section, choose the Textual differences radio button and in the Choose compare report type section, select Side by Side Report. Leave the other settings unchanged, and click OK.

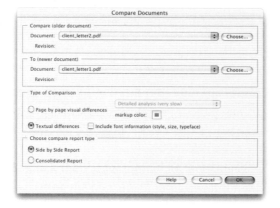

6 Acrobat opens a new document with one letter on the left side of the window, and the other letter on the right side of the window. The initial page provides an overview of the number of words that match or do not match, which provides an understanding of how substantially different the documents are.

7 Scroll down to see the actual letters presented side-by-side. Acrobat underlines words that have been added in one document, and strikes-through those words that have been removed. This provides a clear view of how the document has been changed.

8 Close the document by choosing File > Close.

Congratulations! You have finished this lesson.

Exploring on your own: Using Acrobat's technical features

1 Using the Pages panel, merge the file Client_letter1.pdf into the engineering_finished.pdf file. Because you added security to the engineering file, you will need to use the Document Properties window to remove the security settings before integrating the files.

2 Using the Distance tool and a ratio of 1 in : 8 ft., measure the distance between each of the windows on the side of the house. Annotate these measurements.

3 Using the floorplan and the Layers panel, locate all the layers displaying text, and disable these layers for viewing when the document is initially opened using the layers Properties option.

Review questions

1 Where do layers in an Adobe PDF file originate? How are they added into the file?

2 What tools exist to help navigate through large documents?

3 How is the Cloud Annotation tool useful for technical drawings and illustrations?

Review answers

1 Layers come from the authoring program, such as AutoCAD, Microsoft Visio, Adobe Illustrator, or Adobe InDesign. They are created in these programs and exported as a component of the PDF at the time the PDF file is generated. Layers are not added to a PDF file using Acrobat, but you can merge multiple layers together and edit attributes of the layers, including whether they are visible or print.

2 Acrobat Professional includes both a Loupe tool to focus on smaller portions of a document, and a Pan & Zoom window to easily change the focus of the document window. The Crop tool can be used to remove unnecessary borders around the perimeter of a document.

3 Because the Cloud Annotation tool does not use any straight lines the comments it creates are more visible on documents containing many straight lines. You can change the properties of these comments to adjust the color, thickness, opacity, and cloud style to make them even more visible in your documents.

Lesson 14

Lesson 14

14 Creating PDF Forms

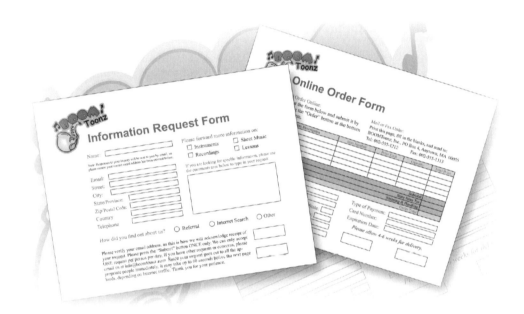

Using Adobe Acrobat 7.0 Professional, you can create dynamic PDF forms to capture and share information electronically.

In this lesson you will learn how to do the following:

- Convert paper forms to PDF and create electronic PDF forms.

- Add form fields including text, numbers, check boxes, and lists.

- Validate and calculate form data.

- Import and export form data.

If needed, remove the previous lesson folder from your hard drive, and copy the Lesson14 folder onto your hard drive.

Note: Windows 2000 users may need to unlock the lesson files before using them. For information, see "Copying the Classroom in a Book files" on page 4.

Getting started

In this lesson, you'll work on two forms for a fictitious music supply business. You'll start by taking an existing paper form and converting it to a PDF. You'll then work with an existing PDF file. This lesson uses the forms tools available within Adobe Acrobat 7.0 Professional. You can also use Adobe Designer for creating PDF forms. Lesson16 provides details on how to use Adobe Designer for creating and editing PDF forms.

1 Start Adobe Acrobat.

2 To see what the finished file looks like, navigate to the Lesson14 folder and open the file info_end.pdf.

3 When you have finished examining the completed PDF file, you can keep the file open for reference while you work on this exercise, or you can close the file by choosing File > Close.

Converting paper forms to PDF forms

With Acrobat you can create electronic forms or convert your paper forms to Adobe PDF files. You will start by opening a paper form that has already been scanned for you, and you will convert it to an Adobe PDF document. You will then add fields to the document, using Adobe Acrobat 7.0 Professional, to turn the file into an interactive form.

1 Choose File > Create PDF > From File. Navigate to the Lesson14 folder and locate the file info_start.tif.

2 Click Open.

Note: *If an alert window opens referencing the Picture Tasks button, simply click the OK button to close the window.*

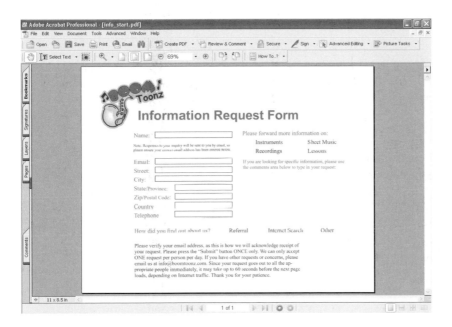

3 After the document appears, choose File > Save. Name the file info.pdf and save it in the Lesson14 folder.

4 Choose Tools > Advanced Editing > Show Advanced Editing Toolbar to access the tools
for creating an electronic form.

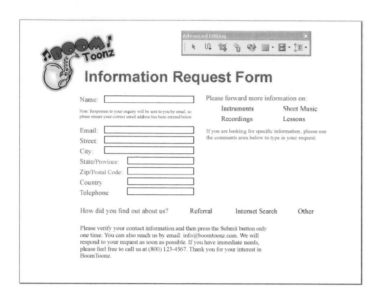

Adding text fields

Users will use text fields to enter letters and numbers that provide information, such as
their name or telephone number. Text fields are represented by boxes on the form, and are
created using the Text Field tool.

1 From the Forms toolbar, choose the Text Field tool ( ).

2 Move your cursor to the box next to the area titled Name.

3 Position the crosshair at the upper left corner of the box. Click and drag downward and to the right to trace the box. The Text Field Properties dialog box opens after you have finished drawing the region for the field.

4 Choose the General tab and set the following:

- For Name, type **Name**.

- For Tooltip, type **Enter your name here**.

Tooltips appear when the cursor is placed over a form field. They provide contextual help or information.

Leave the other settings in this tab at their default values. The Name field is used to apply names to each form field, such as Address or Phone Number. You will use this information about each form field to identify the data if it is exported. The names of form fields should be descriptive.

5 Choose the Appearance tab and for Font Size choose 10. This sets the size of the text entered into this field. Leave the other settings in this tab at their default values.

6 Choose the Options tab and for Alignment, select Center. Leave the other settings in this tab at their default values.

7 Click the Close button to close the Text Field Properties dialog box.

8 Choose the Hand tool (🖐) and click within the Name field you created. Enter your name, and note that the text appears using the attributes you applied.

Formatting multiple form fields

Now you will create the other text fields on this page, and then format them at the same time.

1 Choose the Text Field tool.

2 Using the process from the previous step, create text fields for each of the following fields. Be certain to name each field appropriately in the General tab of the Text Field Properties window:

- Email.

- Street.

- City.

- State/Province.

- ZIP Code.

- Country.

- Phone.

Note: *It is not necessary to close the Text Field Properties window after creating and naming each field.*

3 Position your cursor over the Email field and hold down the Ctrl key (Windows) or Command (Mac OS). Click to select the Email field. While continuing to hold down the Ctrl or Command key, click and select the Street, City, State/Province, ZIP Code, Country, and Telephone fields. Right-click (Windows) or Ctrl-click (Mac OS) on any of the selected fields and choose Properties to open the Text Field Properties dialog box.

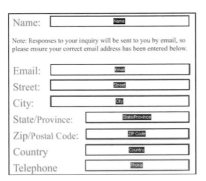

4 Choose the Appearance tab and for Font Size choose 10. This sets the size of the text as it is entered into each field. Leave the other settings in this tab at their default values. Do not close this window.

5 Choose the Options tab, and, for Alignment, select Center. Leave the other settings in this tab at their default values.

6 Click the Close button to close the Text Field Properties dialog box.

7 Choose the Hand tool () and click within the Email field you created. Enter your email address. Then enter information into the other fields by either clicking within them or using the Tab key to move from one field to another. The formatting attributes you specified are applied to the text you enter.

Adding special format restrictions

You can use special formatting to restrict the type of data that is entered into a form field, or convert information into a specific format. For example, you can set fields to accept only numbers, or conform to special formats, such as those used for ZIP codes or telephone numbers.

1 If necessary, from the Tools menu, select Advanced Editing > Show Advanced Editing Toolbar. Choose the Select Object tool (▶) from the Advanced Editing toolbar. Double-click the ZIP code field you created in the previous section.

2 Choose the Format tab and select Special from the Select format category pull-down menu. Choose Zip Code from the list of available formatting choices. This will restrict the user's entry to a five-digit numerical value. Click the Close button to close the window.

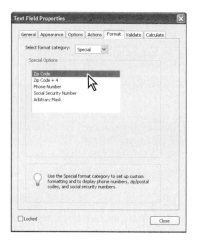

3 Double-click the Phone field you created in the previous section.

4 Choose the Format tab and select Special from the Select format category.

5 Under the Special Options header, choose Phone Number. This will restrict data being entered to a 10-digit numerical value, and will display the field as a conventional North American telephone number.

6 Click the Close button to close the window.

Adding check boxes

Check boxes are useful for responses that allow one or more selections. In this form you will use check boxes to allow users to select multiple items from a list of products.

1 From the Advanced Editing toolbar, select the Check Box tool ( ).

2 Position your cursor to the left of the word Instruments on the upper right side of the form. Click-drag downward and to the right to draw a small box that is approximately the same height as the letter I in the word Instruments. When you release the mouse button, the Check Box Properties dialog box opens.

3 Click the General tab of the Check Box Properties and set the following:

- For Name, type **Instruments**.

- For Tooltip, type **Select to receive more information**.

Leave the other settings in the General tab unchanged, do not close this dialog box.

4 Click the Options tab and for Check Box Style, choose Check. Readers will need to check this box if they wish to make the selection. To leave the check box deselected by default, leave the option for Check box is checked by default, deselected. Click the Close button.

5 If necessary, select the check box you created in the previous steps, and zoom in on the check box by using Ctrl + (Windows) or Command + (Mac OS). Choose the Select Object tool, hold down the Ctrl (Windows) key or Option (Mac OS) key and drag the checkbox downward. While dragging it, continue to press the Ctrl or Option key and also hold the Shift key to maintain the alignment of the duplicate copy. Once the duplicate copy is in place, release the mouse first and then release the keys from the keyboard.

6 Double-click the duplicated field only, and choose the General tab in the Check Box Properties window. Change the name to **Recordings**, then click the Close button.

7 Using the Select Object tool (🠔), Shift-click to select both check boxes. Hold down the Ctrl (Windows) key or Option (Mac OS) key and drag copies of these boxes to the right. You can hold down the Shift key while duplicating to align the duplicated fields with the originals. The duplicate copies should be positioned next to the words Sheet Music and Lessons.

8 Choose Edit > Deselect All and then double-click on each of the two check boxes you've copied. In the General tab of the Check Box Properties dialog box, name the duplicated check boxes **Sheet Music** and **Lessons**, respectively. Each check box must be double-clicked separately.

Creating a multi-line text field

You can establish form fields that allow for more than one line of text to be entered. To accomplish this, you will create a larger text field and adjust the properties of the field to allow for additional lines of text to be entered.

1 Choose the Text Field tool (⬜). Click and drag a text field that fills all the available space under the sentence that begins "If you are looking for specific information… ." The Text Field Properties window opens after you create the text field. Keep this window open.

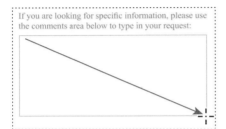

2 Click the General tab of the Text Field Properties dialog box. For Name, enter **Specifics** and for Tooltip, enter **Place your special requests here**. Do not change the other settings within the General tab, and keep the Text Field Properties window open.

3 Choose the Appearance tab and set the following:

- For Border Color, click on the swatch to the right and choose Black.
- For Fill Color, click on the swatch to the right and choose White.
- From the Line Thickness drop-down menu, choose Thin.
- From the Line Style drop-down menu, choose Solid.
- Set Font Size to Auto.

Leave the other settings in this tab at their default values, and do not close the window.

The Auto setting for Font Size allows Acrobat to increase or decrease the size of text as it is entered into a field. With this option, Acrobat changes the font size based upon the amount of space available within the field. If you prefer to use a specific size rather than a variable font size, you can also enter a specific size for the text.

4 Choose the Options tab and for Alignment, choose Left, then click the Multi-line checkbox. This allows the text to expand beyond one line as it is entered. Leave the other settings in this tab at their default values.

5 Click the Close button to close the Text Field Properties window.

Adding radio buttons

Next you will add radio buttons to allow users to indicate how they learned about the company.

1 From the Advanced Editing toolbar, select the Radio Button Tool (◉).

2 Position your cursor to the left of the word Referral. Click and drag downward and to the right to create a small radio button. The radio button should be approximately the same height as the letter R in the word Referral. The Radio Button Properties window opens after you finish drawing the button.

3 Choose the General tab of the Radio Button Properties dialog box, and for Name, enter **Learned About Us From** and for Tooltip, enter **Tell us how you learned about BoomToonz**. Leave the other settings in this tab unchanged, and keep the Radio Button Properties window open.

4 Choose the Appearance tab and set the following:

- For Border Color, click on the swatch to the right and choose Black.

- For Fill Color, click on the swatch to the right and choose White.

- From the Line Thickness drop-down menu, choose Thin.

- From the Line Style drop-down menu, choose Inset.

Leave the other settings unchanged, and keep the window open.

5 Choose the Options tab and for Button Style, choose Circle. For Export Value, type **Referral**. Leave the other settings unchanged, and click the Close button to close the window.

6 Using the Radio Button tool (⊙), select the radio button you created in the previous steps. Hold down Ctrl (Windows) or Option (Mac OS), and drag the button to the right. While continuing to hold down the Ctrl or Option key, also press the Shift key while dragging the field to the right. Place the copy of the radio button to the left of the words Internet Search.

💡 *Using the Shift key along with either the Ctrl (Windows) or Option (Mac OS) you can duplicate form fields and have the duplicated fields remain in alignment with the original fields. The Shift key constrains movement to keep the copy positioned on the same vertical or horizontal path as the original.*

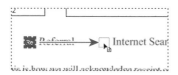

Note: *It may be helpful to increase the magnification of the radio button before duplicating. Use either the Zoom In tool or Ctrl + (Windows) or Command + (Mac OS).*

7 Repeating the process in step 6, duplicate the original radio button and place the duplicated button adjacent to the word "Other."

8 Continuing to use the radio button tool, right-click (Windows) or Ctrl-click (Mac OS) on the radio button adjacent to the words "Internet Search." Choose Properties from the contextual menu and the Radio Button Properties window opens. Choose the Options tab and for Export Value, type **Internet Search**. Leave the other settings unchanged, and click the Close button to close the window.

9 Repeating the process in step 8, right-click (Windows) or Ctrl-click (Mac OS) on the radio button adjacent to the word "Other," and choose Properties. In the Radio Button Properties window, choose the Options tab and for Export Value, type **Other**. Leave the other settings unchanged, and click the Close button to close the window.

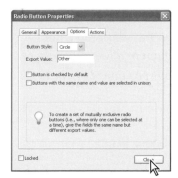

$\bigcirc$ *If you want to give users the choice of selecting multiple options all at once, you can use check boxes instead of radio buttons. Radio buttons allow for only one choice.*

Adding print and reset buttons

With Adobe Acrobat 7 Professional you can create buttons that enhance the functionality of PDF forms. Here you will create two buttons that can be used to clear the data from the form fields and print the form.

1 From the Forms Toolbar, select the Button tool (■).

2 Move your cursor to the blank area below the radio button "Other." Click and drag downward and to the right to draw a box that covers the top half of the empty space. The Button Properties window opens when you release the mouse. Keep this window open.

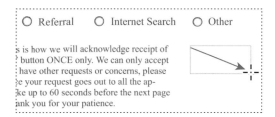

3 Choose the General tab and for Name, enter **Print**. For Tooltip enter **Click to print** form. Leave the other settings in this tab at their default values, and keep the window open.

4 Choose the Appearance tab of the Button Properties dialog box:

• Click on the swatch to the right of Border Color and choose a light red color.

• Click on the swatch to the right of Fill Color and choose a dark red color.

• From the Line Thickness drop-down menu, choose Medium.

• From the Line Style drop-down menu, choose Beveled.

• From the Font Size drop-down menu, choose 14.

• Click on the swatch to the right of Text Color and choose White.

• In the Font drop-down menu, choose Helvetica Bold.

Leave the other settings in this tab unchanged, and keep the window open.

5 Click the Options tab and set the following:

• For Layout, choose Label only.

• For Behavior, choose Invert.

• For Label, enter **Print.**

Leave the other settings in this tab unchanged, and keep the window open.

6 Choose the Actions tab and for Select Trigger, choose Mouse Up. For Select Action, choose Execute a Menu Item, then click Add. The Menu Item Selection window appears.

7 In the Menu Item Selection window, choose File > Print. Click OK to accept this action and close the Menu Item Selection window (Windows) or choose File > Print then click OK (Mac OS).

8 Click the Close button to close the Button Properties window.

Creating a reset button

1 If necessary, choose the Button tool (■) from the Forms Toolbar.

You can use the Grid to help you align buttons and form fields. Choose View > Grid to make the grid visible or to hide it. You can set the size of the grid by choosing Edit > Preferences > Units & Guides.

2 Position the cursor under the Print button created previously. You will create a similarly sized button by positioning the cursor below the lower left corner of the Print button. Click and drag down and to the right, creating a box that is approximately the same size as the Print button. When you release the mouse, the Button Properties window opens.

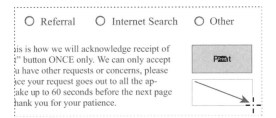

3 In the General tab, locate the Name field and enter **Clear**, then enter **Click to reset form** in the Tooltip field. Leave the other settings in the General tab unchanged, and do not close the window.

4 Choose the Appearance tab of the Button Properties dialog box:

- Click on the swatch to the right of Border Color and choose a light red color.

- Click on the swatch to the right of Fill Color and choose a dark red color.

- From the Line Thickness drop-down menu, choose Medium.

- From the Line Style drop-down menu, choose Beveled.

- From the Font Size drop-down menu, choose 14.

- Click on the swatch to the right of Text Color and choose White.

- In the Font drop-down menu, choose Helvetica Bold.

5 Select the Options tab and make the following selections:

- From the Layout drop-down menu, choose Label only.

- From the Behavior drop-down menu, choose Invert.

- In the Label textbox, type **Clear**.

Leave the other settings in the Options tab unchanged, and leave the window open.

6 Click the Actions tab and choose Mouse Up from the Select Trigger drop-down menu. Choose Reset a Form from the Select Action choices, and click the Add button. The Reset a Form window opens.

7 In the Reset a Form window, confirm that all the fields are selected. If necessary, click Select All to choose all the fields that will be reset. Click OK to close this window, then click Close to close the Button Properties window.

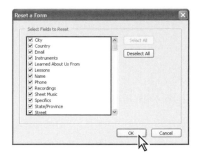

8 From the Toolbar, select the Hand tool ( ).

9 Enter the requested information into each of the form fields that you have not yet completed. You will use this information in the next section, so keep the form open after you have filled in the fields, check boxes and radio buttons.

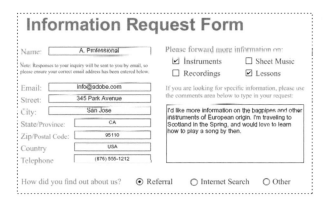

Exporting form data

Adobe Acrobat 7 Professional can be used to extract data from PDF forms. Because the form data that is entered is independent of the form itself, the form data can be submitted into a database or extracted and saved as a separate file. You will extract the form data from the information request form, and then transfer the information into an electronic order form.

1 Choose Advanced > Forms > Export Data from Form...

2 In the Export Form Data As dialog box, navigate to your Lesson14 folder.

3 Confirm that the Save as Type is set to Acrobat XFDF files (*.xfdf), enter **information** as the file name, then click Save. XFDF is an open format that Adobe has developed for storing forms data. The information is extracted from the PDF and saved in the location you specify. Later in this lesson, we will import the form data into another PDF form that you will create.

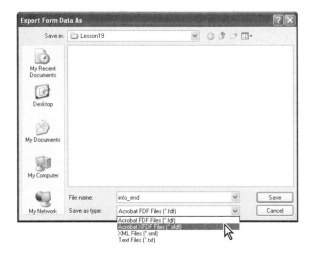

The process of extracting the data can be more automated and transparent to the user of the form. We discuss submitting forms data later in this lesson.

4 Choose File > Save to save the file. Choose File > Close.

Creating an electronic order form

By adding form fields to existing PDF documents you make them interactive and allow for data capture. Here you will use a form that was created using Adobe InDesign CS— but it could have been created using any other software package—and then converted to PDF. You'll be adding interactivity and the ability to capture the form data using Acrobat 7.0 Professional.

1 Choose File > Open and navigate to the Lesson14 folder. Choose the file order_start.pdf.

2 To see what the finished file looks like, navigate to the Lesson14 folder and select the file order_end.pdf, then click Open.

3 When you have finished examining the completed file, you can keep the file open for reference while you work or you can close the file by choosing File > Close.

4 If necessary, choose Tools > Advanced Editing > Show Forms Toolbar to access the Forms Toolbar and its tools for creating electronic forms.

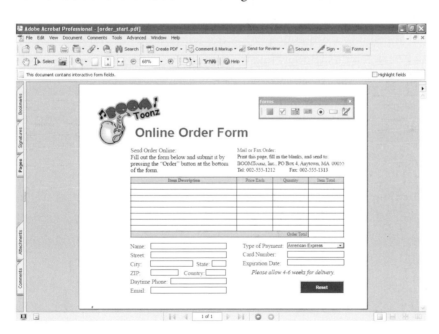

Adding combo boxes

Use combo boxes to create pull-down menus from which users can select a response or choose a specific item. Here you will create a list of musical instruments that can be purchased from BoomToonz.

1 From the Advanced Editing Toolbar, select the Combo Box tool (⊞).

2 Move your cursor to the first column under the heading Item Description.

3 Position the cursor approximately one-third of the way across the first empty cell in this column. Click and drag down and to the right, creating a box that covers the middle one-third of the cell. The Combo Box Properties window opens after you have completed drawing the box. Keep this window open.

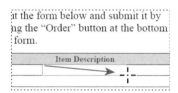

4 Choose the General tab. For Name, enter **Item** and for Tooltip, enter **Choose first item**. Leave the other settings unchanged and keep the window open.

5 Choose the Appearance tab. For Font Size, select 10 and leave the other settings in this tab unchanged. Keep this window open.

6 Choose the Options tab. In the Item textbox, enter **Make Selection**, and then click the Add button.

7 Return to the Item textbox and enter **bagpipes**, then click the Add button. Repeat this procedure, adding the following items:

- **drums**

- **guitar**

- **saxophone**

- **trombone**

- **tuba**

Confirm that Make Selection remains highlighted, as the highlighted text is used as the default selection. Leave the other settings in this tab unchanged.

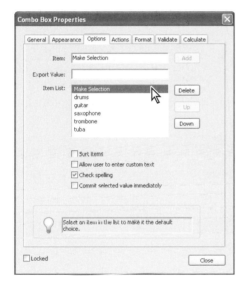

8 Click Close to close the Combo Box Properties dialog box.

Duplicating fields

1 If necessary, select the combo box you created in the previous section using either the Combo Box tool (▤) or the Select Object tool (▶).

2 Right-click (Window) or Ctrl-click (Mac OS) the combo box and choose Create Multiple Copies. The Create Multiple Copies of Fields window appears.

3 For Copy selected fields down, enter **8**. For Copy selected fields across, enter **1**. If necessary, click the Preview checkbox to view the duplicate fields.

💡 *You can use the Overall Size (All Fields) to adjust the amount of space between each field affected by the duplication. Additionally, use the Overall Position (All Fields) to move the field being duplicated and all the copies. If all the fields are either too high or too low within each cell, click the Down or Up button to move the fields on the page. Click the OK button to close the window.*

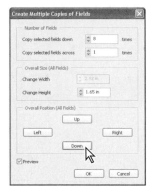

4 Double-click the original form field that was duplicated, and click the General tab. Note that Adobe Acrobat added a period and number following the form field name. When fields are duplicated using this method, Acrobat automatically renames each field so that it is unique by adding a consecutive number at the end of each form field name. Because of this, it is not necessary to rename each of the duplicate fields—this time-consuming work has been done for you.

5 Click Close to close the Combo Box Properties Box.

💡 *After duplicating form fields, the individual fields can be moved using the Select Object tool (▶).*

Validating text/numeric fields

To ensure that correct information is entered into form fields, use Acrobat's field validation feature. For example, if a response needs to be a number with a value between 10 and 20, you can restrict entries to numbers within this range. Here you will limit the price of instruments to no more than $1,000.

1 From the Forms toolbar, select the Text Field tool (▭).

2 In the Order Form table, move your cursor to the second column from the left, with the heading of Price Each. Position the crosshairs at the upper left corner of the first empty cell at the top of this column. Click and drag downward and to the right to create a field that completely fills the cell. The Text Field Properties window opens after drawing the field.

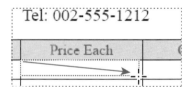

3 Click the General tab of the Text Field Properties window. For Name, enter **Price** and for Tooltip, enter **Price per item**. Leave the other settings in this tab unchanged, and keep the window open.

4 Click the Appearance tab and for Font Size, choose 10. Leave the other settings in this tab unchanged, and keep the window open.

5 Click the Options tab and for Alignment, choose Center. Leave the other settings in this tab unchanged, and keep the window open.

6 Click the Format tab and set the following:

- For Select format category, choose Number.

- For Decimal Places, choose 2.

- For Separator Style, choose 1,234.56 (the default).

- For Currency Symbol, choose Dollar ($).

Leave the other settings unchanged, and keep the window open.

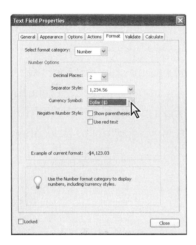

7 Click the Validate tab, then choose the radio button to select Field value is in range. In the range fields, enter a value of **0** into the From field and **1000** for the To field.

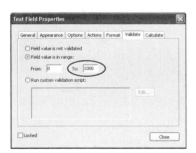

8 Click the Close button to close the Text Field Properties window.

9 Right-click (Windows) or Ctrl-click (Mac OS) the text field price you have just created, and then choose Create Multiple Copies from the contextual menu. The Create Multiple Copies of Fields window opens.

10 In the Create Multiple Copies of Fields window, choose the following:

- For Copy selected fields down, enter **8**.

- For Copy selected fields across, enter **1**.

Leave the other settings in this dialog box unchanged, and click OK.

More numeric fields

Formatting is another method for ensuring that data entered into form fields is appropriate. By specifying a field's contents as a number, you can prevent users from entering letters or any other characters.

1 If necessary, select the Text Field tool.

2 Move the cursor to the third column, with the heading Quantity.

3 Select all the fields in this column by Ctrl-clicking (Windows) or Command-clicking (Mac OS) each one of them. Right-click (Windows) or Ctrl-click (Mac OS) on any of the selected fields, and choose the Properties command from the contextual menu. The Text Field Properties window opens.

Be careful not to click or drag while holding down the Ctrl key (Windows). Ctrl-clicking is used to select multiple fields. Ctrl-clicking and dragging will duplicate a field.

4 Click the Appearance tab and for Font Size, choose 10. Leave the other settings in this tab unchanged, and keep the window open.

5 Click the Options tab and for Alignment, choose Center. Leave the other settings in this tab unchanged, and click the Close button to close the window.

6 Select the Quantity.0 field. Right-click (Windows) or Ctrl-click (Mac OS) and choose Properties. The Text Field Properties window opens. Click the Format tab and set the following:

- For Select format category, choose Number.

- For Decimal Places, choose 0.

- For Separator Style, choose 1,234.56 (the default).

- For Currency Symbol, choose None.

Leave the other settings in this tab unchanged, and click the Close button to close the window. The other Quantity fields have already been formatted for you.

Calculating numeric fields

In addition to verifying and formatting form data, Acrobat can be used to calculate values used in form fields. For your PDF order form, you will calculate the cost for each item, based on the quantity that has been ordered. You will then have Acrobat calculate the total cost of all items that have been ordered.

1 If necessary, select the Text Field Tool.

2 Move your cursor over the top field in the Item Total column, labeled Total.0.

3 Right-click (Windows) or Ctrl-click (Mac OS) and choose Properties. The Text Field Properties window opens.

4 Click the Calculate tab and set the following:

• Select the Value is the radio button, which is the second from the top.

• Choose product (x) of the following fields:

• Press the Pick button. The Field Selection window displays a listing of fields that can be used in the calculation. In the Field Selection window, check the boxes to the left of Price.0 and Quantity.0. Click the OK button to close the Field Selection window and the Close button to close the Text Field Properties window.

5 Right-click (Windows) or Ctrl-click (Mac OS) the Total 1 field. Choose Properties from the context menu.

6 Repeat step 4 to establish the calculation for this field, changing the fields selected in the Field Selection window to Price.1 and Quantity.1.

7 Repeat the process described in steps 5 and 6 to format the remaining Total fields so that they include the appropriate calculation. Each Total field should include a calculation that is the product of the Price and Quantity in its row.

Do not format the last field in the Item Total column, Order Total, as it will perform a different calculation.

8 Right click the Order Total field and choose Properties. Click the Calculate tab. You will establish a calculation that adds the totals on each line to create the entire cost of the order. In the Calculate tab, set the following:

• Select the Value is the radio button, which is the second from the top.

• Choose sum (+) of the following fields:

• Press the Pick button. The Field Selection window displays a listing of fields that can be used in the calculation. In the Field Selection window, check the boxes to the left of all the Total fields. After selecting the fields, click the OK button to close the Field Selection window and the Close button to close the Text Field Properties window.

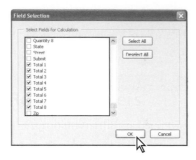

When selecting all the fields that use the same prefix for a calculation, you can choose the base name in the Field Selection window, rather then choosing each individual field name. For this exercise you could have selected the Total option in the Field Selection window.

Formatting a date field

1 With the Text Field tool, right-click (Windows) or Ctrl-click (Mac OS) on the Expiration Date field and choose Properties from the context menu. The Text Field Properties window opens.

2 Click the Format tab.

3 Choose Date, from the Select format category drop-down list.

4 Choose mm/yy from the list of date formatting options.

5 Click the Close button to close the Text Field Properties window.

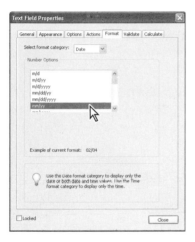

Adding a submit button

As you discovered in the Information Request Form you created earlier in this chapter, buttons can add functionality to electronic forms, making it easy to print or reset a form. Here you will explore creating a submit button.

Because every organization has different needs and security concerns relating to electronic data, Acrobat supports a variety of methods for extracting data from PDF forms and routing it electronically. In our example, we will create a button that will submit data to a fictitious URL. Because we are not actually submitting the data to an online server, the data will not leave your computer.

Submitting Form Data

If you have a server that is capable of receiving data from electronic forms, such as those posted on the Internet, you can use PDF forms to submit data to your own server. For example, you can use Perl, CGI, ASP, or JSP scripts to route form data created from PDF files. The routed form data can be sent via email or entered automatically into a database.

1 From the Advanced Editing Toolbar, choose the Select Object tool (↖). Move the cursor over the Reset button.

2 Ctrl-click and drag (Windows) or Option-click and drag (Mac OS) the Reset button, dragging the duplicate button directly to the left. When the left edge of the duplicate button is aligned with the word Expiration, release the mouse, and then release the Ctrl or Option key,

💡 *While dragging the copy of the button, you can hold down the Shift key to keep the copy of the button aligned with the original.*

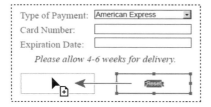

3 Position the cursor over the duplicated button and Right-click (Windows) or Ctrl-click (Mac OS) and select Properties from the contextual menu. Be certain to select the copy and not the original when choosing Properties. The Button Properties window opens.

4 Click the General tab of the Button Properties window. For Name, enter **Submit** and for Tooltip, enter **Click to submit form**. Leave the other settings unchanged, and keep the window open.

5 Click the Options tab and set the following:

- For Layout, choose Label only.

- For Behavior, choose Invert.

- For Label, type **Submit.**

Leave the other settings unchanged, and keep the window open.

6 Click the Actions tab and set the following:

- For Select Trigger, choose Mouse Up.

- For Select Action, choose Submit a Form.

Click the Add button, the Submit Form Selection window appears.

7 In the Submit Form Selections window, leave the URL empty.

This is the location where you would enter the Internet address of any script or server that would receive and route your form data. Because we are only simulating the submission of forms data, we will leave this blank.

8 In the Export Format portion of the window, choose HTML.

About Acrobat form data

Acrobat can submit data from PDF forms in a variety of formats:

• FDF exports as an FDF file. You can choose to export the form fields data, comments, incremental changes to the PDF, or all three. The Incremental Changes to the PDF option is useful for exporting a digital signature in a way that is easily read and reconstructed by a server.

Note: *If the server returns data to the user in FDF, or XFDF formats, the server's URL must end with the #FDF suffix, for example, http://myserver/cgi-bin/myscript#FDF.*

• HTML exports as an HTML file.

• XFDF exports as an XML file. You can choose to export the form fields data, comments, or both.

• PDF exports the entire PDF file that is your form. Although this creates a larger file than the FDF option, it is useful for preserving digital signatures.

—From the Complete Acrobat 7.0 Help.

9 In the Field Selection portion of the window, choose specific fields you want to submit if you only want a portion of the form submitted. As an alternative, choose All Fields to submit all the fields from the form. Also, choose whether you want dates converted to a standard format.

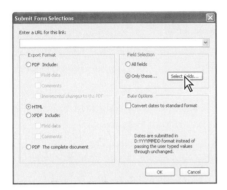

10 Click OK to close the Submit Form Selections window. Do not close the Button Properties window.

11 In the Actions panel of the Button Properties window, click on Submit a form, then press the Up button. This causes that action to occur first.

Buttons may contain multiple actions. The sequence in which they occur is decided by their order in the Actions portion of the Buttons Properties window.

12 Click the Close button to close the Button Properties window.

When you test the Submit button, you will receive an alert message from Acrobat because you have not specified an actual location where the form data can be sent. If you have a database administrator, an information technology professional or an Internet Service Provider that hosts your web server, they can establish an address where you can submit your forms data for testing purposes.

Exporting form data to a spreadsheet

If you've received PDF form data from multiple sources, you can use Acrobat to easily convert the data into a spreadsheet for use in programs such as Microsoft Excel. Acrobat 7.0 Professional makes it easy to organize form data into a comma-delimited spreadsheet file (.csv). To convert form data into a .csv format, use the following procedure:

1. Choose File > Form Data > Create Spreadsheet From Data Files.

2. Click on the Add Files button and select one or more files with the extension .fdf, .pdf, .xfdf, or .xml. Click Select to add them to the Files To Export Data From list. If necessary, files can be removed from the list by selecting the file and clicking on the Remove Files button.

3. If you've previously added form data to the Data Files list, select Include Most Recent List of Files To Export Data From to automatically include it.

4. When you're finished adding files, click on the Export button.

The Select Folder To Save Comma Separated File window opens.

5. Choose a location to save the file, then click Save. The Export Progress dialog opens, displaying Done! when Acrobat is finished building the spreadsheet.

6. To open the new spreadsheet file, click the View File Now button, or click Close Dialog to end the process.

Importing form data

Just as data can be submitted and extracted from PDF files, it can also be imported. You will import the form data from the Information Request form that you completed earlier in the lesson.

1 Select the Hand tool (🖐).

2 Choose Advanced > Forms > Import Data to Form... The Select File Containing Form Data window opens.

3 Navigate to the Lesson14 folder and choose information.xfdf. This is the file you exported earlier in this lesson.

4 Click the Select button.

5 The fields in the order form that share the same name as those in the information request form are automatically populated with the form data that you imported.

Fields must share the same name, including capitalization, to input correctly.

Using automatically calculated form fields

To complete the testing of the order form, you will select several items, and then enter their price and quantity.

1 If necessary, select the Hand tool (🖐).

2 In the first row of the order form, choose drums from the Item Description column. Enter a price of **10** and a quantity of **2**. Press the Enter or Return key on your keyboard.

Acrobat automatically calculates the total price for these items based upon the quantity and the cost per item that you specified. The calculation occurred immediately after your cursor left the field. Whether you click in another field, use the Enter or Return key or use the Tab key, Acrobat completes the calculation when you finish entering the data necessary for the calculation.

Item Description		Price Each	Quantity	Item Total
drums	▼	$10.00	2	$20.00
Make Selection	▼			$0.00
Make Selection	▼			$0.00

3 In the second row of the order form, choose Guitar from the Item Description column. Enter a price of 20 and a quantity of 1. Press the Return or Enter key on your keyboard.

Note the Order total at the bottom of the form now reflects the total cost of these two lines of the order. As items are added to the order, the total will continue to update and reflect any changes to the order.

Item Description		Price Each	Quantity	Item Total
drums	▾	$10.00	2	$20.00
guitar	▾	$20.00	1	$20.00
Make Selection	▾			$0.00
Make Selection	▾			$0.00
Make Selection	▾			$0.00
Make Selection	▾			$0.00
Make Selection	▾			$0.00
Make Selection	▾			$0.00
			Order Total	$40.00

4 Choose File > Save As and save your file as **order.pdf** in the Lesson14 folder.

Congratulations! You have completed the lesson.

Exploring on your own: Enhancing PDF forms

Open the Information Request Form you completed in the first part of this lesson, and enable the Grid by choosing View > Grid. If necessary, choose Edit > Preferences and choose Units and Guides to change the Grid increments and use the grid to align the left and right sides of the form.

Open the Online Order Form you just created. Using the Select Object tool, Ctrl-click (Windows) or Command-click (Mac OS) to select the fields Name, Street, City, and ZIP. Right-click (Windows) or Ctrl-click (Mac OS) and from the contextual menu that appears, choose Align > Left.

Click on the Pages tab to access the Pages panel of the Order form, and right-click (Windows) or Ctrl-click (Mac OS) on the page thumbnail for the first page. Choose Page Properties from the contextual menu. In the Page Properties window, click the Tab Order tab and choose Use Row Order to have the form tab move naturally from left to right.

Review questions

1 Why would you use Adobe PDF forms?

2 What options exist for presenting users with several choices from which they can choose when completing a form?

3 Can you separate form data from the PDF itself?

Review answers

1 With Adobe PDF forms you can maintain the look and feel of existing paper forms. Users making the transition from paper to electronic forms will maintain familiarity with the appearance of the forms. Because PDF forms can be viewed and filled out using the free Adobe Reader, they are the perfect option for placing forms on line.

2 Acrobat provides several options for presenting various choices. Combo boxes provide a drop-down list of choices, from which a user can select one. Radio buttons are used when there are several options, but only one can be selected. For options that allow several choices, use check boxes or list boxes, as these allow for more than one choice. For more information, see "Elements of an Adobe Acrobat PDF Form" in the Complete Acrobat 7.0 Help.

3 Form data can be extracted manually and saved using the Advanced > Forms > Export Data from Form... command. Using a Submit action, which can be attached to a button, the data can be routed to a script that will send the form information into a database or direct it to an email address.

15 | Using Adobe Acrobat for Professional Publishing

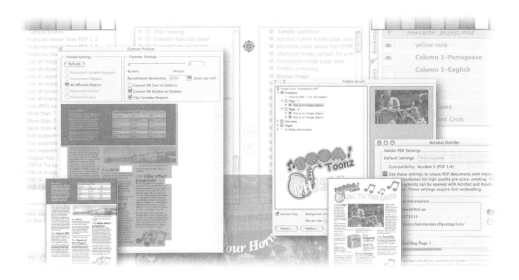

Use Adobe Acrobat Professional 7.0 to create high-quality PDF files. Acrobat's specialized prepress tools allow you to check color separations, preflight PDF files to check for quality concerns before printing, adjust how transparent objects are imaged, and color-separate PDF files.

In this lesson you will learn how to do the following:

- Create Adobe PDF files suitable for high resolution printing.
- Preflight Adobe PDF files to check for quality and consistency.
- Use layers from Adobe Illustrator and Adobe InDesign.
- Check how transparent objects impact a page.
- Use Acrobat to generate color separations.

If needed, remove the previous lesson folder from your hard drive, and copy the Lesson15 folder onto your hard drive.

Note: Windows 2000 users may need to unlock the lesson files before using them. For information, see "Copying the Classroom in a Book files" on page 4.

Getting started

In this lesson, you'll convert an Adobe PostScript file to a high-quality PDF file using Adobe Acrobat Distiller 7.0. You will then check the file using Acrobat's preflight tools, and view its color separations. You will also work with a file that contains transparency and layers, and generate a color separated proof.

1 Start Adobe Acrobat Professional 7.0.

2 To see what the finished file looks like, open the file newsletter_end.pdf located in the Lesson15 folder. This two-page PDF file is a full-color brochure that will be delivered to a printer, where it will be color separated to either a film imagesetter or a computer-to-plate device.

3 When you have finished examining the completed PDF file, you can keep this file open for reference while you work on this exercise, or you can close the file by choosing File > Close.

About Adobe PostScript Files

Adobe PostScript is a page description language that is used by software applications to provide imaging instructions to output devices, such as laser printers, ink jet printers, high resolution imagesetters, and platesetters. These imaging devices use the PostScript information to determine how text and graphics are plotted onto a page.

Instead of sending the PostScript imaging information directly to an output device, you can have it saved on your computer's hard drive. These files are sometimes called print-to-disk files, or .prn, because the printing information is stored on the hard disk instead of being sent to a printer. Adobe PostScript files are a special type of print-to-disk file, because they contain high quality imaging information. PostScript files are typically designated by a .ps file extension on the end of their name.

To create a PostScript file

1. Choose File > Print.

2. In the print window, select a PostScript print driver, such as the Adobe PDF printer.

You can also use other PostScript print drivers to create PostScript files. You can obtain the latest Adobe PostScript print driver for both Windows and Macintosh computers at the downloads section of Adobe.com.

3. Choose the Print to file check box (Windows) or select Save as File check box in the Output Options section and choose PostScript as the format (Mac OS).

4. Click OK (Windows) or Save (Mac OS), name the file and specify the location where it should be saved.

Creating PDF files for print & prepress

You will start by converting an Adobe PostScript file to PDF using Acrobat Distiller 7.0. Acrobat Distiller converts PostScript files and EPS files to PDF. The quality and size of the PDF file are determined by the settings that you specify.

1 Choose Advanced > Acrobat Distiller. Acrobat Distiller starts, and a window opens.

2 From the Default Settings drop-down, choose Press Quality. This establishes the kind of PDF file that will be created.

3 In the Acrobat Distiller window, choose File > Open. Navigate to the Lesson15 folder and choose newsletter.ps.

4 Click Open. The PostScript file is processed by Acrobat Distiller and is converted into an Adobe PDF file.

Acrobat Distiller creates a new file called newsletter.pdf. You will use this file you have created in the next exercise.

5 From the Acrobat Distiller window, choose File > Exit.

There are several PDF settings that can be used to create PDF files generally suitable for high resolution printing and publishing.

- **High Quality Print** *creates PDF files that have higher resolution than the Standard job option file. It downsamples color and grayscale images to 300 ppi and monochrome images to 1200 ppi, prints to a higher image resolution, and preserves the maximum amount of information about the original document. PDF files created with this settings file can be opened in Acrobat 5.0 and Acrobat Reader 5.0 and later.*

- **PDF/A:Draft** *checks incoming PostScript files for compliance to the proposed ISO standard for long-term preservation (archival) of electronic documents. These files are primarily used for archiving. PDF/A-compliant files can contain only text, raster images, and vector objects; they cannot contain encryption and scripts. In addition, all fonts must be embedded so the documents can be opened and viewed as created. PDF files created with this settings file can be opened in Acrobat 5.0 and Acrobat Reader 5.0 and later.*

- **PDF/X-1a:2001** *checks incoming PostScript files for PDF/X-1a:2001 compliance and only creates a file that is PDF/X-1a compliant. If the file fails compliance checks, Distiller creates a PDF/X.log file that describes the errors in the document. PDF/X-1a is an ISO standard for graphic content exchange. PDF/X-1a:2001 requires all fonts to be embedded, the appropriate PDF bounding boxes to be specified, and color to appear as CMYK, spot colors, or both. PDF/X-compliant files must contain information describing the printing condition for which they are prepared. For the PDF/X-1a:2001 settings file, the default output intent profile name is U.S. Web Coated (SWOP). PDF files created with this settings file can be opened in Acrobat 4.0 and Acrobat Reader 4.0 and later.*

- **PDF/X-1a:2003** *checks incoming PostScript files for PDF/X-1a:2003 compliance and only creates a file that is PDF/X-1a:2003 compliant. If the file fails compliance checks, Distiller creates a PDF/X.log file that describes the errors in the document. PDF/X-1a_2003 is an ISO standard for graphic content exchange. PDF/X-1a requires all fonts to be embedded, the appropriate PDF bounding boxes to be specified, and color to appear as either CMYK, spot colors, or both. PDF/X-compliant files must contain information describing the printing condition for which they are prepared. For the PDF/X-1a:2003 settings file, the default output intent profile name is U.S. Web Coated (SWOP). PDF files created with this settings file can be opened in Acrobat 5.0 and Acrobat Reader 5.0 and later.*

- **PDF/X-3:2003** *checks incoming PostScript files for PDF/X-3:2003 compliance and only creates a file that is PDF/X-3:2003 compliant. If the file fails compliance checks, Distiller creates a PDF/X.log file that describes the errors in the document. Like PDF/X-1a, PDF/X-3 is an ISO standard for graphic content exchange. The main difference is that PDF/X-3 allows the use of color management and device-independent color in addition to CMYK and spot colors. For the PDF/X-1a:2003 settings file, the default output intent profile name is Euroscale Coated v2. PDF files created with this settings file can be opened in Acrobat 5.0 and later.*

Note: For both PDF/X-1a and PDF/X-3, you can modify only those export options that conform to the selected standard. For example, for PDF/X-1a:2001, the Color option is unavailable. For PDF/X-1a:2003 and PDF/X-3:2003, the Compatibility setting in the General panel is Acrobat 5.0 (PDF 1.4). Any change to the Compatibility setting changes the Compliance Standard setting to None.

• *Press Quality creates PDF files for high-quality print production (for example, for digital printing or for separations to an imagesetter or platesetter), but does not create files that are PDF/X-compliant. In this case, the quality of the content is the highest consideration. The objective is to maintain all the information in a PDF file that a commercial printer or prepress service provider needs in order to print the document correctly. This set of options downsamples color and grayscale images to 300 ppi and monochrome images to 1200 ppi, embeds subsets of fonts used in the document (if allowed), and prints a higher image resolution than the Standard settings. Print jobs with fonts that cannot be embedded will fail. These PDF files can be opened in Acrobat 5.0 and Acrobat Reader 5.0 and later.*

Note: Before creating an Adobe PDF file to send to a commercial printer or prepress service provider, find out what the output resolution and other settings should be, or ask for a .joboptions file with the recommended settings. You may need to customize the Adobe PDF settings for a particular provider and then provide a .joboptions file of your own.

• *Smallest File Size creates PDF files for displaying on the Web or an intranet, or for distribution through an email system for on-screen viewing. This set of options uses compression, downsampling, and a relatively low image resolution. It converts all colors to sRGB, and does not embed fonts unless absolutely necessary. It also optimizes files for byte serving. These PDF files can be opened in Acrobat 5.0 and Acrobat Reader 5.0 and later.*

• *Standard creates PDF files to be printed to desktop printers or digital copiers, published on a CD, or sent to a client as a publishing proof. This set of options uses compression and downsampling to keep the file size down, but also embeds subsets of all (allowed) fonts used in the file, converts all colors to sRGB, and prints to a medium resolution. Note that Windows font subsets are not embedded by default. PDF files created with this settings file can be opened in Acrobat 5.0 and Acrobat Reader 5.0 and later.*

—From the Complete Acrobat 7.0 Help

Preflighting

Preflighting a document checks the file's content against a set of standards to determine whether the file is suitable for print publishing. Preflighting does not correct documents, but it does alert you to concerns such as fonts that are not embedded in a PDF document, colors that may not print correctly, or other objects that may not print as intended.

1 Open Adobe Acrobat Professional.

2 Choose File > Open and navigate to the Lesson15 folder. Choose newsletter.pdf and click Open.

Note: A completed file newletter_end.pdf has been provided for you to use if you did not have access to Acrobat Distiller to complete the previous exercise. If necessary, use this file instead. Be certain to use either newsletter.pdf or newsletter_end.pdf for this exercise.

3 Choose Advanced > Preflight. The Preflight: Profiles window opens.

Preflight analyzes the contents of a PDF and compares the results against a set of values that are defined within a profile. Acrobat reports any items within the document that are examined as a part of the profile.

4 Select the PostScript 3 support required profile and then click Execute.

5 In the Preflight window, review the information presented.

Acrobat confirms that this file should print successfully on a PostScript® 3™ output device—the most current version of PostScript used by a variety of printers and plotters.

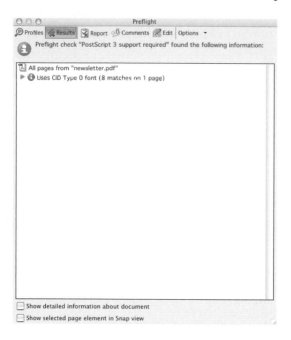

6 Select the Profiles tab of the Preflight window. Select the List all images profile and then click Execute.

Examining the quality of the images used in a PDF file helps identify possible quality concerns before the file is printed. Acrobat's Preflight capability can also be used to examine the resolution of graphics used in a PDF. In the Preflight window, a list of all images in the file can be displayed.

7 If necessary, click the plus sign (+) (Windows) or the triangle (▶) (Mac OS) immediately to the left of the info icon to expand the page contents. This displays a list of all graphics found in the pdf file and the resolution of each image.

The first image found on page one is approximately 200 pixels per inch (ppi). This resolution is appropriate for printing to a laser printer, high speed copier, and many newspapers. But this does not contain enough information for most high quality commercial printing methods.

If your print service provider has suggested that you provide images of a certain resolution, use the Preflight option to confirm the resolution of graphics that are used within a PDF.

8 Select the graphic indicated on page 1, then choose the Show selected page element in Snap view checkbox in the bottom left of Preflight window. This opens the Preflight: Snap View window. The item selected in the Preflight window is displayed in the Preflight: Snap View window.

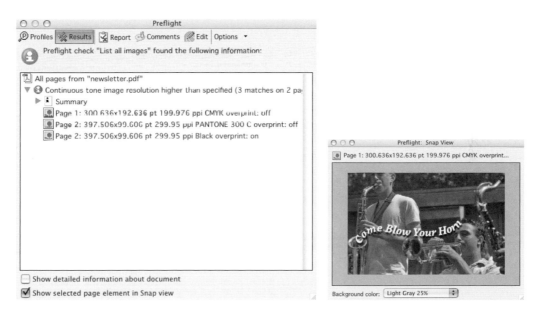

9 Click the Close button of the Preflight: Snap View window to close it. Keep the Preflight window open.

Creating a custom preflight profile

The default preflight profiles provide a good foundation for identifying possible concerns within a PDF file. Acrobat can also search for nearly 100 criteria within PDF files, based upon custom profiles that you create. You will develop criteria that will search for page elements that use a specific Pantone spot color. Because spot colors often require additional preparation in the printing process, they can be problematic if they have been unintentionally included in a PDF file.

1 In the Preflight window, click the Edit tab.

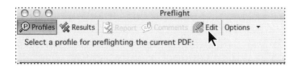

2 At the bottom of the Profiles list, click the New Profile button ( ), creating a New Profile 1 style.

3 In the General portion profiles window, for the Name for this profile enter **List elements using PMS 300c**. For Purpose, enter **Lists elements using PMS 300c**. The new profile is listed in the Profiles column of the Preflight window.

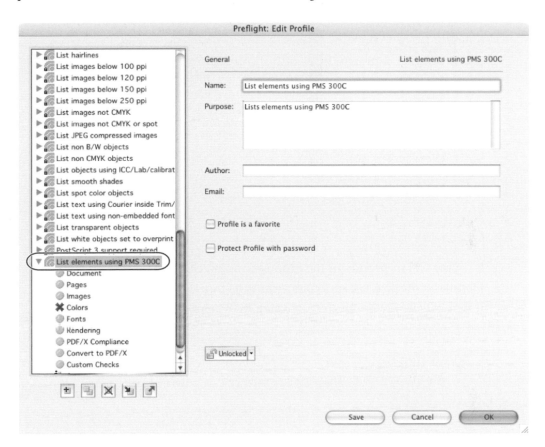

4 Confirm the new profile is selected in the Profiles column. Scroll to locate the Colors option. Click on the Color option, causing the window to display color-specific options for this profile.

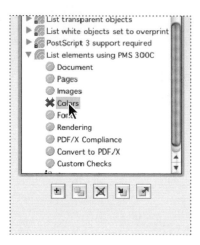

5 In the Colors portion of the Profiles window, click the downward facing arrow for Objects on the page use spot colors whose name is. Select Error. An error will be displayed if Acrobat encounters an element using RGB color when using this profile.

6 Click the Add button to select from a list of available PMS colors. Select PMS 300c and click OK. Click OK closing the Preflight: Edit Profile window.

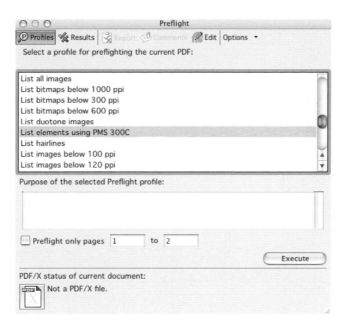

7 In the Preflight window, select the Profiles tab and then select the List elements using PMS 300C profile you've just created, and click Execute. The document is then analyzed against the rules in the profile. The Preflight: Results window appears. The Preflight: Results window displays information about the document relating to the preflight profile criteria.

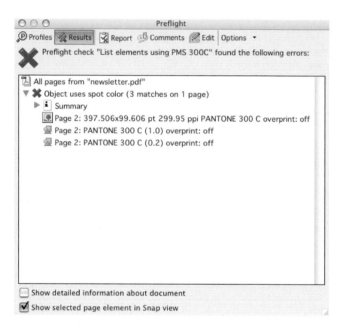

8 In the Results window, click the plus sign (+) (Windows) or the triangle (▶) (Mac OS) next to Object uses spot color. Then click to select the item listed on page two. If necessary, select the Show selected element in Snap view option. The items using Spot Color are displayed.

The Snap view visually displays page elements that are listed in the Preflight: Results window.

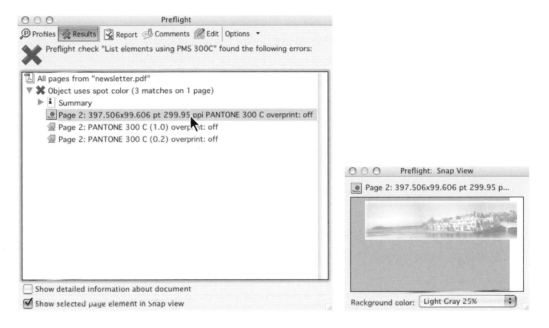

9 Click the Close button to close the Preflight: Snap View window, and click the Close button in the upper corner of the Profiles window to close it.

10 Choose File > Close to close this document.

Use custom profiles to identify areas of problem or concern. You can then return to the original source document—in this case an Adobe Photoshop image that was placed into an Adobe InDesign layout—and correct the concern before printing.

Layers

Adobe PDF files created from some graphics software, including Adobe InDesign CS and Adobe Illustrator CS, may include layers that were built in the original document. You will use the Layers tab to enable and disable certain layers within a brochure that was created using Adobe InDesign CS and exported to the Adobe PDF file format.

1 Choose File > Open. Navigate to the Lesson15 folder and choose the file newsletter_export.pdf. Click the Open button.

2 Click the Layers tab on the side of the document window or choose View > Navigation Tabs > Layers. Click on the (+) sign next to newsletter_project.indd.

3 Click the Eye icon ( ) to the left of the Column 1–English. Clicking on the eye hides it and turns off the layer for viewing and printing.

4 Click the empty box to the left of the Column 1–Portuguese. The Eye icon becomes visible. The elements on this layer are displayed on screen, and will print if the document is printed. You can use layers in your design software to create separate versions of documents, or to control which elements are visible or will print.

5 Click the Eye icon to toggle the Illustrations layer off and click the Eye icon again to make the layer visible. Layers can include both text and graphics.

All the layers in this document were created in the original file before it was converted to PDF. Programs that can export directly to the PDF file format, such as Illustrator and InDesign, can often include more robust information in the PDF document, such as document layers and transparency. Layers and transparency are not preserved when files are converted to PDF by printing using the Adobe PDF printer, nor are they maintained when creating most PDF files using Acrobat Distiller.

Output preview

To determine which portions of this document will print on each of the color separations, you will use Acrobat's separation preview.

1 Click the Fit Page icon (⬍) or choose View > Fit Page.

2 Click the Next Page button (▶) or choose View > Go To > Next Page.

3 Choose Advanced > Output Preview. The Ouput Preview window opens.

The Output Preview window shows all the colors that are included in this document for printing. The four subtractive primary colors used in color printing are displayed: Cyan, Magenta, Yellow, and Black (CMYK). Also, any special colors that will print are listed.

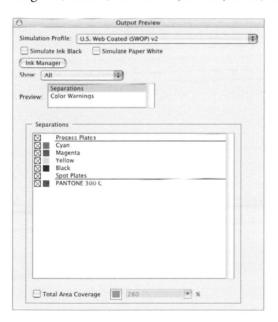

These special colors, called spot colors, are printed in addition to the four subtractive primary colors. This typically increases the cost of a print job. Because of the extra cost associated with spot colors, you may want to check PDF files to confirm that none are used in your documents if you did not intend to use them. The Separation Preview window can be used to confirm the colors used in Adobe PDF files. You can also use the Preflight process, described earlier in this chapter, to check for spot colors in PDF documents.

4 In the Output Preview window, click once on the check box located to the left of the Pantone 300 C color swatch. The check box becomes deselected. All items on the page that would be printed using this color are hidden from view.

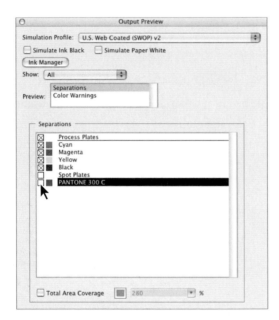

The Pantone 300 C color swatch is only used on page 2. If you are not viewing page 2, or if you have not opened the newsletter_export.pdf file, you will not see any changes to the file when enabling or disabling this color separation in the Output Preview window.

5 Click to deselect the Process Cyan and also the Process Magenta check boxes in the Separation Preview window. Objects using these colors are then hidden from view.

6 Click the Process Plates check box to display all the CMYK plates.

7 Click the Spot Plates check box for the Pantone 300 C spot color to be displayed on your monitor.

Note: *Unless you use a color management system (CMS) with accurately calibrated ICC profiles, and have calibrated your monitor, the on-screen separation preview colors may not provide an exact match of the final color separation output.*

8 Click the Close Window button in the upper right corner of the Output Preview window (Windows) or the upper left corner of the window (Mac OS). Keep the file open.

Working with transparency

Adobe applications offer the ability to modify objects in ways that can affect the underlying artwork, creating the appearance of transparency. This can be accomplished by using the Transparency palette's opacity slider in applications such as InDesign, Illustrator, or Photoshop, or by changing the blending mode in a layer or with an object selected. Transparency works across Adobe applications, and you need to be aware of a variety of settings and preparation steps before printing documents containing transparency.

Previewing transparency

When printing, objects with transparency are broken down, so any overlapping objects are converted into either separate vector shapes or rasterized pixels. This retains the look of the transparency. This process of converting transparent objects into vectors and pixels is referred to as flattening. Flattening essentially eliminates the transparency while maintaining its appearance.

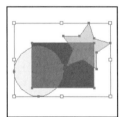 

Objects before flattening.   *Objects after flattening.*

Before flattening occurs, you can determine how much of the transparent area remains vector, and how much becomes rasterized. Some effects, such as drop shadows, must be rasterized in order to print correctly.

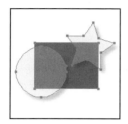 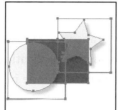

What is Rasterization?

Rasterization is the process of changing vector objects, including fonts, into bitmap images for the purpose of displaying and printing. The amount of ppi (pixels per inch) is referred to as the resolution. The higher the resolution in a raster image, the better the quality. When flattening occurs, some objects may need to be rasterized, depending upon flattening settings.

Vector Object *Rasterized at 72 ppi* *Rasterized at 300 ppi.*

If you received a PDF file but did not create the file, you may not know if, or where, transparency has been applied. Acrobat's transparency preview shows you where transparency is used in a document. This feature can also help you to determine the best flattener settings to use when printing the document.

1 If necessary, click the Next Page button (▶) to navigate to page 2. If the entire page is not visible, press Ctrl+0 (Windows) or Command+0 (Mac OS) to fit the entire page in your window.

2 Choose Tools > Print Production > Transparency Flattening. The Flattener Preview window opens.

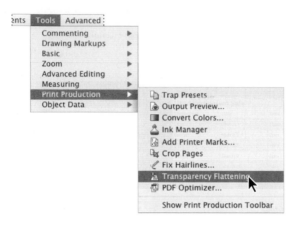

3 In the Preview Settings section, click the Refresh button. The Refresh button scans the content of the current PDF to identify if transparency features have been used. In this document, it recognizes transparency and outlined strokes. The Flattener Preview now shows a preview of the newsletter on the right side of the window. Keep this window open.

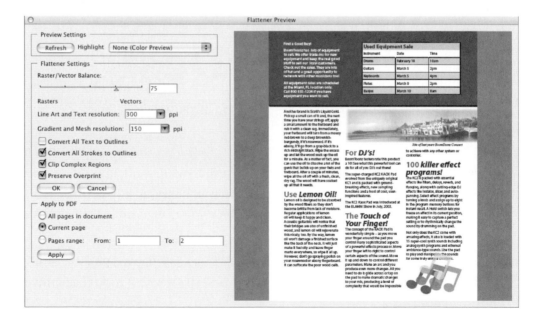

Setting flattener preview settings

1 In the Flattener Preview window, choose Transparent Objects from the Highlight drop-down menu. The photo image and three of the musical notes are highlighted in red, indicating that they have transparent properties.

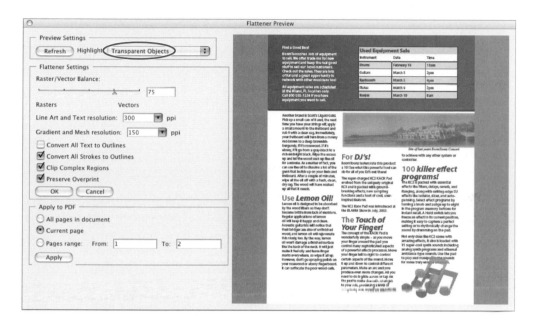

2 In the Flattener Preview window, use the Flattener Settings to choose how much of the artwork you wish to retain as vector artwork and how much you want to rasterize. Click and drag the Raster/Vector Balance slider to the farthest position to the right. This maximizes the amount of artwork to remain as vectors.

Note: The preview disappears as you select new settings. It becomes visible again after you click the Refresh button.

The settings vary from complete rasterization, which is obtained by dragging the slider completely to the left, to maximum retention of vectors, obtained by dragging the slider completely to the right.

3 From the Line Art and Text drop-down menu, choose 300 pixels per inch.

Note: *The Gradient and Mesh resolution is used to get the rasterization resolution for gradients and mesh objects. This document does not contain these objects, so no adjustments are necessary.*

4 Click the Refresh button and a new preview appears. Position your cursor over the image of the musical notes in the lower right corner of the window, and click to increase magnification.

Use the zoom capabilities to better identify smaller objects that are affected by transparency. If necessary, hold down the spacebar, then click and drag, to scroll within the preview area.

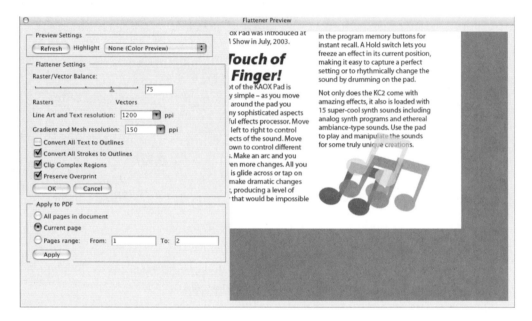

5 To zoom out, click the Refresh button to see the entire page.

6 In the Flattener Settings portion of the window, click and drag the slider entirely to the left. This causes Acrobat to preview which objects will be rasterized if this setting is used when printing.

7 Click the Refresh button, then choose All Affected Objects from the Highlight drop-down menu. Note that a significantly larger portion of the page is now covered in red. If a lower Raster setting is used, the majority of the document will be rasterized—or converted to a bitmap.

Note: Documents that contain many transparent objects may take longer to print when higher Flattener settings are used, which rasterizes fewer page elements.

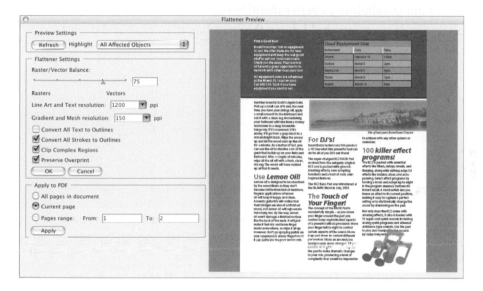

8 If you want to use the selected transparency flattener settings when printing, click the Apply button. When you are finished previewing how the various transparency flattening settings affect different portions of your document, click the close button in the upper corner of the window to close the Flattener Preview window.

About flattening options

Convert all text to outlines

This option ensures that the width of all text in the artwork stays consistent. However, converting small fonts to outline can make them appear noticeably thicker and less readable (especially when printing on lower-end printing systems).

Convert all strokes to outlines

This option ensures that the width of all strokes in the artwork stays consistent. Selecting this option, however, causes thin strokes to appear slightly thicker (especially when printing on lower-end printing systems).

Clip complex regions

This setting ensures that the boundaries between vector artwork and rasterized artwork fall along object paths. This option reduces stitching artifacts that result when part of an object is rasterized while another part of the object remains in vector form (as determined by the Raster/Vector slider). Keep in mind that selecting this option may result in extremely complex clipping paths, which take significant time to compute, and can cause errors when printing.

Preserve Overprint Settings

Retains any overprint settings in files being converted to PDF. Overprinted colors are two or more inks printed on top of each other. For example, when a cyan ink prints over a yellow ink, the resulting overprint is a green color. Without overprinting, the underlying yellow would not be printed, resulting in a cyan color.

About rasterization resolution

Gradient and meshes

Use the Gradient and Meshes drop-down menu to determine the ppi of gradients and meshes—which are sometimes called blends. These will be rasterized, and should have a resolution appropriate to your specific printer. For proofing to a general purpose laser printer or inkjet printer, the default setting of 150 ppi is appropriate. When printing to most high-quality output devices, such as a film or plate output device, a resolution of 300 ppi is sufficient for most work.

Line art and text

Because line art and text involves a more sharp contrast around its edges, it needs to be rasterized at a higher resolution to maintain a high quality appearance. A resolution of 300 ppi is sufficient when proofing, but this should be increased to a higher resolution for final high-quality output. A resolution of 1200 ppi is typically sufficient for high-quality output.

Advanced printing controls

Use Acrobat Professional's advanced printing features to produce color separations, add printing marks, and control how transparent and complex items are imaged.

1 Choose File > Print. The Print window opens.

2 Choose a PostScript printer to which you would like to print this document. If you do not have a PostScript printer available, choose Adobe PDF as the Printer, as this uses a PostScript print driver and can be used for this lesson.

Acrobat is capable of printing to most output devices for general printing purposes. Because you are creating color separations, it is necessary to choose a PostScript printer for this portion of the lesson.

3 For Print Range select All.

4 For Page Handling (Windows) or Page Scaling (Mac OS), choose Fit to paper and choose Auto-Rotate and Center. Keep all the other settings unchanged.

5 Click the Advanced button. The Advanced Print Setup window opens. Note that there are four options along the left side of this window: Output, Marks and Bleeds, Transparency Flattening, and PostScript Options.

6 Confirm the Output tab is selected along the left side of the Advanced Print Setup window, and choose Separations from the Color drop-down menu.

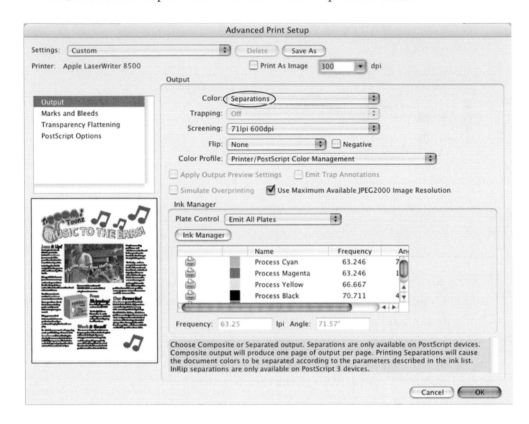

7 Click the Ink Manager button. Scroll through the listed inks of the document and locate Pantone 300 C. Click the spot color icon to the left of the Pantone 300 C name. The check box changes into a CMYK color swatch, indicating that this color will be printed as a combination of CMYK color values.

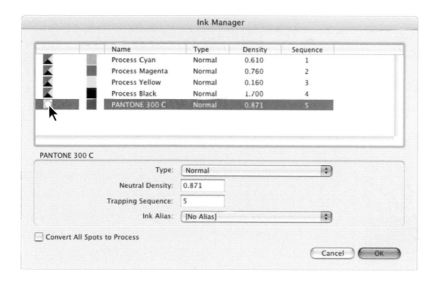

For Pantone 300 C, a close approximation of the color is made by mixing Cyan and Black. Because you converted this color to a CMYK mixture, Acrobat will mix these two colors to simulate the dedicated ink that is used to produce Spot colors. Because these two colors are already used throughout this newsletter, it is more cost-effective to use them to represent a spot color, rather than adding an entirely new ink in addition to the CMYK colors that are being used.

Acrobat also lets you globally convert all spot colors to their CMYK equivalents by choosing the Convert All Spots to Process check box. Click OK to close the Ink Manager window.

8 Click OK to close the Ink Manager window, then choose the Marks and Bleeds option. Click the All Marks check box to turn-on a variety of marks that are created outside the edges of the document. Keep the Advanced Print Setup window open.

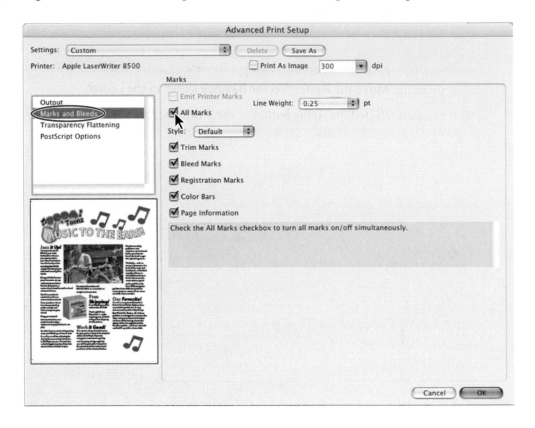

Flattening transparency

Determine the flattening settings for your PDF in the Advance section of the Print window.

1 In the Advanced Print Controls, click once on the Transparency Flattening option on the left side of the Advanced Print Controls window.

2 Acrobat displays the same options that you reviewed in the Flattener Preview window prior to printing. Move the Raster/Vector Balance slider to the center.

Note: *If you had selected the Apply button in the Flattener Preview window, it is not necessary to make any additional changes.*

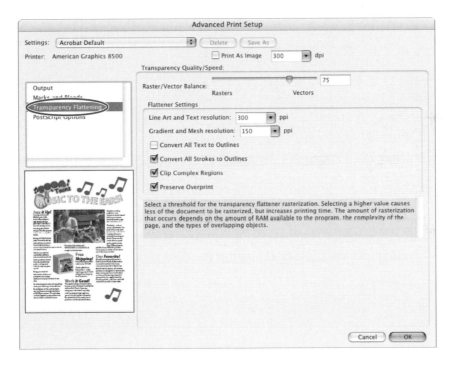

3 Choose the Save As button at the top of the Advanced Print Set-up window to save these flattening settings.

When settings are saved, you can re-use them on future jobs, avoiding the repetition of re-entering the settings you use for certain jobs or specific output devices.

4 In the Save Print Settings window, type newsletter and click OK.

The settings are now available from the Settings drop-down menu at the top of the Advanced Print Setup window.

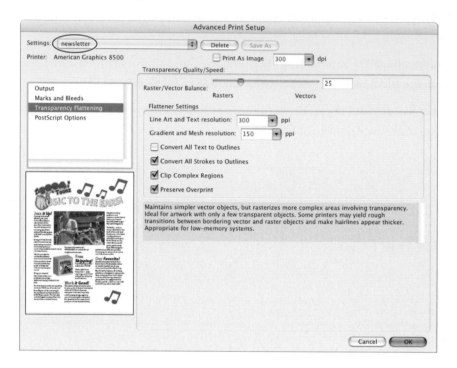

5 Click OK to exit the Advance Print Setup window. Then click either the OK button to print this document, or click Cancel if you prefer to not print at this time.

Setting up color management

Using color management can help you to control color consistency throughout your workflow. Color management essentially assigns profiles, or characteristics, for different devices to your document so that you get more consistent results throughout the entire production process—on screen when printing proofs, and on a printing press.

1 If the newsletter PDF is not open, choose File > Open. Navigate to the Lesson15 folder and choose the file newsletter_export.pdf. Click the Open button.

2 Choose Edit > Preferences (Windows) or Acrobat > Preferences (Mac OS) and click the Color Management tab along the left side of the Preferences Window.

In the Color Setup section, several presets are available to make color management less complicated.

3 From the Settings drop-down menu, choose U.S. Prepress Defaults. This selection allows Acrobat to display colors as they generally appear when printed using North American printing standards. By using a Settings selection, all the options in this window are changed.

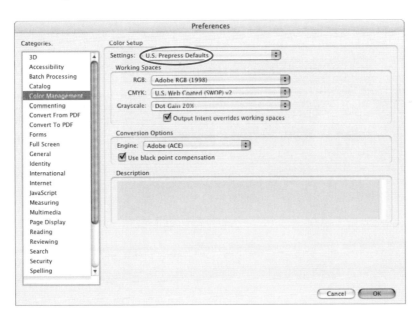

4 Under Conversion Options, confirm Adobe (ACE) is selected for the Engine.

The Adobe ACE is the same color management engine used by Adobe's other graphics software, so you can be confident that color management settings applied in Acrobat will mirror those applied in your other Adobe software.

5 Click OK to close the Preferences window.

6 Navigate to Page 1.

7 Use the Zoom-in tool (🔍) to focus on the picture of the band.

8 Choose Advanced > Output Preview. The Output Preview window opens. In the Output Preview window choose U.S. Web Uncoated v2 from the Simulation Profile drop-down menu. Notice the subtle shift in colors when you choose a new output profile, as Acrobat attempts to represent how the document will appear when printed on this type of printing device. Return to the default Simulation Profile and click the Close Window button.

The proof on your monitor is called a Soft Proof. The reliability of the soft proof is highly dependent upon the quality of your monitor, your monitor profile and the ambient lighting conditions of your workstation.

9 Choose File > Close to close the document.

Congratulations! You have finished this lesson.

Exploring on your own: Acrobat's prepress features

1 Print one copy of the English language version of the newsletter, and one copy of the foreign language version. Use the Layers pane to switch between these layers before printing. Use the layers to print text-only versions of the document, or to print only the graphics.

2 Open the Transparency Flattener Preview window and test various settings to determine how increasing the amount of Raster or Vector content impacts different portions of the document. Try these same settings when printing, and note that when more vectors are used, the print time increases. But these settings generally provide a higher quality output.

3 Create a custom preflight profile to identify if fonts are not built into a PDF document. Also create a preflight profile to identify images below 200 pixels per inch.

Review questions

1 What is the purpose of Acrobat Distiller, and how is it useful for high resolution printing?

2 What problems can Preflight detect within a PDF? Does it always correct the problems it encounters?

3 How are layers useful for print and prepress? What concerns arise when printing a document with layers?

Review answers

1 Acrobat Distiller is used to convert PostScript files to PDF. PostScript files are generally created by using the Print to File option with a PostScript print driver. Any document that can be printed to file can be converted to PDF with Acrobat Distiller.

Because you can easily convert a PostScript file to PDF with Acrobat Distiller, you can use the same PostScript file to generate multiple PDF files for various uses. You can convert the same PostScript file to PDF using the various Default Settings for experimentation, or to meet the needs of posting a PDF on-line and also delivering a different PDF to your printer.

2 Use the Preflight command to check for all areas of concern within a PDF. For example, if you are posting PDF files on-line, you can look for items that might make a PDF file too large—such as embedded fonts, or graphics that have too high a resolution. If you are using PDF files for print and prepress, you can check for fonts that are not embedded, low-resolution graphics, and incorrect colors.

3 Layers provide the ability to easily create various versions of a PDF document. But not all prepress workflows accept layered PDF files, and they introduce the possibility of printing the wrong layer if your printer or service provider is not expecting to receive a layered PDF file. It is a good idea to always communicate with your printer or service provider before using layers within a PDF document.

16 Creating Forms with Adobe LiveCycle Designer

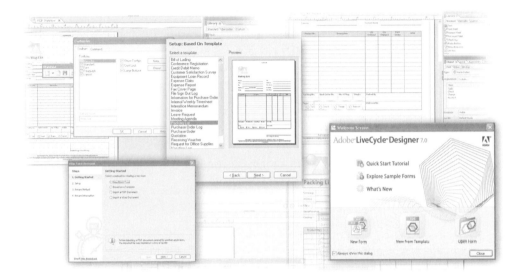

Adobe Acrobat 7.0 for Windows also includes Adobe LiveCycle Designer. You can use Adobe LiveCycle Designer to create powerful PDF forms.

Adobe LiveCycle Designer provides extensive control over form design and presentation. It includes a unified design and development environment for form building, so you can layout form templates, incorporate business logic, and preview forms in real-time.

Adobe LiveCycle Designer makes it easy to create interactive forms that combine the high-fidelity presentation of Portable Document Format (PDF) and HyperText Markup Language (HTML) forms with powerful eXtensible Markup Language (XML) data handling. With Adobe LiveCycle Designer, you can streamline form-driven business processes, and design XML form templates that can be deployed as Adobe PDF or as HTML.

In this lesson you'll learn how to do the following:

• Use Adobe LiveCycle Designer to create a complete PDF form.

• Use the grid layout and drag-and-drop libraries to position graphics.

• Enter text and add graphics to a form design.

• Add form objects such as list boxes, drop-down lists, command buttons, and check boxes.

If necessary, copy the Lesson16 folder onto your hard drive from the CD located inside the back cover of this book.

Note: *Windows 2000 users may need to unlock the lesson files before using them. For information, see "Copying the Classroom in a Book files" on page 4.*

Getting started

This lesson uses Adobe LiveCycle Designer. Adobe LiveCycle Designer is included with Adobe Acrobat 7.0 Professional for Windows. If this is not the version of Adobe Acrobat you are currently using, you can download an evaluation copy of Adobe LiveCycle Designer from the Adobe.com web site at http://www.adobe.com/products/server/adobe-designer/tryreg.html.

You will start the lesson using Adobe Acrobat 7.0 Professional and then move into Adobe LiveCycle Designer to create a PDF form that will be distributed as a PDF.

1 Start Adobe Acrobat 7.0 Professional.

2 To see what the finished file looks like, open the file form_complete.pdf, located in the Lesson16 folder you copied to your hard drive. You can keep this file open for reference while you work on this exercise, or you can close the file by choosing File > Close.

3 Choose Advanced > Forms > Create New Form. If this is the first time this command has been used on your computer, a Create New Form message may be displayed, informing you that Adobe Designer will be used to create the form. If necessary, click OK to allow Adobe LiveCycle Designer to open. The New Form Assistant is displayed.

4 In the New Form Assistant window, choose Based on a Template to create a form that uses the overall design of a pre-existing template. You will still be able to customize the form. Templates save time by avoiding the need to recreate many commonly used form objects. Click the Next button.

5 The New Form Assistant displays a list of templates. Choose Packing List and then click the Next button.

6 The New Form Assistant now displays options for the Return Method. The Return Method indicates how the form will be completed and returned to you. Forms may be completed manually using a pen or completed electronically using Adobe Acrobat or Adobe Reader. The completed form can then be returned to you via fax, mail, or electronically. Specifying the Return Method helps Designer create the correct form for your needs. Choose the Print option, click the Next button, and then click the Finish button. The Packing List template is used to create a new, untitled form.

7 Go to the Window menu and choose Manage Palettes, and then choose Reset Palette Locations. This ensures that you have the default palette configuration. You can use this command at any time while you are working in Adobe LiveCycle Designer to return the palettes to their default location.

Getting to know the work area

Form creation and editing is done using the Layout Editor. This is the area where you create and maintain a form design. The Layout Editor includes several tabs which provide different views of a form for either editing or preview purposes. For example, the Body Pages tab is used primarily for editing form design, while the PDF Preview tab is used to view how a form will look when converted to an Adobe PDF file.

There are also tabbed palettes arranged around the Layout Editor that provide access to editing and layout tools. These palettes can be attached to either the left or right side of the Layout Editor, or they can be free-standing palettes that are positioned anywhere within the work area.

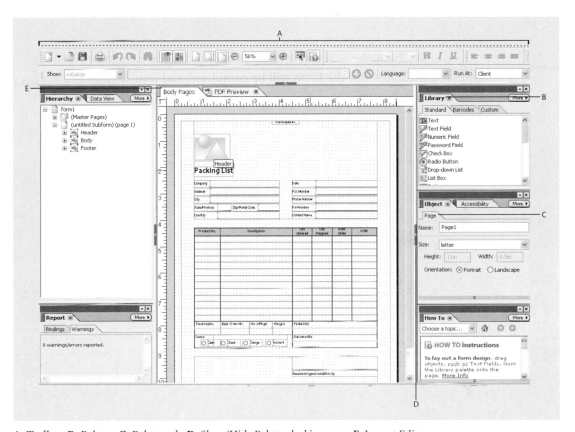

A. Toolbar. B. Palette. C. Palette tab. D. Show/Hide Palette docking area. E. Layout Editor.

1 Click on the blue bar at the top of the Library palette. Notice how the palette expands to reveal more of its content. Click on the blue bar at the top of the Object and Accessibility tabs, and notice how these palettes are also expanded.

2 Double-click on the blue bar on top of the Object and Accessibility palette. The palette is no longer attached to the docking area along the right side of the Layout Editor. Position your cursor over the blue bar at the top of the Object and Accessibility palette and then click and drag the palette to the center of the Layout Editor.

3 Click on the Object tab and drag away from the Accessibility tab. The palette separates into two separate palettes. Tabbed palettes can be attached to the docking areas on either the left or right side of the display. Additionally, tabbed palettes can be grouped together or separated based upon your needs.

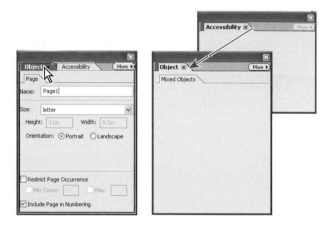

4 Click on the Object tab and drag it to the center of the Accessibility palette. When you release the mouse, the two palettes become one. You can click on either tab to switch between the Accessibility tab options and the Object tab options. Joining the editing tools you use most frequently into a grouped tab makes it easier to access the tools in one central location.

5 Click on the blue bar on top of the Accessibility and Object palette and drag the palette to the Library palette. When dragging an entire palette into the docking area on either side of the Layout Editor, the palette group is attached to the docking area. Note that the tabs did not become part of the Library palette, but when you dragged the Object tab into the Accessibility tab, the two tabs were joined. Adobe LiveCycle Designer differentiates between whether you are looking to move a palette or join together tabs based upon whether you click and drag a tab, or click and drag the blue bar at the top of a palette.

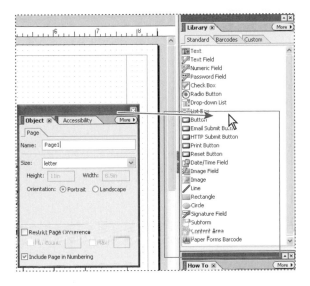

6 Choose Window > Manage Palettes > Reset Palette Locations to reset the palettes and tabs to their default locations.

7 Locate the toolbars positioned across the top of the Layout Editor, positioned directly beneath the menu commands. Click the Fit Page icon ( ) and the entire form is displayed within the Layout Editor.

The toolbars are very similar to those used in Adobe Acrobat 7.0, and like Acrobat, include options for opening and saving forms, changing the display view percentage and printing. Additional options specific to the needs of creating and editing a form are also included. You will work with these specific options later in this lesson.

8 Position your cursor over the far left side of the top toolbar, to the left of the New icon (▢). Click and drag the toolbar to the center portion of the Layout Editor. Similar to Acrobat, toolbars can be positioned anywhere within your layout. Click and drag the top of the Standard toolbar palette to return it to its original position, at the top of the window below the menu.

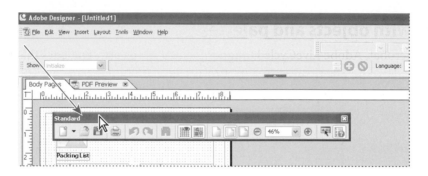

9 Click the Customize Toolbars button (▩) located on the right side of the toolbar. The Customize window opens.

10 In the Customize window, click the Standard checkbox to deselect this option and note that the Standard toolbar disappears. Click the Standard checkbox and the Standard toolbars are once again displayed. Click the Cancel button to close the Customize window.

Note: The Reset Palette Locations command does not cause hidden toolbars to become visible. You must use the Customize command to make hidden toolbars visible.

11 Choose Window > Script Editor. The Script Editor, positioned beneath the Standard toolbars, is hidden from view. Choose Window > Script Editor again and the Script Editor is displayed. Palettes can be displayed or hidden from the Window menu. Palettes that are currently displayed show a check mark next to their name in the Window menu.

Keep the untitled document open, as you will use it in the next exercise.

Working with objects and palettes

Like Adobe Acrobat, Adobe LiveCycle Designer includes a variety of palettes that make it easy to manipulate and create form objects. While some of these palettes are similar to those found in Acrobat, many will be new to you. Here you'll become familiar with some of the essentials of the LiveCycle Designer workspace.

1 Choose Window > Manage Palettes > Reset Palette Locations to reset the palettes to their default location. Position your cursor over the image at the top left corner of the untitled packing list form you created earlier in this lesson. Click once to select the image.

2 Examine the Object palette, which indicates that the object selected is an Image, and displays the location of the image file that is being used in the URL field of the Object palette.

3 Choose Window > Layout. The Layout palette appears and displays the location of the image on the page as X and Y coordinates along with the width and height of the image. These values can be adjusted numerically in this palette, or you can use your cursor to adjust the size and position of the object.

4 Position your cursor over the text which reads Packing List and click once. As with the image, the Layout palette displays information about the size and location of the text. Click on the Object tab and the object is identified as Text.

5 Choose Window > Font and the Font palette is displayed. The typeface and size of the text in the selected text frame are shown, along with any attributes applied to the type, such as text color or underlining.

Note: *To edit text attributes, you must first select either the text to be modified or the box containing the text.*

6 Click the Paragraph tab located adjacent to the Font tab. Additional information regarding the text attributes is displayed, including vertical and horizontal alignment and indent spacing.

When text is selected, information about text attributes is also displayed in the toolbars at the top of the display area. Much of the information in the toolbars is identical to the options in the Font and Paragraph palettes, and either location can be used to edit the appearance of the text.

7 Move your cursor over the text Company, beneath the Packing List text. Click the Company text and then click to select the Object palette. The Object palette displays three new tabs within the Object tab: Field, Value, and Binding. These three tabs allow you to define attributes that are unique to Text Fields used in the form. The Field tab of the Object palette identifies this as a Text Field.

The Object palette, like many of the other palettes, is contextual. Its display may change based upon what type of object is selected or what operation you are performing.

8 If necessary, scroll to the bottom of the form. Click to select the Cash radio button, located within the Terms section in the lower left portion of the form. Note that the Object palette changes to reflect the attributes of the selected radio button.

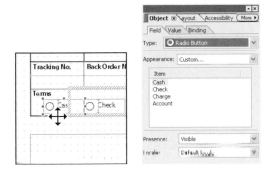

9 Choose Window > Hierarchy. The Hierarchy palette is displayed. In the Hierarchy palette, click the plus sign (+) next to Header. The items displayed under the Header section are grouped elements, making them easier to manipulate as a single item when being moved or edited.

10 Choose Window > Manage Palettes > Reset Palette Locations to reset the palettes to their default layout. Keep the form open.

Changing views

The Layout Editor includes different options for previewing a completed form and for viewing form master pages. These display options are accessed via tabs, located along the top of the form and from the View menu. The four possible views are Body Pages, Master Pages, XML Source, and PDF Preview.

1 Click the PDF Preview tab to view how the form will appear when rendered as an Adobe PDF file.

Clicking the PDF Preview renders an Adobe PDF file that is then displayed within the PDF Preview window using Adobe Acrobat. If Adobe Acrobat is not already running, the program starts, facilitating the PDF Preview within Adobe LiveCycle Designer.

The Packing List is displayed.

2 Click in the Company text field, beneath the Packing List headline. Enter the text **ABC Company**.

3 Click the drop-down option to the right of the Date field, and a calendar is displayed. Click to choose a day from within the calendar and the selected date is placed in the Date field.

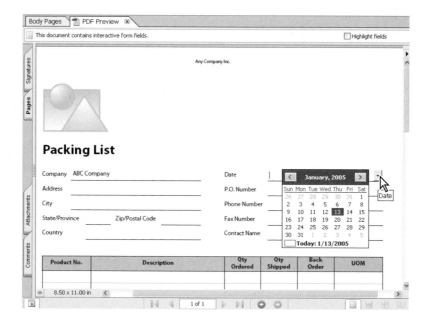

4 Choose View > XML Source. The XML Source tab is displayed along with the PDF Preview and Body Pages tab. The currently selected field is highlighted within the XML code that makes up the form file. Click the Body Pages tab.

5 Choose View > Zoom Area. The cursor changes to a magnifying glass. Click and drag the cursor to create a marquee surrounding the Date field and the four fields beneath it. The view changes to focus on this area of the form.

6 Click the Fit Width icon ( ) in the toolbars. Additional magnification options in the toolbars, located to the right of the Fit Width icon, provide other methods for changing the zoom level of the form.

7 Choose File > Close. Click the No button when asked if changes to the file should be saved. After closing the Packing List form, the Adobe LiveCycle Designer Welcome Screen is displayed. Keep this window open.

Building a new form

In this exercise you will create a product registration form, including a questionnaire for a fictitious company, LPH Technology.

1 In the Welcome Screen, click the New Form button. If the Welcome Screen is not displayed, choose File > New to access the New Form Assistant. The New Form Assistant is displayed. Click to select the New Blank Form radio button and then click the Next button.

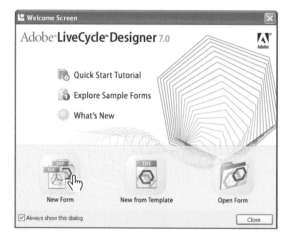

2 In the Setup portion of the New Form Assistant, choose letter from the Page Size drop-down menu, leaving the Orientation and Number of Pages options unchanged. Click the Next button.

3 In the Return Method portion of the New Form Assistant, choose the Print radio button, then click the Next button. Adobe LiveCycle Designer reminds you to include submission information with your form. Click the Finish button. A new form is displayed.

Based upon the Return Method that you select, various buttons and other logic may be automatically added to the form you create. For example, the form can be set-up to automatically return the contents to your Email address.

4 Choose Window > Drawing Aids. The Drawing Aids palette is displayed.

You'll use the Drawing Aids palette to create guidelines to assist in the form design process.

5 In the Guideline Definition section of the Drawing Aids palette, click the green plus sign (+) in the Horizontal section of the window, and then type **2.75**. Press the Enter or Return key on your keyboard. A guideline is added at the 2.75 inch position. This guideline will be used to separate the header from the body portion of the form during the design process.

6 Once again click the green plus sign in the Horizontal section of the Drawing Aids palette. Type **3** then press the Enter or Return key on your keyboard. Another guide is added at the 3 inch position. Repeat this process to create two more horizontal guidelines at the **9.75** inch and **10.25** inch positions.

7 Click once on the green plus sign in the Vertical section of the Drawing Aids palette and then type **.5**. Press the Enter or Return key to add the guideline. Repeat this process to add a second Vertical guideline at the **8** inch position and add two more vertical guides at the **4** inch and **4.5** inch positions.

8 In the Drawing Aids palette, click the Color option, located in the center portion of the palette located under the Grid & Ruler Settings section. Choose the color red, and the guides are updated to reflect the new color.

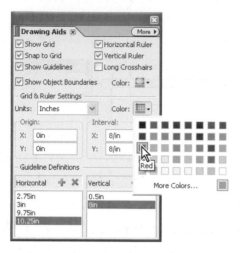

9 Close the Drawing Aids palette by clicking the x in the upper right corner of the palette.

10 Confirm that there is a check mark next to the Snap to Grid command by examining the View > Snap to Grid command. If necessary, select this command to make it active. You can tell the command is active if a check mark appears next to the command name. This causes objects to align with the grid.

The grid can be displayed or hidden by choosing View > Grid.

11 Choose the Save button (🖫) in the toolbars. The Save As window is displayed. Name the file **RegistrationForm**, and confirm the Save as type is set to Static PDF Form File (*.pdf). If necessary, navigate to the Lesson 16 folder on your hard drive and then click the Save button to save the file.

Adding text to a form

In the header section of the form you will include the company name, logo, and the form name. These individual items will then be joined together as a group.

1 In the Library palette, locate and click on the Standard tab. Click and drag the Text icon from the Standard tab of the Library onto the top, center portion of the page.

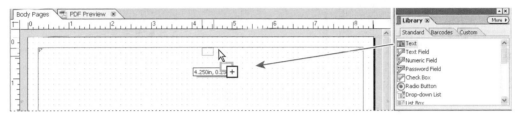

Note: You can also click to select the Text icon in the Library palette, then click and drag on the form to define the size of the text frame.

2 Position your cursor over the text frame that you added to the page in the previous step and double-click to select the default text inside the frame. Enter the text **LPH Technology** to replace the default text. Keep the text frame selected and click the Actual Size icon ( ) in the toolbar.

3 Choose Window > Font and the Font palette is displayed. Click and drag across the LPH Technology text so that it is selected. You can also triple-click to select all the text. In the Font palette, change the font to Myriad Pro Black and set the size to 16 point.

4 Click the Layout palette. If the Layout palette is not visible, choose Window > Layout. From the Anchor drop-down menu in the Layout palette choose Top Middle.

The Auto-fit checkboxes are selected for both Width and Height. This allowed the text box to expand as you entered additional text.

5 In the Layout palette set enter the Anchor X value of **4.25** and enter the Anchor Y value of **.25**. Press the Enter or Return key after entering these values. The text box is aligned with the top margin and centered horizontally on the page.

Adding graphics to a form

Your forms may contain graphics and design elements. Adobe Designer makes it easy to add graphics to your forms. Here you'll add a logo for our fictitious company.

1 In the Library palette, locate and click on the Standard tab. Click and drag the Image icon from the Standard tab of the Library onto the top, center portion of the page, below the text you entered in the previous section. You may need to scroll through the available choices in the Standard tab to locate the Image icon.

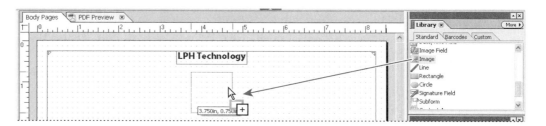

2 Click the Object tab. In the Object tab locate the URL: option and click the folder icon (🖿) to the right of the URL: option. The Browse for Image File window opens. In the Browse for Image File window, navigate to the Lesson16 folder, and import the file logo.tif.

Adobe LiveCycle Designer can import a variety of graphic file formats, including .bmp, .jpg, .gif, .png, and .tif files.

3 Click to select the Layout tab. In the Layout tab, choose Top Middle from the Anchor drop-down menu and enter the Anchor X value as **4.25** and the Anchor Y value as **.75**. Press the Enter or Return key after entering these values.

4 Press the Save button (🖫) in the toolbar to save the file.

Adding more text

Here you will add a text banner across the top of the form, creating the form name.

1 In the Library palette, locate and click on the Standard tab. Click and drag the Text icon from the Standard tab of the Library onto the top portion of the page under the logo you added in the previous exercise.

2 Position your cursor over the text frame you added in the previous step and double-click to select the default text inside. Enter the text **Warranty Registration and Questionnaire** to replace the default text.

3 Triple-click the Warranty Registration and Questionnaire text so that it is selected. You can also click and drag across the text to select it. After selecting the text, use the toolbar at the top of the window to set the text size to 24 points. The text frame extends beyond the right edge of the page. Keep the text selected.

Warranty Registration and Questionnaire

4 Click to select the Layout palette. If the Layout palette is not visible, choose Window > Layout. In the Layout palette, enter the Width as **7.5** and the Height as **.6**. Press the enter or return key. Keep the text selected.

5 In the Layout palette, confirm that the Anchor option is set to Top Middle and for the Anchor X value, enter **4.25**, and for the Anchor Y value, enter **2**.

6 Click to select the Paragraph palette. If the Paragraph palette is not visible, choose Window > Paragraph. Choose the second alignment icon from the left side, aligning the text to the center of the frame from left to right. Keep the text selected.

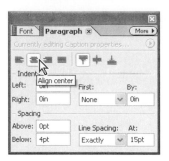

7 In the Paragraph palette, click the second icon from the right side, aligning the text in the middle of the frame, from top to bottom.

8 Click to select the Border palette. If the Border palette is not visible, choose Window > Border. In the Background Fill section, located at the bottom of the palette, choose Solid from the Style drop-down menu.

9 In the Border palette, to the right of the Style drop-down menu, click the paint bucket icon ( ) and choose the light-green color. The text banner is filled with the color you select.

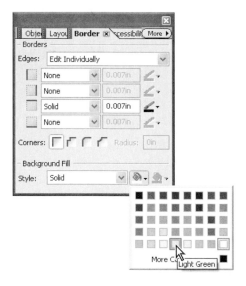

Grouping Objects

Grouping multiple objects into a single grouped element ensures that all the items move as one, and that their relationship and location remains constant.

1 Choose Window > Hierarchy. The Hierarchy palette is displayed. The elements you created for the top of the form are listed under the section titled (untitled subform) (page 1).

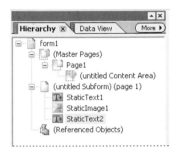

2 Click to select the Warranty Registration and Questionnaire text box. Press and hold the Shift key and then click to select the logo and click to select the LPH Technologies text box. All three objects should be selected.

3 With the three objects selected, choose Layout > Group.

In the Hierarchy palette, all three items now appear under a Group designation.

4 In the Hierarchy palette, right-click the Group object and choose Rename Object from the context menu. Enter the name **Head**.

5 Click the Save button (■) in the toolbar to save the file.

Adding content to the form body

The body of the form contains most of the data input by the user. For this form, it includes the personal information of the form user.

1 Click on the Custom tab of the Library palette and scroll to locate the library item titled Address Block. Click and drag the Address Block object from the Library palette into the body section of the form, below the head section. If necessary, you can close the Hierarchy palette to expand the work area.

As you move the Address Block, the current position of the object is displayed. Move the Address Block object until it snaps to the upper left corner of the red guides, at the .250 in., 3.00 in. position. The position is displayed at the bottom of the object as it is moved onto the page.

The label adjacent to the Address Block label indicates that this library item is a group of objects. Placing commonly used groups of objects in the library makes it easy to add commonly used fields to forms you create.

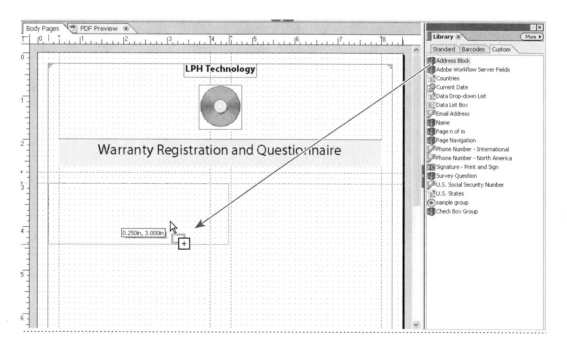

2 Confirm that the Address Block boxes are still selected. Choose Layout > Group. Grouping these objects makes it easier to select them using the Hierarchy palette.

3 Click to select the Name text field and then click to select the Object Palette, then click the Field tab. In the Field tab, choose the Appearance drop-down menu and select Underlined.

4 In the Object Palette, click the Value tab. In the Value tab, click the Type drop-down menu and choose User Entered – Required.

Choosing User Entered – Required establishes this field as being required before the form can be submitted.

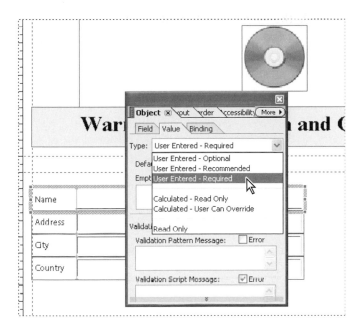

5 Repeating the process from the previous step, set the following fields as User Entered – Required:

- Address
- City
- State
- Zip Code
- Country

6 Select the Actual Size button () in the toolbars to view the form at a 100% scale, and then click to select the Group object in the Hierarchy palette. The group of objects on the form becomes selected. Click the center handle along the right side of the group, and drag it to the left. Align the right edge of the group with the guide positioned at the 4 inch location.

When the group is selected, all the objects in the group are modified when using the handles to adjust their size. In this example, all the form fields are slightly smaller.

7 Click on the Custom tab of the Library palette and scroll to locate the library item titled Address Block. Click and drag the Address Block object from the Library palette into the body section of the form, below the head section. Position the Address Block so it is located at the coordinates X: 4.00 in. and Y: 3.00 in. If necessary, scroll or choose the Fit Page icon () to see the entire head section of the form.

8 Confirm that the Address Block boxes that were added to the form in the previous step are still selected. If necessary, select all these boxes and then choose Layout > Group to create a group from the individual objects. Keep the group selected.

9 Click the center handle along the left side of the group, and drag it to the right. Align the left edge of the group with the guide positioned at the 4.5 inch location.

10 In the Hierarchy palette, right-click the first item labeled Group under the Head section and choose Rename Object from the contextual menu. Change the name of the group to **PersonalInfo**.

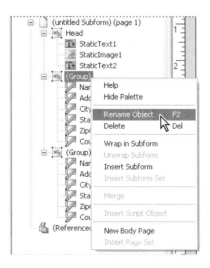

11 Right-click the second item labeled Group In the Hierarchy palette and choose Rename Object from the contextual menu. Change the name of the group to **CompanyInfo**.

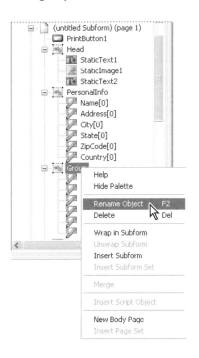

12 Hold down the Shift key and click to select the text fields in the CompanyInfo group located in the Hierarchy palette. In the Object palette, click the Value tab and from the Type drop-down menu choose User Entered – Required. Because all the fields in the CompanyInfo group were selected when you made this choice, they all have been labeled as fields that must be completed before the form can be submitted.

13 Click the close window button in the upper right corner of the Hierarchy palette to hide the palette. You can always choose to display a palette by choosing its name from the Window menu.

Creating a radio button

Radio buttons allow for mutually exclusive choices, where the user is provided with many choices but only one can be selected at any given time.

1 From the Standard tab of the Library palette, click and drag a Text box onto the form, positioning the box so that its location is X: 0.5 in. and Y: 4.5 in.

Be certain to use the Text and not the Text Field box. The Text box adds static text onto the page that is not changed by the user of a form and does not require or allow a user to enter any text. This text will serve as the label for the radio-button choices the form user will select.

2 Double-click to select the default text in the text frame you added to the form in the previous step. In the toolbars at the top of the window, change the font to Myriad Pro Black, and change the font size to 11 point. Keep the text selected and enter the text **Age Group**.

Note: You can also change the text attributes, including font and size, using the Font palette, which is available by choosing Window > Font.

3 From the Standard tab of the Library palette, click and drag a Radio Button onto the form, placing it adjacent to the Age Group field, at the position of X: 1.5 in. and Y: 4.5 in.

4 Click and drag to select the Radio Button text and enter the text 18-25.

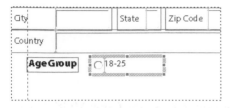

Duplicating an object

Adobe LiveCycle Designer makes it easy to generate multiple copies of similar objects on a form.

1 Click onto the outside edge of the radio button for the 18–25 age group and choose Edit > Copy Multiple. The Copy Multiple window opens.

If the Copy Multiple command is not available, it is because the text inside the radio button is selected, instead of the button itself. If necessary, try to select the button again by clicking on the blue line on the outside edge of the radio button.

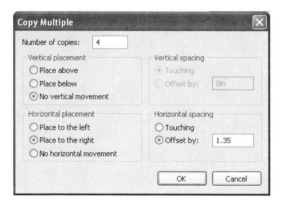

2 In the Copy Multiple window, set the following values:

- Number of copies: 4.

- Vertical Placement: No vertical movement.

- Horizontal placement: Place to the right.

- Horizontal spacing: Offset by: **1.35 in**.

After entering these values, press the OK button to close the Copy Multiple window.

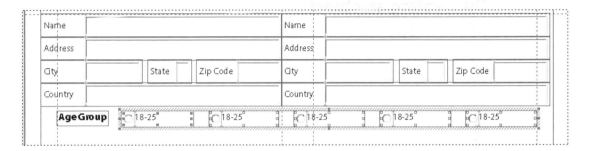

3 Double-click the radio button located immediately to the right of the original button. The text inside of this duplicated button becomes selected. Change the text to: **26–35**. Repeat the process of selecting and then renaming the text in the three remaining radio buttons, entering the names **36–45**; **46–55**; and then **56 and Over.**

Adding and duplicating a check box

Like radio buttons, check boxes allow you to present a form user with multiple choices. Unlike radio buttons, check boxes allow for more than one selection at a time.

1 From the Standard tab of the Library palette, click and drag a Text box onto the form, positioning the box so that its location is X: 0.5 in. and Y: 5 in.

2 Double-click to select the default text in the text frame you added to the form in the previous step. In the toolbars at the top of the window, change the font to Myriad Pro Black, and change the font size to 11 point. Keep the text selected and enter the text **How did you hear about this product?**

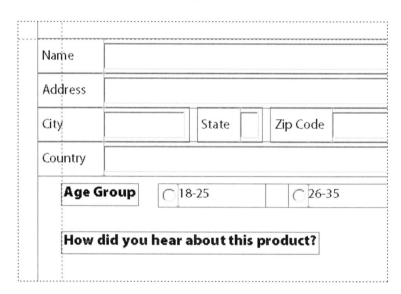

3 From the Standard tab of the Library palette, click and drag a Check Box onto the form, placing it under the How did you hear about this product? text, locating the check box at the position of X: 1 in. and Y: 5.25 in.

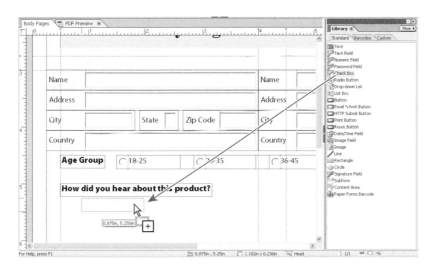

4 Click and drag to select the Check Box text and enter the text **Dealer**.

5 Click to on the outside edge of the Check Box labeled Dealer and choose Edit > Copy Multiple. The Copy Multiple window opens.

6 In the Copy Multiple window, set the following values:

- Number of copies: **3**.

- Vertical Placement: No vertical movement.

- Horizontal placement: Place to the right.

- Horizontal spacing: Offset by: **1.75 in**.

After entering these values, press the OK button to close the Copy Multiple window.

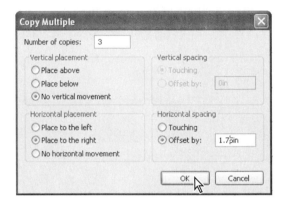

7 Double-click the check box located immediately to the right of the original check box. The text inside this duplicated check box becomes selected. Change the text to: **Friend**. Repeat the process of selecting and then renaming the text in the two remaining check boxes, entering the text **Internet** and **Ad** for the two remaining check boxes.

8 Click the Save button in the toolbar to save the file.

Adding and using Custom Library items

Use the library to store frequently used objects and groups. Objects can be pulled from the library and placed onto any form, saving the time of recreating objects that you use frequently.

1 Click on the text box that contains the text How did you hear about this product? and then hold down the Shift key and click to select all the check boxes on the form. Keep all the objects selected.

2 Click and drag the selected items to the tab labeled Custom in the Library palette. A white arrow with a plus sign is displayed ( ), indicating that the objects are being added to the Library. Release the mouse when the white arrow with the plus sign is displayed. The Add Library Object window is displayed.

3 In the Add Library Object window, enter the Name as **Check Box Group**. For Description enter **How client learned about us**. Click the OK button to close the Add Library Object window.

4 From the Custom tab in the Library palette, click and drag the Check Box Group onto the form. Position it under the existing check boxes at the coordinates of X: 0.5 in. and Y: 5.75 in.

5 Triple-click on the How did you first hear about this product? text in the group you added to the form in the previous step. The text becomes selected. Enter the text **What product features most influenced your decision to make this purchase?**

6 Triple-click on the description of the first Check Box. With the text selected, type Styling. Repeat this process for the three other check boxes, entering the text Performance, Value, and Engineering for these three check boxes.

Adding shapes

You can use shapes as design elements to draw attention to specific portions of a form or to separate one part of a form from another.

1 From the Standard tab of the Library palette, click and drag the Rectangle to the lower left corner of the form. Keep the rectangle selected.

2 In the Layout palette, enter the following values to adjust the size and position of the rectangle: X: **0.5 in**, Y: **6.5 in**, Width: **2.75 in**, Height: **3 in**. Keep the rectangle selected.

3 In the Object palette, click the Line Style drop-down menu and choose None. Click the Fill drop-down menu and choose Solid.

4 Click the Fill Color button (✎) and choose the same light green color you selected earlier in the lesson.

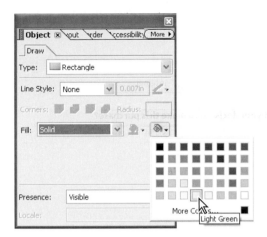

Adding a drop-down list

Create a drop-down list to provide multiple choices for users in which multiple options are displayed at the same time. Drop-down lists can also allow for multiple selections from a list of choices.

1 From the Standard tab of the Library palette, click and drag a drop-down List onto the green box in the bottom-left corner of the form.

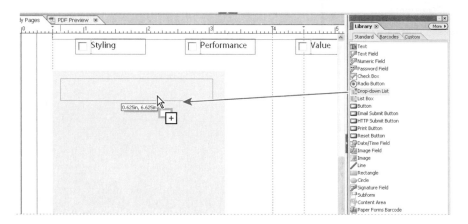

2 In the Layout palette, enter the following values to adjust the size and position of the drop-down list: X: **0.5**, Y: **7**, Width: **2.75**, Height: **0.354**.

3 Double-click the drop-down List text on the form so it becomes selected. Use the toolbars to change the Font to Myriad Pro Black, and the size to 11 pt. Keep the text selected.

4 Change the drop-down list text to read **Model**.

5 In the Field tab of the Object palette, click the green plus sign (+) in the List Items section. This allows you to add an entry to the available choices of the drop-down list. Type **Please Choose One** and press the Enter or Return key on your keyboard. The next line of the List Items section becomes active.

6 Add the following three entries, pressing the Enter or Return key after each entry: **Model 123**, **Model 456**, **Model 789**.

Note: You can change the order of items in the list by selecting an item and then clicking the up or down arrows. You also have an option to allow the user to add a custom entry if they can't find an option in the list you provide.

7 In the Value tab of the Object palette, click the Type drop-down and choose User Entered – Required.

Adding another text field

Now you will add a text field for the user to input the serial number.

1 From the Standard tab of the Library palette, click and drag a Text Field onto the green box in the bottom-left corner of the form.

2 In the Layout palette, enter the following values to adjust the size and position of the text field: X: **0.5**, Y: **7.75**, Width: **2.75**, Height: **0.354**.

3 Triple-click the text field so it becomes selected. Use the toolbars to change the font to Myriad Pro Black, and the size to 11 pt. Keep the text selected.

4 Change the selected text to read **Serial No**.

5 In the Field tab of the Object palette click the Appearance drop-down menu and choose Underlined.

6 In the Value tab of the Object palette click the Type drop-down menu and choose User Entered – Required.

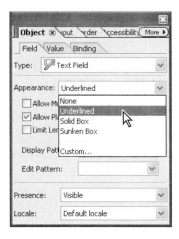

7 Click the Save button (🖫) in the toolbar to save the file.

Copying a text field

You will duplicate the serial number text field and then use it as to collect the user's email address.

1 Click to select the outside edge of the Serial No. text field and then choose Edit > Copy Multiple. The Copy Multiple window opens.

2 In the Copy Multiple window, set the following values:

- Number of copies: **1**.
- Vertical Placement: Place below.
- Vertical spacing offset by: **.75**.
- Horizontal placement: No horizontal movement.

After entering these values, press the OK button to close the Copy Multiple window.

The Copy Multiple command is useful when duplicating a single object if it needs to be positioned precisely on a form.

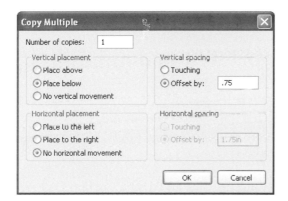

3 Triple-click the duplicate box that was created in the previous step. The Serial No. text becomes selected. Type **Email:** to change the selected text.

4 Position the cursor over the vertical red line that separates the Email text and the data entry field which follows it. The cursor changes to a vertical line with arrows pointing to the left and right. Click and drag to the left, enlarging the size of the data entry field and reducing the space for the text describing the field. This provides additional space for the user to input his or her email address.

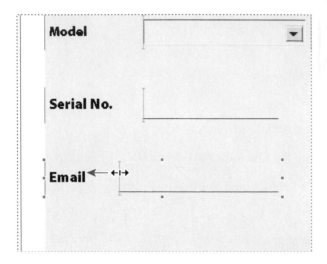

5 In the Value tab of the Object palette confirm that User Entered – Required is selected from the Type drop-down menu.

Adding the current date

Adobe Designer can automatically add the current date to a form field, automating this portion of the form completion process.

1 From the Custom tab of the Library palette, click and drag a Current Date object onto the form, under the Email field.

2 In the Layout palette, confirm the Expand to fit options are both selected and then enter the following values to adjust the size and position of the Current Date field: X: **0.5**, Y: **9.125**, Width: **2.75**, Height: **0.25**.

3 Triple-click the Current Date field. The text inside the field becomes selected. Use the toolbars to change the font to Myriad Pro Black. Keep the size unchanged, and keep the text selected.

4 In Field tab of the Object palette, click the Appearance drop-down menu and choose None. This removes any borders or underlines from the perimeter of the area that will contain the date.

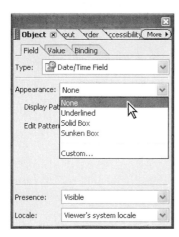

5 Click the Value tab of the Object palette. Confirm that Type: is set to Calculated-Read Only. This ensures that the user will not be making any entries in this field and that it will be automatically calculated.

Adding a list box

You'll add a list box to collect the user's listening preferences.

1 From the Standard tab of the Library palette, click and drag a List box onto the bottom of the form.

2 In the Size & Position portion of the Layout palette, enter the following values to set the location and size of the list box: X: **3.5**, Y: **6.5**, Width: **1.5**, Height: **2.75**.

3 In the Caption portion of the Layout palette, enter a Reserve value of **.6** and confirm the Position is set to Top.

4 Triple-click the list box caption. The text becomes selected. Use the toolbars to change the font to Myriad Pro Black, and the size to 11 pt. Keep the text selected.

5 Enter the text **Select the type of music you listen to most often:**, which becomes the caption over the list box.

6 In the Field tab of the Object palette, click the green plus sign (+) in the List Items section. This allows you to add an entry to the available choices of the list box.

7 Type **Please Choose One** and press the Enter or Return key on your keyboard. The next line of the List Items section becomes active.

8 Add the following entries to the list box, pressing the Enter or Return key after each entry: **Rock, Popular, Classical Blues, Jazz Country, Ambient Dance, Hip Hop, Rap**.

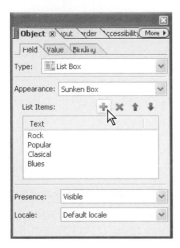

Adding the last Text Field

The last text field will allow the user to enter suggestions. Because they may have multiple suggestions, you'll allow for multiple lines of text to be entered.

1 From the Standard tab of the Library palette, click and drag a Text Field onto the form, positioning it next to the list box.

2 In the Caption portion of the Layout palette, click the Position drop-down menu and choose Top.

3 In the Size & Position portion of the Layout palette, enter the following values to adjust the location and attributes of the text field: X: **5.25**, Y: **6.5**, Width: **2.75**, Height: **3**.

4 Triple-click the text field so it becomes selected. Use the toolbars to change the font to Myriad Pro Black, and the size to 11 pt. Keep the text selected.

5 Change the selected text to read **Product Suggestions:**.

6 In the Field tab of the Object palette click the Allow Multiple Lines checkbox so it is selected.

Creating a Submit button

When creating the form, the New Form Assistant inquired about the type of form we were building, and how we wanted to receive the form data. Our response indicated that the form would be submitted. We have now decided to add a button to allows the form data to be submitted electronically to an email address.

If we had indicated that the form would be submitted electronically in the New Form Assistant, a Submit button would have automatically been added to the form at the time it was created.

1 From the Standard tab of the Library palette, click and drag the Email Submit Button onto the form, positioning it under the list box.

2 In the Size & Position portion of the Layout palette, enter the following values to adjust the location and size of the submit button. X: **4.25**, Y: **9.75**, Width: **2**, Height: **0.5**.

3 In the Field tab of the Object palette, enter your email address in the Email Address field. In the Email Subject field enter **Warranty Registration**.

This will cause the form to be submitted to your email address with the subject line of submitted forms set to Warranty Registration Response.

Previewing and exporting the form

You can use the PDF preview capability to confirm the form includes all the design elements you need.

1 Click the PDF Preview tab. The form is displayed as an Adobe PDF file. If the form is acceptable, you can create an Adobe PDF version of the form.

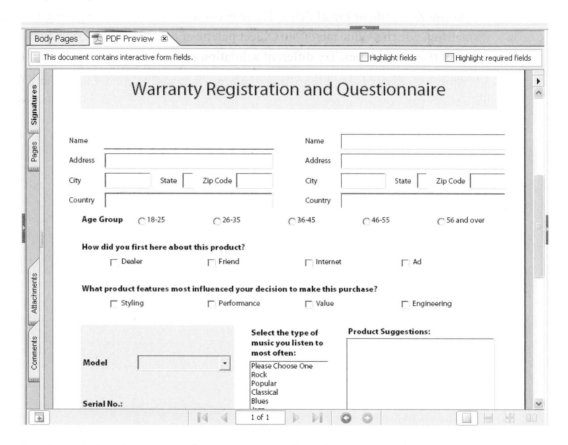

2 Choose File > Save As. In the Save as type: drop-down menu, choose Acrobat 6 Compatible (Static) PDF form file (*.pdf).

This allows users with an older version of Adobe Acrobat or Adobe Reader to view and complete the file electronically.

Congratulations! You have completed this lesson.

Exploring your own: Using Adobe Designer

1 Use the Field tab of the Object palette to change the Appearance of some of the fields in the form. Explore the various options to change the appearance of the form fields.

2 Adjust the red line that divides the description of each field with the user-entry section of the field. Modify fields so they include more or less space for user entries.

3 Choose Zip Code or Email fields. These fields will contain data requiring specific formatting. Use the Value tab of the Object palette and choose a validation pattern for either of these field types. Try different validation patterns for these fields. In the Validation pattern, the letter A represents locations where letters will be considered valid input, while the number 9 represents locations where numbers will be considered valid input.

Review questions

1 When would you use Adobe LiveCycle Designer to create a form instead of the form tools available in Adobe Acrobat 7.0 Professional?

2 How can you save an object or group of objects to re-use on one form or on many forms?

3 What is the difference between these objects found in the Standard tab of the Library palette: Text, Text Field, Numeric Field?

Review answers

1 Use Adobe LiveCycle Designer to create forms that use intelligence, forms that need to integrate into Adobe LiveCycle server solutions, or forms need to be repurposed in a variety of formats, such as XML, HTML, accessible HTML, or Adobe PDF.

2 An object or group of objects can be saved for re-use by dragging them to the Custom tab of the Library palette. Objects stored in the Custom tab of the Library palette can be accessed in any document, not just the document in which they were added to the Library palette.

3 The text object is used to add static text onto a form. This text is not modified by a form user. A text field allows the end-user to enter form data into a field that is provided. The text field option provides both descriptive text and a field for user entry. The numeric field is like the text field, although it only allows numbers to be input into the field and does not allow letters. Text fields allow for both letters and numbers to be input into their fields, unless a specific validation requirement has been established.

Index

Production Notes

The *Adobe Acrobat 7.0 Classroom in a Book* was created electronically using Adobe InDesign and Adobe FrameMaker. Art was produced using Adobe InDesign, Adobe Illustrator, and Adobe Photoshop. Proofing was completed using Adobe Acrobat 7.0 Professional using Adobe PDF files.

We would like to thank the Chesapeake Bay National Estuarine Research Reserve in Virginia for permission to use the poster in Lesson 8. All other references to company names and telephone numbers in the lessons are for demonstration purposes only and are not intended to refer to any actual organization or person.

Typefaces used

Adobe Minion Pro and Adobe Myriad Pro.

Update team credits

The following individuals contributed to the development of new and updated lessons for this edition of the *Adobe Acrobat 7.0 Classroom in a Book*:

Lessons 1 through 11:

Project coordinator, production: Lisa A. Fridsma

Technical writer: Jo Davies

Proofreading: David Davies

Testing: Dawn Dombrow

Lessons 12 through 16:

Project coordinator, technical writer: Christopher G. Smith

Production: Luis Mendes

Proofreading: Jay Donahue, Cathy Auclair

Testing: Greg Heald, Sean McKnight, Jeremy Osborn, Eric Rowse, Jennifer M. Smith, Greg Urbaniak

official
Theatrical
lettering
flexible
excellent

OpenType allows
automatic substitution of
ligatures and alternates,
which can be controlled by
contextual rules.

Překrásný
Ωραίος
ПРЕКРАСНЫЙ
奇麗なフォント

Worldwide scripts and
languages are supported with
Unicode character encoding –
all within a single font.

SMALL CAPITALS
12345 67890
ITALIC SMALL CAPITALS
½ ⅞ ³⁵⁹/₄₆₀

Typographic refinements such as
small capitals, old style figures, and
fractions are easily applied.

a agH
a agH
a agH
a agH

Optical sizes are designed to
optimize text appearance in a
full range of sizes.

Brioso
Warnock
Chaparral
Ex Ponto

Adobe Originals offer a complete
range of sophisticated composition
and display typefaces, crafted for
advanced typographic usage.

At Adobe®
the future of typography
is here today.

SINCE ESTABLISHING ITS TYPE PROGRAM in 1984, Adobe Systems has brought state-of-the-art type technology and design to a worldwide audience, leading major advancements in typography that have revolutionized publishing, exemplified by award-winning Adobe Originals composition families with sophisticated typographic features like expert sets and optical sizes.

Today, the OpenType® font format offers new features, cross-platform flexibility, and multilingual support. Typographic refinements such as old style figures and stylistic alternates are readily available and, where appropriate, can appear automatically. With Unicode, OpenType makes multilingual typography easier by allowing multiple language character sets in a single, cross-platform font.

The addition of OpenType technology to Adobe's type program is the beginning of an exciting new chapter in digital typography. Now and in the future, the Adobe Type Library will remain the best choice for typographic quality.

For more information on the Adobe Type Library and Adobe Originals, please visit: www.adobe.com/type

ADOBE
ORIGINALS